Praise for Slash Coleman:

"Good offbeat company."
—*Washington Post*

"It's hard to get stranger than the Sedarises, but Slash Coleman's family could give them a run for their money."
—*Backstage* magazine

"A refreshingly joyful view of a child's world, discovering love, savoring hero worship, and the thoughtful realization of just how far we will go to accomplish a cherished dream."
—TheatreOnline.com

"Laugh-out-loud funny and genuinely touching."
—*Willamette Week*

"Full of charm and writing that shines."
—*Portland Mercury*

"Uplifting, inspirational, and full of theatrical catharsis."
—*The Vanguard*

"Completely mesmerizing, pure and honest."
—*The Happiest Medium*

"Daringly thoughtful!"
—NYTheatre.com

"Whimsical and playful."
—StageBuzz.com

The greatest thing you'll ever learn is just to love and be loved in return.

—Henri de Toulouse-Lautrec in
Moulin Rouge!

the bohemian love diaries

a memoir

slash coleman

LYONS PRESS
Guilford, Connecticut
An imprint of Globe Pequot Press

For Elizabeth

Lyons Press is an imprint of Globe Pequot Press.

Project editor: Meredith Dias
Layout: Justin Marciano

Library of Congress Cataloging-in-Publication Data

Coleman, Slash.
The Bohemian Love Diaries : a memoir / Slash Coleman.
    pages cm
  ISBN 978-0-7627-8698-5
1. Coleman, Slash. 2. Authors, American—21st century—Biography. I. Title.
  PS3603.O4363Z46 2013
  814'.6—dc23
  [B]
                                                    2012051750

Printed in the United States of America

10 9 8 7 6 5 4 3 2 1

contents

author's note

This memoir is a work of nonfiction. While much of it was re-created from memory, other parts were pieced together with photographs and shaped through interviews with family and friends. To be clear, I am not a historian, and it is not meant to be taken as narrative research into events that happened in the past.

Locations, dates, and events remain as true to memory as possible, but many if not all of the names of primary characters have been changed to protect the privacy of those individuals. In some cases, identifying characteristics have also been altered to meet this end as well.

Faced with the decision of how to chronicle public events, such as Evel Knievel's jump or Howard Cosell's reaction to his jump, I erred on the side of creativity rather than actual reports as documented through YouTube or Wikipedia. Why? My passion for this work comes first and foremost from the re-creation of truth as an artist and bohemian rather than as a transcriber of fact.

part one

love me

1

the great escape

chesterfield, virginia
july 11, 1974

It's seven minutes after midnight, and I'm standing in a silver shopping cart with a bad wheel in Harvey's Meat Market and Grocery, facing a Standoff Sandwich.

My dad stands to one side, shirtless, wearing bleach-spotted jeans with a deerskin loincloth on the front and his Nazi soldier helmet with fake pigtails on his head. He holds an open can of Schlitz in his hand and a cigarette in his mouth. With his thick black beard and roadkill clothing, he looks like a cross between Ringo Starr and Daniel Boone.

Harvey, with his crazy red hair and greasy face, stands on the other side, the rest of my father's case of Schlitz under his arm, a cigarette also in his mouth.

A cashier—a Mexican woman with a red and white name tag that says ROSARIO—stands between them. She resembles a stick of beef jerky in a maroon apron and is chewing a big wad of bright pink gum. She holds a phone receiver in one hand, her other hand frozen on the rotary dial, ready to call the *policía* when given the signal. I open the black cover on my Moleskine sketchbook and write her name down with my pencil.

At this exact moment, the scene is silent except for the Muzak: Tony Orlando and Dawn's "Tie a Yellow Ribbon Round the Ole Oak Tree." My father's chest heaves up and down to the synthesizer and soft drumbeat while spittle drips from his beard. Harvey hums with revenge. As a John Wayne devotee, I know exactly what's going on here. Neither side is willing to shoot for fear of being shot in return, yet neither side wants to relinquish his weapon for fear that his opponent will shoot. If my dad attempts to grab the case of beer, the manager may take off running, leaving Rosario free to call the *policía*—which will put a damper on our trip to Alaska.

I'm not thinking about where my sisters are or where my mom is or how many times I've been in this same exact place before. For all I know, this is how every seven-year-old kid across America spends Saturday nights with his father, and I'm determined to make the most of it.

My bets are placed on a preemptive strike by my father because, with him, after midnight all bets are off when it comes to diplomacy and surrender. Harvey follows the No Beer on Sunday law to the letter. But he also knows what my father is capable of doing. Last month, the argument ended with the stock boy flying into the candy rack. His price gun flew through the air in slow motion, and all the Mars bars and Juicy Fruit gum and *People* magazines fell on his head.

I'm wearing my orange, glitter-flaked motorcycle helmet with a plastic orange visor snapped on the front. My father decoupaged a loinclothed, sword-toting, muscle-bound *Conan the Barbarian* on the back of the helmet with a naked woman and a large skull at his feet. Because of the visor, my entire world is orange: orange soup cans, orange cereal boxes, orange Standoff Sandwich. I tighten my grip on the grocery cart.

"Why do you always come in here and want to cause a scene?" Harvey says.

"Why do I always come in here and want to cause a *scene?*" my father repeats, agitated.

3

"You know that is what he already said," Rosario says. Her eyes shift from side to side, watching the tennis match of wills between them.

"Yeah, why do you always come in here and want to cause a scene?" Harvey says a little louder.

"*Yeah?* Why do I always come in here and want to cause a scene?" my father says louder yet.

"I want you both to stop it right now," Rosario says. She smiles at me. I smile back. This beats the hell out of getting dropped off at my grandparents' house, which is what my mom usually does with me and my sisters when Dad decides to drink in the afternoon.

"You want me to call the *policía*, Mister Harvey?" Rosario asks.

Suddenly Harvey swipes the open can of beer out of my dad's hand and makes a run for it. My father dashes after his beer. I turn to the page near the back of my sketchbook where I've drawn a map of the store beside the page where I write down the license plate numbers of suspected murderers and kidnappers. Ever since the book *Helter Skelter: The True Story of the Manson Murders* ended up on our kitchen table, I've been extremely suspicious of all adults. I often fantasize about turning my sketchbook over to the *policía* to become the world's youngest hero.

"Kiss my honkey ass!" my father yells in hot pursuit.

This is the dumbest thing ever. My father can't run at all, and he has a huge plumber's butt. Rosario hangs up the phone, looks at me, lights a cigarette, and ducks down under the counter. Her orange head vanishes behind plumes of orange smoke.

Near the back of the store, Harvey yells something as he crashes, and my dad yells something else as he crashes, then someone from another part of the store yells something and crashes. After a sharp but short silence, Harvey shouts in a high-pitched voice, "*Sell him the goddamn beer, Rosie!*" Rosie quickly stands and throws her cigarette to the floor. I follow my father's return with my finger on the map. He has just entered the frozen meat section and is about to approach the cereal section. He rounds the jars of peanut butter and jelly, smiling and sipping from his can of Schlitz, his case of beer tucked under one arm.

"If his brain was in his asshole, he'd know where it was," my father mumbles. He puts the beer in the cart with me, smiles, and pushes us up to the register. I smile back, pretending like I've succeeded at some great task while he was away. I feel the exact same way when he asks me to hold the ladder for him or hand him a nail when he's fixing something.

I put the beer and the rest of our goods onto the orange register belt, which slowly moves them toward Rosario: a box of orange banana-flavored Frosted Flakes, a bag of orange red-rope licorice, a box of orange instant potatoes, and a jar of Tang.

"You know, I think you dye your beard, don't you?" Rosario says, eyeing my father.

"Pardon?" he says, adjusting his crooked helmet.

"I notice it last time. Your beard is not the same color as you hair," she says. She reaches out and tugs at one of my father's pigtails. He swats her hand away but catches it at the last minute and brings it to his lips. They look at each other for a moment while she rings up the beer with one hand. This thing that my father does with women forever gives me a stomachache. She hands him the bag. My dad gives her the money, hands me the bag, and pushes us away.

"What's your name, cutie?" Rosario calls to me.

I tilt my head back so when I look at her under my visor she's no longer orange. "Fuck you," I say and then blow her a kiss.

My father knocks my helmet askew with the back of his hand.

Out in the parking lot, he lights another cigarette and loads the food into the saddlebags on the chopper.

"We'll live up in the Yukon," he slurs, "in an ol' skewl bus. We'll hunt for Kodiaks, fish for Kings, and make a killin' working on the pipeline."

I want to believe him because he's my father, but the farthest we've gotten to the Yukon is the Fredericksburg rest stop, about an hour away.

This is where my dad invariably pulls over before he passes out. As a result, I've grown used to living the Yukon life vicariously both through his consistent promises to get us there and through my Yukon Jack comic books about an Indian superhero who wears a Speedo and has the power to emit light from his hand due to telekinetic bone manipulation.

"What?" he says.

I shrug my shoulders. He doesn't say anything else, just hands me the bag of licorice and puffs away on his cigarette.

I stare at him. He acts differently when he drinks; he slumps more, and slurs more, and his eyes appear darker, and something happens to his hands, but I only know it by my mother's reaction to him. "Get your hands away from me," she always yells, wiggling her hands away from his. He always responds by trying harder to grab her hands.

She always refuses. She hates holding his hand when he drinks. To him, her reaction is a full-blown insult. As a sculptor, who creates every-thing with his hands, he shows his love that way. She screams at his hands when he drinks, then he gets offended and tries to grab her hands and screams back at her until she cries, which makes my twin sisters cry, and then the air in our house becomes so thick that escaping to the Yukon seems like the only reasonable option.

He stares down the empty highway like he's looking across a river. Neon signs flash like stars as far as the eye can see. He rearranges his painting easel on the back of the bike and straps the case of beer to it with a rubber cord. When I was younger, their fights used to scare me. I'd lie awake with eyes squeezed shut and try to make it all go away. Then my father left for days. Now that I'm older, he always yells for me to get my shit—which means my helmet and coat and my sketchbook—and he always takes me with him.

He kick-starts the bike, and we pull away. Just beyond the foot peg, the lines in the road blur beside me, my jacket pressed flat with the wind, and my thoughts weave in and out through the constant drone of the

6

engine. There is no visible sign that my father feels triumphant in any way. But I know with a son's intuition that he is proud of himself for his accomplishments in the store and proud of me for the "fuck you" to Rosario at the very end. I am proud of both of us as well.

Many years later, when I end up sleeping in the streets of Chicago for a few weeks, he'll hide that same sense of pride—as if having a son who is living like a bum equals having one accepted to Harvard Law School. We are bohemians. It's an unspoken understanding that will remain an important part of our connection.

The Yukon. Our destination sounds so big, so vast, so full of possibility. It creates the template for travel that I will carry with me through the rest of my life: one saturated with abandon and testosterone and bound with some kind of twisted love plot. Eventually I find a map of the Yukon in an old *National Geographic* and redraw it in my sketchbook.

Until I finish high school, my father keeps me stocked with black Moleskine sketchbooks. He continually tells me two important things about the sketchbooks: first, that tiny moles shed their skins for the sake of artists the world over, and, second, that Pablo Picasso wrote down his thoughts and sketched out his ideas in the same kind of book and that, if he had had a father who understood the importance of art and creativity half as much as Picasso's did, he wouldn't have gotten stuck in Chesterfield, Virginia, with a wife and kids and an art studio in the basement of a rancher house.

He guns the bike to pass an eighteen-wheeler. The motorcycle howls, and I tighten my arms around him. I feel my sketchbook, squeezed into the front of my jacket, wiggle. The pigtails on my dad's helmet fling out behind him and flap against mine. I rest my head against his back and feel safe. I fall asleep within minutes.

2

major league pop fly

chesterfield, virginia
june 24, 1975

I BEGIN TO MAKE MY REQUESTS IN JANUARY IN THE FORM OF HANDWRIT-
ten notes on white note cards. "Baseball tryouts on August 15," I write. I
leave each note card in an inconspicuous place: taped to the pint of half-
and-half in the refrigerator where my mom, a first-grade teacher, will find
it as she makes her coffee and looks over her lesson plans each morning; on
the saw blade in my father's art studio; within the current roll of toilet paper,
where it is sure not to be overlooked.

My parents never mention the notes, which is unusual because I use
an entire 50-pack of note cards. Weeks come and go. The season is about
to come and go. I feel invisible.

One morning, the countdown to tryouts looming, I slip into the chair
at the kitchen table beside my mother, pour Pepsi into a coffee cup, sip, and
count to ten and ten again, building the courage to bring up the subject. How
do I tell her that I feel like a jock trapped in an artist's body? That there is no
greater joy in life than getting beaned in the head during dodgeball at school
because I like seeing stars? That playing baseball will make me feel alive?

"Baseball me try out Saturday is good," I finally blurt out. It's more
like a sports haiku by Boris Karloff.

In an instant, my mother's beautiful European complexion turns yellow. She's barely five feet tall, but she suddenly seems taller than a skyscraper. "If you playe spots, you vil ghat *pair of lies!*" she says, standing and repeating the same phrase with the same accent that her own German-born mother used with her brothers.

With her accent, it sounds like she's just said, "Pair of Lies" instead of "paralyzed," and immediately I think she's talking about some horrible plague from the Old Testament. I see myself stepping onto the baseball diamond as a huge *Pair of Lies* descends from the sky like pants and squeezes me until I can't breathe. I subsequently break out in spots.

"But JP and his brother play sports all the time, and they don't get any pair of lies," I say.

"The spots! The spots! All you do is talk about this ridiculous obsession with the spots!" she says, pushing open the back door and yelling into the backyard. "Michael, tell your son about the spots."

The back door opens into what looks like a cross between a Wonderbread Thrift Store graveyard and a Joseph Mengele petting zoo. My father, who is taking taxidermy classes and experimenting with bread-baking techniques, loves to work on his roadkill sculptures in the backyard just as the sun is rising. All year, he's been bringing home dead animals from the side of the road and reconfiguring them with bread bodies. One snapping turtle found himself in his afterlife with the feet of a blue bird, the ears of a deer, and a pumpernickel body.

"If you can't fish it, hunt it, or build it, it's a daggon waste of time," my father yells back.

This is his typical response. He's always making art and athletics seem as unlikely a combination as fish and bicycles. At his feet, his personal assistant, Roosevelt, a large brown and orange Bantam rooster, which he's trained like a dog to sit on his sculptures, looks at me and nods.

"See, danger is sumting that increases exponentially the closer a boy gets to spots," my mother says as she's putting on her helmet.

As she starts up her motor scooter and drives off to work, there's no denying it: Keeping me from sports makes me want to play them even more. My father and I share a rare mutated gene related to all things masculine. It just doesn't make sense why he won't support me.

Hanging on his studio wall is a reminder of that gene, a newspaper clipping, ripped from the 1973 *Richmond News Leader*. The headline reads: Freaks vs. Pigs. Underneath the article a photo shows my shirtless father standing beside his shirtless, freaky artist friends on the softball field. To his right is Frank Creasy, a painter who shaved the hair off the entire right side of his body. This includes the hair on his head, face, eyebrows, eyelids, armpits, chest, arms, and legs. To my father's left is Britta Garrison, a tiny printmaker who rides a pink miniature horse to class and looks like a thirteen-year-old girl.

In one of my earliest sports memories, the VCU sculpture department—aka. The Freaks—beat the City of Richmond Police Department—aka. the Pigs—in a fund-raising softball game that changes the way the city relates to itself and my father relates to sports.

Something about how the players on both teams interact with one another touches me at my core. When a Pig drops his bat, another Pig hands it to him. Between innings, one of the Freaks carries another Freak's glove out to him. Whenever the Pigs are up to bat, the Freaks howl like hungry hyenas to distract them from hitting the ball.

The Freaks win 8–7. My father scores the winning run, and his plumber's butt becomes famous, but he dislocates his shoulder during a collision with the catcher in the process. After the game, a celebration ensues that lasts months. For the next year, his arm in a sling, and he has to do everything with his left hand: drink beer, zip up his pants, create art. The game is all anyone at the studio talks about, and, although it lessens the extent of his injury, it also leaves a bad taste in his mouth in terms of sports. Beyond the bad taste, I see a perfect community of spirit. I want something like this for myself—but something all mine.

Which is why, with baseball tryouts only hours away, I steal my father's softball mitt, sneak out of the house, walk the three and a half blocks to the baseball field, and prepare to change my destiny.

The spring air blends with the smell of grass-stained denim, freshly oiled gloves, and watermelon Hubba Bubba. The coach joins us, and his own profound smell bounds into ours like a slobbering bulldog. Wearing Brut by Fabergé—made famous by Muhammad Ali, Wilt Chamberlain, and James Bond—I know the instant I smell it that this man is our pre-destined leader. This is the smell that screams, "Go where no man has gone before!" If anyone can turn this group of ten naive boys into a team, it's Coach Walt.

He's a sight to behold. He stands seven towering feet tall—although three of them consist of his white-man perm. To a group of seven-year-olds no taller than lamp shades, Coach Walt's hair, which actually seems to touch the sky, has its own weather system and satellites. We look up to him in awe as he describes the art of catching the "major league pop fly"—a concept so manly and scientifically advanced that none of us understands it.

"Gentleman," Coach Walt says, which I like, even though we all still sleep in Underoos, "I'm a-gonna hit y'all the highest, longest, and hardest-hit baseballs imaginable. Balls that mighten rise so high they'll most likely leave the earth's atmosphere and burn up 'fore they reach y'all's mitts. Balls that are known as the Major League Pop Fly. By doing this on day one, I assure you that anything else in this sport will be easy. Relativity speakin'."

A few of us giggle. Coach Walt is a very smart man.

Honestly, I don't think any of us is able to tell the difference between a major league pop fly and a major league fruit fly. As latchkey kids with blue-collar parents too busy working to have time to play with us, none of us even tried on a baseball mitt before today. One of the kids is wearing his mitt on his head.

"And gentlemen? You do not simply catch a major league pop fly. Nawsir. It's y'all's job to stand still, hold your mitt out, and look invitin'.

The invited ball will find its way into y'all's mitt just as sure as hot tea from a teakettle finds its way into a teacup."

The last statement confuses me, and I look to my immediate left and right for confirmation. Two boys picking their noses and staring off in the distance confirm my suspicions.

As true-blue sweet-tea diehards, hot tea is a completely unknown species to us. To southern boys, sweetened ice tea means you take a tall glass and fill it to the very top with sugar, then you dilute it with a little water, add ice, and stick a Lipton tea bag in your mouth and suck on it as you drink the sugary concoction. Hot tea just doesn't compute.

"Now, take to the field!" he says.

Just like that, we trot off, no more sure of what we're getting ourselves into than before his speech. As I jog, all I can think about is Coach Walt's hair. It looks like he has a bowl of macaroni salad on his head. A big bowl, like you would bring to a Fourth of July picnic to share with seventy-five relatives. It has to be big because when the beautician puts the curler in at the beauty shop, there has to be enough hair there to take the curl. The hairdo gives the illusion that his hair is shorter than it actually is, which causes a unique phenomenon.

If a man like Coach Walt exerts himself enough, coaching under the hot August sun, the macaroni gets soggy and droops over his eyes. Because of this, men in the white-man perm clan develop a tic called the macaroni shake. They shake that bowl of salad to move the long macaroni out of their eyes. As a result, the coach always appears to say, "No," when he actually isn't saying, "No," which makes it even more confusing when he actually is saying, "No."

As all ten of us walk to the outfield, one of us occasionally looks back and sees Coach Walt shaking his macaroni, which means we haven't quite walked far enough. Gentlemen that we are, we keep walking and walking . . . and walking. We walk through the teacher parking lot, past the play-ground, and right up to the school. We would have walked right in, but the kid wearing his mitt on his head checks the door and finds it locked. We finally stop.

We just stand around until the tallest boy in the bunch says, "My name is Kent Williams, and my ma-maw is a Yankee, and she drinks hot tea out of a kettle."

Kent walks a couple steps away, puts one hand on his hip, and raises his gloved hand to the sky, which, I have to admit, makes him look very much like an *invitin'* teakettle. He looks like he knows what he's doing, so the rest of us copy him, ten teakettles spread out in a straight line. I'm starting to feel like we're quickly becoming something quite community-like.

From where we stand, Coach Walt looks like a tiny dot, and the baseball bat looks like a toothpick, and the ball that he keeps tossing up in the air and trying to hit looks like a tiny dot that has been erased. Evidently, hitting the major league pop fly is a complicated process. It takes so long for the first ball to arrive that a couple of us get distracted. Johnnie Ford, one of the boys with freckles all over his face, sits down and looks for four-leaf clovers. Another boy named Bo "Butter Bean" Ligon because his family owns a butter bean farm starts making squishing sounds.

I look at the sun. I love what happens when I look at the sun and then look away: A kaleidoscope of lights dances before my eyes. *Look. Look away. Kaleidoscope. Look. Look away. Kaleidoscope.* This reminds me of my *Saturday Night Fever* album back home. *Look. Look away. Kaleidoscope.* Although I wasn't allowed to see the movie, starring John Travolta as the disco king, I begged my father for the album because it included a sixty-page dance instruction booklet inside. *Look. Look away. Kaleidoscope.* On every page red and yellow shoe prints move in different directions. *Look. Look away. Kaleidoscope.* I follow the red and yellow spots swirling in front of my eyes. *Look. Look away. Kaleidoscope. Dance.*

I barely notice the first faint clank of Coach Walt's bat or the two balls that drop from the sky and land on top of the school. *Look. Look away. Kaleidoscope. Dance.* The third ball hits the side of the building so hard that it chips away part of the brick, but I am lost in spotted footprints. Someone screams. It's obvious to everyone but me and the kid with his mitt on his head that the balls seem to gain speed like torpedoes as they near us.

"Incoming!" Kent yells, but I am totally distracted from the task at hand. *Look. Look away. Kaleidoscope. Da—*

Thwump!

I'm the first to go down. A ball hits me right between the eyes, and I face-plant into the grass. Then Butter Bean gets hit on the arm and falls into the bushes. Everyone scatters. In a haze of stars and footprints, someone pulls me around the corner of the building as balls continue to fall from the sky.

I wake up in Coach Walt's arms, which makes for a great ending to a love story, especially one about baseball. He carries me to my house as the team follows. My mom is going to kill me, but with the team behind me I can conquer anything.

"Vhat is this?" she says, greeting Coach Walt at the front door. Coach Walt doesn't answer. He just puts me in my mother's arms, turns around, and walks away. Before my mom takes me into the house, Johnnie Ford comes up and buckles a leather bracelet around my wrist. His freckles look like chips of paint, and I vaguely remember that it was he who pulled me around the building to safety. I look at the bracelet and notice his name is spelled funny. It's Johnnie rather than Johnny. His face also seems softer than the rest of the boys'. Then I realize that Johnnie is no boy at all—he's a she.

Johnnie kisses her hand and presses it onto my arm. As my mother shuts the door, a strange mixture of surprise and warmth washes over me.

The next morning, just after Roosevelt wakes up the entire neighborhood, my dad goes over to Coach Walt's house to give him a piece of his mind. When he comes home late that night, he has a surprise. He, too, has a white-man perm now and also something more: a new creative cohort. Coach Walt invites him to become his assistant coach. I've found a way to bring my dad into my world after all.

And my mom? She liked my dad's hair so much that she went to the same beautician and asked for a white-man perm herself.

3

the last american gladiator

chesterfield, virginia
september 11, 1977

AMERICA IS STILL RECOVERING FROM A RARE DISORDER KNOWN AS
bicentennial fever. Symptoms include the sudden need to collect anything
marked with the number 1976. Lost in a haze of red, white, and blue, I
continue to collect bicentennial quarters, bicentennial Pepsi bottles, and
bicentennial Happy Meal toys from McDonald's.

Most of my weekends unfold with Johnnie at the Southside Speed-
way. Surrounded by her seven sisters, Johnnie and I wear matching leather
name bracelets and watch her dad, Mr. Ford, race his loud red, white, and
blue Ford Mustang Mach 1.

Although Mr. Ford's racing number is 76, my grandest bicentennial
obsession involves a middle-aged man with a motorcycle and a mission.
The infamous daredevil Evel Knievel adds a crisscross swatch of stars and
stripes to his classic white jumpsuit and, in the ultimate display of American patriotism, decides to jump his motorcycle across a 76,000-gallon
tank full of 76 Great White sharks. I start a new sketchbook just for him
and add a new drawing of him and his motorcycle each day, tracking the
days, hours, and minutes until his bicentennial jump. For weeks preceding
the event, a huge buildup takes place. I watch TV fanatically for hours just

to glimpse the commercials advertising the event on ABC's *Wide World of Sports.*

Every commercial shows Evel Knievel flying through the sky in slow motion. John Philip Sousa's "Stars and Stripes Forever" plays in the background. Then the screen fades to black, and an image of an ominous shark swims across the screen. The words "Don't Miss the Bicentennial Event of the Bicentennial" scroll across the screen. It's like a kid wrote the commercial for other kids.

For weeks, I imagine myself as Mr. Knievel. Wearing a red pillowcase around my neck, I set up a little ramp in the street with a brick and piece of plywood and jump over it again and again on my bicycle.

The day of the jump, I plant myself in front of the TV. It's a whirlwind of excitement. "Hello, sports fans, and welcome to the Bicentennial Event of the Bicentennial!" Shot of Evel Knievel. Shot of the Shark Tank. Shot of the fans. Commercial. "Welcome back, sports fans!" "Star Spangled Banner." Shot of Evel Knievel. Commercial. The Jump. Close-up of Evel Knievel gassing his motorcycle. Countdown. He takes off. I hold my breath. He jumps. He leaves the ramp. He flies over the sharks. He hits the ramp on the other side. Perfect. Then the motorcycle veers to the left. He goes down. His cameraman goes down. Chaos. Ambulance. Commercial.

The next day, ABC's *Wide World of Sports* sends Howard Cosell into the hospital to interview our hero. "Mr. Knievel," Howard Cosell says. "Yesterday marked a verifiable tragedy in American sports. A dark cloud now hangs over your long and noble daredevil career. You were injured, something we've come to expect. But your cameraman lost his eye. With rumors adrift as to where you will go from here after this shocking tragedy, sports fans everywhere would like to hear from you, *The Last American Gladiator,* if you feel it's finally time to hang up your jumpsuit, your valor, and retire?"

I hold my breath. The camera slowly zooms out and reveals two beautiful assistants on either side of the hospital bed. Mr. Knievel looks directly into the camera at me and says, "I dunno. I guess we're gonna just have to waiiiiiiiiit it out."

For the rest of the interview, I can't quit staring at him, and I don't hear a word he says. In that moment, I want a cast on my leg more than anything else in the whole world. I had a cast on my arm a couple of years ago. The chalky white gauze strips that the doctor dipped in water and laid on my arm turned hard as steel, like a warrior's shield. After I showed up at school with my cast, everyone lined up to sign it. I especially loved the saw the doctor used to cut off the cast. It sliced right through and barely tickled my skin. It gave just a tiny little tickle like a cat's tongue, and I actually closed my eyes and imagined the doctor holding an electric cat, its tongue going *lick, lick, lick, lick.*

But the real reason that I want a cast on my leg is that I feel it will help me attract the sympathies of Ms. Ottenbrite, my gorgeous, single, second-grade teacher. My attention-starved heart craves being noticed by Ms. Ottenbrite more than anything else in the world.

My attention deficit stems from my twin sisters. Nicknamed Mac 1 and Mac 2 because that's what their initials spell (Melissa Andra Coleman and Michelle Angela Coleman), my sisters speak a strange Martian-like language called twin speak or idioglossia. Mac 1 sounds like the teacher from Charlie Brown, Mac 2 like a squeaky car door. When they laugh, they sound like a broken cotton candy–spinning machine. I often listen to them talk through the house's thin walls, scared out of my mind. It's like listening to a cross between early Herbie Hancock and living with real, live circus freaks.

When *The Shining* comes out years later and the Redrum Twins make their debut, I see what identical girls are capable of doing, and I develop an acute case of insomnia. I lose sleep for nearly a year. So with all the appointments my sisters have with speech therapists and doctors and meetings with family friends doing research on their behalf, I often wait in the wings. Hence my determination to win the affections of Ms. Ottenbrite. As such, I develop a sophisticated plan.

Each morning I brush my teeth with Ultrabrite toothpaste. This is a subtle karmic message. Then every day after school until dinner and on weekends until dark, I put on my Baltimore Colts football helmet. (The Colts are still in Baltimore rather than Indianapolis, but the helmet still has the big, blue, lucky horseshoes on the side.) My father found it at a thrift store, and it doesn't have any padding inside. When I wear it, I look like one of those ceramic NASCAR bobbleheads. I tie it on using one of my father's macramé belts under my chin.

Next I shove a hundred-foot-long orange extension cord out the bathroom window. (I asked my parents for it on my seventh birthday, and to date it is still my favorite present.) I pull the cord into the back-yard. Next I attach my reel-to-reel recorder to it, place the little square microphone next to my leg, and lie down beside a huge stack of old car tires. I stack the tires one at a time onto my right leg. My theory runs that if I can distribute the weight of the tires in just the right way for long enough, I can get my leg to break. It's far less dramatic than jump-ing off the roof of the house and way less painful than getting hit by a car.

My helmet makes me feel brave, like a gladiator. I record the process because the doctors or even my parents might need proof. Each night, I take my recorder back into my room. I put on my huge headphones and rewind the recording, listening for the distinct and promising crack through the audio fuzz and silence.

Besides school, dinner, and baths, this is my life: lying there for hours as my legs, hands, back, and parts of my body that I didn't even know could fall asleep fall asleep. All the while I think about Ms. Ottenbrite—her thin, pretty nose, her frosted hair, she and I on a green hill, a picnic basket between us, my hand in hers, her hand on my cast.

One day as I'm lying there, a dark shadow passes over me. The image of being interviewed on ABC's *Wide World of Sports* immediately comes to mind. I imagine Howard Cosell standing over me.

"Mr. Coleman, do you think you will get your leg bone to break?" Cosell asks.

"I dunno," I say. "I guess we're gonna just have to waiiiiiiiit it out."

Then I smell it—Glade Air Freshener. I open one eye. I think I see a microphone. But an upside-down Mrs. Schneider—my very old next-door neighbor in her loosely fitted pink day robe and pink day slippers— is jabbing it into me.

Then, as my eyes adjust, it turns out that the microphone is actually a stick. Mrs. Schneider, inches from my face, has some kind of greasy medicine smeared all over her lips. Her mouth is open, and her teeth are gone, and her tongue is swishing back and forth. She looks like one of those horrible sea creatures that lures unsuspecting fish by wiggling its tongue like a worm and, when a curious fish swims up, it gobbles it down.

I scream. I fling out my arms. Mrs. Schneider screams and flings out her arms, her stick sailing across the yard. With an "Oh, Dear!" her Andy Warhol wig falls over her eye, and she falls on top of me.

"Mrs. Schneider, what are you doing? Get off me. I can't breathe!"

"Who's that talking to me?" she says.

"It's Jeffrey, your next-door neighbor. I can't breathe."

"Jeffrey? Oh, dear. I was taking out the garbage and thought you were one of your father's weird sculptures back here. So I started poking it with a stick." Considering our backyard, it was an easy mistake to make. "Why are you out here under all these tires?" Mrs. Schneider says, wiggling.

"I'm trying to break my leg. Why are you still lying on top of me?"

"I dunno, it's my low blood pressure," she says. "I guess we're just gonna have to waiiiiiit it out."

We wait for what seems like hours, which would have traumatized gladiators twice as old as me. Then, without warning, Mrs. Schneider grunts, stands, and waddles away. Her weight removed from my chest, oxygen rushes into my lungs like rainwater breaching a flood wall. My head feels light.

Suddenly two ideas overwhelm me. First, I'm willing to go to the ends of the earth to suffer for Ms. Ottenbrite's affection. Second, my reel-to-reel recorder suddenly feels dirty with the sound and smell of Mrs. Schneider. I need to scrub it down.

———

At dinner a few nights later, my dad announces that we'll be going to the Mermelsteins' for Shabbos dinner. Shabbos happens every week in the Jewish faith. From Friday at sundown to Saturday at sundown it's the Sabbath.

Herbert and Louis Mermelstein are artist friends of my father. Louis shared a studio space with my dad in grad school, and Herbert stayed on at the school as an algebra instructor. Louis is most famous for the little golf courses that she makes out of plaster torsos. She makes a plaster cast using a naked model, and once the cast dries she covers the mold in AstroTurf and sticks a tiny flag near the belly button and a clay golf ball beside it. My favorite is *Par 3*. Given to my father as a gift, it lives on our kitchen counter beside the cookie jar.

As soon as my dad tells my mom that we've been invited to the Mermelsteins', she doesn't want to go. Since they met, my father has always been trying to please her. Unfortunately, he insists on utilizing a specific and very southern method of trying to impress her called "puttin' on the dawg," a technique that employs over impressing that rarely works.

For instance, on their first date, after he finds out that she's Jewish, he picks her up in a stolen car with five bottles of Manischewitz wine and a 24-pack of Styrofoam cups. My father, not realizing that Manischewitz is cheap, ceremonial Jewish wine that tastes like a cross between prune Kool-Aid and liquid SweeTarts, doesn't understand why she gives him the cold shoulder, which is why he drinks all the wine himself. By the end of the night, he passes out at a stoplight, and my mom has to walk back to the dorm rooms alone.

His Manischewitz consumption impresses my mother so much that she offers him a second date. She invites him to my grandparents' house for Passover and more Manischewitz. By the end of the night, he has made out with my mom's learning-disabled cousin and lost a horseradish-eating contest with my uncle Bernie during which he loses consciousness. When he comes to, my grandfather is standing over him, completely distraught.

"If you continue to let yourself be pursued by this hoodlum," my grandfather says, "I will disown you like Tevye disowns his daughter in *Fiddler on the Roof*. A *cholearya af dir*. A plague on you!"

They immediately elope.

—⁓—

My dad reminds my mom that Herbert and Louis are Jewish, which is supposed to work in his favor, but then my mom *really* doesn't want to go.

"Bee-zides," she says, "aren't the Mer-mulsteens zee peoples zat kees everyone own thay lips?"

"It's a dag-gone custom," my dad says. "They're from Israel."

"Mmmm, I do not tink I like zee customs," she says. "Do you vant sum man kissing zhou on dee lips?" my mother says, looking at me.

I look at my sisters, who laugh. I'm not even sure they understand the question.

"No way," I say. "That's gross!"

"Y'all are all a bunch of closed books. The whole lot of y'all," my father says. He sticks his tongue out of the side of his mouth and bites down on it. "If you'd come out your Jew closet every now and again, maybe, just maybe, you'd get some civilizationing in ya."

"Zat is not a word, Michael," my mother says. "Civilizationing."

My dad is always complaining that my mom isn't civilized because she has decided to hide herself in the Jewish closet, which means she doesn't like anyone to know she's Jewish—especially other Jewish people. He jokes that the closet has a pull-string light and a couple shelves with snacks, and she spends most of her waking hours inside.

"Well, hellfire! We're going," my dad says. "It's cultural!"

On Saturday, we go. My dad puts on his skunk-skin jacket and his dragon-skin pants (real dragon, not imitation). My mom brings her closet and her snacks. I get my Colts football helmet and my reel-to-reel recorder. Mac 1 and 2 bring their Herbie Hancock soundtrack. Although we're only a family of five, we barely fit in the van with all of our idiosyncrasies.

At the Mermelsteins, I record everything, including not one but *three* rounds of kisses, which equals sixty kisses total because the Mermelsteins do a warm-up kiss before placing the actual kiss, sort of like how a dog circles a few times before it actually lies down. My dad takes all his kisses right on the lips. My mom turns her head each time so the kisses hit the hinges of her closet door. Mac 1 and Mac 2 take theirs on the top of their heads. I take mine squarely on the face mask of my helmet.

When we enter the house my father shouts, "Man, Louis, your pad is Jewcy!" It's true, too. Hanging from the ceiling in every room are stars of David. Entire solar systems of stars. On the walls hang paintings of great rebbes, Jewish holy men with beards, curly sideburns, and skullcaps. As far as the eye can see sit menorahs, the candleholders used for Hanukkah: silver ones, ceramic ones, misshapen ones.

The only thing Jewish we have in our house is a menorah wrapped in an old rag in a mop bucket underneath the sink. It sees the light of day only during the few precious hours of the holiday when we stand around it and sing the prayers and embrace our Jewish identity. Then it goes right back in the bucket underneath the sink for another year.

Right before we eat, Mr. Mermelstein stands at the head of the table and announces in Yiddish, "*Mir Vellen Ben shen*," which I think means something about a new TV show he likes to watch on CBS. Mrs. Mermelstein stands and, holding her fork out like a musketeer, extends her arm so it's in the middle of the table. Everyone holds their forks out until they meet in the middle and clang. I'm so excited.

"*A gezunt dir in pupik!*" Mrs. Mermelstein says, laughing. "Good health to your belly button!"

The food goes around, but it's all a mysterious version of beef stew, and I don't like it. I push my sweet stew into my red tangy stew and lift a little of the yellow stew and fold it into my bread stew. The rest of dinner is a snorefest. Mr. Mermelstein loves the way his voice sounds as it travels through his paranasal sinuses. He uses his plate as a podium, his fork as a conductor's baton, and lectures us ad nauseam about algorithms in Israel.

Then Mrs. Mermelstein surprises me. She brings out a silver serving tray. Under the lid is an orange hundred-foot extension cord. She says I can take my reel-to-reel into the backyard and record noises. I'm ecstatic. Cartoon hearts rise up from my helmet.

Filled once again with romantic purpose, I plug in the cord, plug in my reel-to-reel, and disappear into the evening. I only need to find something heavy to stack on my legs and I'll be back in business.

To be honest, I wasn't expecting to see the kid-size house in the backyard. But near the edge of the yard, as far as the extension cord will stretch, there it is, a little Cape Cod house, five feet tall, a kid-size door with a plastic flap over it, two little windows painted on either side, one with a flower box, the other with a sleeping cat.

The more I look at it, the more perfect it seems. It's sitting on cinder blocks, and I know I can easily slide my legs underneath. I picture the Wicked Witch of the West, her legs sticking out from under Dorothy's house.

I'm deep in contemplation when the owner of the house emerges from the front door. When I turn around, he stands inches from my face. When you're thirty-seven inches tall and weigh a little less than forty-nine pounds, a Great Dane in your personal space gives a totally new meaning to the word "great."

The monstrous dog looks deep into my eyes, and he knows that I know that everything he sees he falls in love with and everything he loves belongs in his mouth. I'm a centerfold torn from the pages of *Chew Toy Heaven*. I look deep into his eyes, and I know that he knows that he's the essential missing piece to my long-standing obsession with winning Ms. Ottenbrite's attention.

Realizing this, I remove my helmet and offer my tiny ball of a head in supplication. He snatches me up, and suddenly I'm as weightless as an astronaut eating sponge cake on the moon. *Roger, Houston, the sponge cake tastes delicious.* Then, just as mysteriously as I rise up, I return to Earth, and the Great Dane disappears.

I clutch the top of my head. A tear of joy rolls down my cheek. In another time, in another dimension, this would have been the perfect Hallmark moment. I can't wait to go back in and tell the adults about the joy of flight without mechanical motor. I follow the extension cord toward the house. I stand at the head of the table and wait for Mr. Mermelstein to finish. He's stabbing his napkin with his fork, driving home an important point about interval notations on the Wailing Wall.

"What's wrong with you?" my dad says.

"Chu git stung bya bee?" my mom asks. "Bzz, Bzz!"

I drop my hands to my side. A huge smile stretches across my face as my hairline drips down over my left eye like an eye patch. Blood pours over me.

Mr. Mermelstein faints and falls to the floor. Mrs. Mermelstein screams in Yiddish *"Oi Shlamzel! Oi Shlamzel!"* which means "Oh my salami! Oh my salami!" I think. My mother jumps up and down like water bugs have crawled into her underwear. Mac 1 and Mac 2 screech. My father, the only one who thrives in this type of situation, snatches me up in his arms like an oversized art book and rushes me outside to the van.

My family and our idiosyncrasies pile back in, and we speed away, running red lights, dodging cars, driving on the wrong side of the road. To stop the bleeding, my mom stuffs anything her shaking hands can find into the hole in my head: oil rags, used tissues, even an old gardening glove. The sheer magnitude of the reaction convinces me that I'm going to die.

In the hospital, I hear myself moan like I'm listening to my voice underwater, like it's a separate part of me. It reminds me of spending the night at my grandparents' house. Sometimes late at night, my grandmother screams, "The Stormtroopers! The Stormtroopers! The Stormtroopers are here!" and then runs throughout the house. It always sounds like hundreds of people are chasing her. In the morning, no one ever talks about it—not even when I ask—and so I feel like my voice and my thoughts are two different parts of me.

I keep asking the male nurse if I'm going to die. He holds my hand and whispers, "You're gonna be just fine, kid, just fine. Head wounds look worse than they really are. You need to think 'bout something nice."

"But my head hurts too much to think about something nice, mister," I say.

"Well, even if you can only get a glimmer of something nice, that would help."

For the first time, I come to understand the importance of glimmers. A glimmer is for that moment when you reach the bottom, when things get so bad that you need a little something extra to keep going. It gives you something you can push against to get back to the surface, so you can take a breath, like pushing off the bottom of a swimming pool. There's just no telling who or what that glimmer might be or when you might need it. For me that glimmer is Ms. Ottenbrite. I see her thin, pretty nose, her frosted hair, she and I on that green hill, a picnic basket between us, my hand in hers, her hand on my cast.

I wake up at home. When I touch my head it feels much bigger than normal, like maybe the doctor left in all those things my mother stuffed into my head. When I spy myself in the mirror, my gauze turban looks like the top of a vanilla soft-serve cone. I'm excited. This is much more cultural than a cast.

My dad hears me wake and comes into my room. He shows me where the Great Dane's top jaw dug into the top of my head and where his bottom jaw got me where my eye bone meets my nose bone. "An inch lower, Champ, and you would have been a one-eyed pirate. *Arggh!*"

That afternoon, Mr. Mermelstein stops by. He sets my reel-to-reel and helmet on the kitchen table and tells us how a sheriff has been assigned to watch Folger, aka the Great Dane, for thirty days. "After thirty days, the sheriff is going to decide if he should put my boy to sleep."

After he leaves, I take my reel-to-reel into my room and rewind it to the day of the accident. "Is this thing on?" Mrs. Mermelstein says, and "What should I say?" Mr. Mermelstein says. "Just say anything," my dad says.

Then, right after that, comes something new, something I've never heard before, something that wouldn't have sounded like much. Folger's collar jingles a few times. I say, "Oh, wow," as I'm lifted up. You can hear me land with a soft thud, the sound of Folger's tongue licking my cheek, the scrape of his toenails as he walks into his house. After a long pause, Folger sighs, and then in the background if you listen carefully you can hear the screams, the van starting, Folger sighing, and then just before the tape runs out you can hear him snoring.

I draw a picture of Folger in my sketchbook. I'm riding on his back like he's a rocket ship taking me through outer space.

Late that night, I go into my parent's room. I try to tell them that it wasn't Folger's fault, that he was helping me. But I'm too young to explain what I mean, and they're too old to hear what I'm trying to say. I even show them the picture, but all my mom can say is, "Nice," and my dad has his own story about how you can never really trust a wild animal.

"Dad, do you really think they'll kill Folger?" I ask, turning to leave.

"I don't know, Champ," he says. "I guess we'll have to just waiiiiit it out."

~

On Monday, back in school, I'm living my dream, holding hands with Ms. Ottenbrite. Our hands are the same size and fit together perfectly as if made for each other. She takes my hand between classes, out on the playground, and at lunch. The entire time I sway beside her with my huge gauze soft-serve cone head, promising myself I will always be gentle with her. I won't ever try to insist that she hold my hand like my father some-times does with my mom.

When I get home from school that day, my dad has a surprise for me. He has transformed my bike into a chopper. He welded fourteen forks onto the front, making it nearly eighteen feet long. It has a banana seat, a huge sissy bar, two flags with Jewish stars on them, ape hanger handlebars, purple hand grips with pink tassels, and on the back a license plate that reads: THE DREAM MACHINE. When he changes my head bandages that day, he paints red, white, and blue stripes on the sides. I take the wobbly bike for a spin around the yard like a miniature mutant Evel Knievel.

When the stitches come out, I bring the wiry wisps into *Show and Tell*, 144 in all. They represent the end of a special time, and like seeds they embody my potential to dream of bigger and more beautiful things to hold in my hands. That day, in Mrs. Farmer's class, Johnnie and I hold hands while watching a filmstrip about the job of a welder. It's quite excit-ing—as exciting as trying to catch those major league pop flies.

At the end of the month, Mr. Mermelstein calls the house. "The sh-sh-sheriff says my b-b-boy Folger can stay," he says in tears. His cries leap out of the phone receiver.

Above me, on the underside of the top bunk, I tape the X-ray of my skull. Late at night, I sometimes shine my flashlight on it and touch the strange plastic paper. With one hand I trace the notch on the X-ray, in the shape of a comma, where Folger's tooth dug deep and scraped my skull. With my other hand I touch my scar. It's an indelible, irremovable reminder that proves that anything is possible. In some ways I feel lucky to have it because I know a lot of adults have lost this mark. It also rep-resents my secret glimmer, a scar to prove that things aren't always what they seem. With life, as with dreams, sometimes you don't really know how things are going to turn out. Sometimes, things turn out even better than you can even imagine and sometimes, I dunno, I guess you just gotta waiiiiit it out.

4

perpetual underdog

chesterfield, virginia
february 19, 1978

I WANT THE ATARI 2600 SO BADLY THAT I ACTUALLY CONSIDER RUNNING away if I don't get it. I even go as far as jotting down my runaway plan the night before my eleventh birthday. In my sketchbook, beside a reminder not to forget my canteen, I list spices from the kitchen that I might need: dill weed, allspice, garlic salt, and arrowroot.

Like a campfire that attracts people to sit around it for hours for some mysterious reason, the little square Atari box encased like a burrito in stylish fake wood paneling attracts my friends and me to it like moths for the entire winter. Johnnie, Kent, Butter Bean, and I spend nearly all our waking hours huddled around Kent's basement television, our faces painted like members of the rock band KISS, joystick controllers in our hands, laboring through hours of Pong.

On my birthday, my father reaches over the cake and slides a gift-wrapped box the exact same size and shape as an Atari box across the table. A part of me dies when I discover an electric typewriter inside.

I understand this to be unrequited love, a term I heard Kent use when Johnnie got bumped up to a better team and her family moved away. "If she really loved you, she would have stayed with us instead of going to

Chalkley," he said. I'm not sure that I really understand the definition, but the way Kent uses the word makes sense to me. In terms of my father's gifts, it makes more sense. When I want a rock tumbler, he buys me a belt with a removable skull buckle. When I want a motorcycle, I get a surfboard.

"He vants to give you tings that vil make you into a creatif and well-rounded man," my mother says.

The largest and most substantial dose of disappointment arrives four years after the Atari typewriter incident. I ask for the Rick Springfield album *Working Class Dog* for Hanukkah. On it, the song "Jessie's Girl"—a tale, appropriately enough, about unrequited love—speaks to the part of me that can't wait to go out into the real world and get a broken heart of my own.

When my father reaches over the menorah and slides the flat wrapped gift—the exact same size and shape as the album I want—across the kitchen table, I am dismayed once again. Inside is the album *Double Fantasy*.

"John and Yoko?" I say, reading the album name and smiling a fake smile. "Cool."

I am crushed. Which he senses.

"You need to become cultured, Champ," he says. Perhaps he also senses that a kid with a Barry Manilow poster hanging in his room needs something more substantial, or maybe he's just talking out of his ass like always. "You don't wanna end up runnin' around as a redneck kid your whole life. Besides, when you become top dog and can tell the difference 'tween what you need and what you want, you can make the decisions."

He's right of course, but in the moment I'm too young to understand.

He passes my next gift to me. "It's a Billy the Kid suit," he says before I open the box. "It's named after the infamous outlaw. That's white denim. I special-ordered it from the JCPenney catalog. It's exactly like mine."

"Try it on, sweetie," my mother says.

Like he did to his own, my father has altered my suit by running mushroom-shaped copper tacks along the pant legs and attaching silver conchos with leather straps to the jacket pockets. I take a good look at myself in the living-room mirror and I can't believe the transformation. I suddenly feel like I belong to a special club—a dangerous and powerful one.

"It's soft," I say, coming back into the kitchen. "It ain't itchy or nothing."

"Good!" my father says, reaching out and adjusting my collar. "In the morning, once Roosevelt gets you up, you put it on. We got somewhere to be early."

In the morning I put my suit and motorcycle helmet on, get back into bed, and wait for my father in my orange world. In my sketchbook, I draw the robot from *Lost in Space*. I'm obsessed with the show because the boy, Will Robinson, is nine years old like me. I'm even more obsessed with the robot, though, because he's like a father to young Will. Like a faithful Labrador retriever, the robot is always looking out for him and warning him of danger by saying, "Danger, Will Robinson! Danger!"

I fill every page in my newest sketchbook with wobbly drawings of the robot. His head is basically a light bulb in a fishbowl, his body a square washing machine with two Slinky arms, his legs a metal file cabinet.

I jump out of bed when my father knocks on my door and follow him through the house like a little bug. It's amazing the way I feel in my suit. It's like a superhero outfit. My mom often says that God cast my dad from the same mold used for barbed wire, horse shoes, and hot fire. I don't often feel like I'm cast from this mold. My mom says it's because I was born softer from her side, but in this moment I feel tall and strong, like my father. I feel like a tough guy, an outlaw . . . top dog.

"Damnit!" he says, stopping at the front door. I run into his orange butt. He puts one hand on his hip and the other on my head.

"Look at me, Champ."

I look up at my orange father.

"I gotta take the van to the studio. I forgot something. You wait by the bike and don't be runnin' off and gettin' all dirty. I'll be back in thirty minutes."

He doesn't come back for two days.

Early the next morning, just after Roosevelt wakes up the neighborhood, a tow truck backs my father's van into our driveway. My mom jumps onto her scooter. I meet her down by the road.

"I vant you to watch your sisters," she says. "Your father has been shot."

I bite my bottom lip as she drives away and then run to the van. As I touch the dark, bloody hand print on the driver's side door, my stomach drops. As I pull open the door with both hands, my body starts to shake as if the air has suddenly turned cold. There's so much blood on the green seat, green steering wheel, and green dashboard that it looks like a bucket of red paint has exploded inside. When I press my finger into the carpet underneath the brake pedal, it feels like wet wool, firm and squishy.

I climb into the back, careful not to touch anything. I catch myself in the rear-view mirror. I'm still in my suit. My hair, like my mind, is going in a million different directions. What if my father never comes home? Will my mother be able to stop the bleeding by holding her hands over the bullet hole? What if my arms and legs outgrow my suit? I exhaust myself with possibilities and begin to cry.

With tears streaming down my face, I flip my sketchbook open to a new page. As I draw, I hear my dad's voice. "Everything is either a square or a circle. If you can draw a square or a circle you can draw anything."

I draw the robot from *Lost in Space* over and over again. Slowly I come to understand his body as a collection of circles and squares. I try to perfect the shapes. The task makes me feel incredibly close to my father. Consoled after hours of circles and squares, I finally go into the house and make dinner for my sisters. Just before dark I climb into the van, curl up in the back like a tiny moon, and fall asleep.

My dad picked up the hitchhiker in the area around the college. He said the guy was clean cut: short hair, glasses, tie, a young student who needed a ride. My dad always has heart for those who need a hand up.

The hitchhiker climbed into the passenger seat, and my dad steered them onto 95 South to head home, but the hitchhiker said, "No," and my father said "No, what?" and the hitchhiker said, "No, you're going to take me all the way to the beach," and my father said, "I ain't going that way," and the hitchhiker said, "You are tonight," and he pulled out a pistol and my dad started heading toward the beach.

The hitchhiker kept the pistol pointed at my dad, though he didn't know what my father was capable of doing. It was like one outlaw picking up another. Even behind the gun, the guy should have been afraid. My dad made small talk while he slowly began pushing his foot deeper and deeper against the acceleration pedal. By the time the speedometer hit 100 miles per hour, my dad was probably in his element. When it maxed out at 125 and started to shake, the hitchhiker was probably shaking as well. My dad knew the guy would never pull the trigger while they were traveling so fast. If he did, they'd both end up dead.

Up ahead, they neared the weigh station. My dad had planned his escape. He counted to ten, and when he reached ten he simultaneously slammed his foot on the brake and reached over and slammed the hitch-hiker's head into the dashboard. The van fishtailed as he pulled the hitch-hiker across his lap, opened his door, steered for a moment with his knee, and threw the guy out.

As my dad drove on, he noticed that his feet felt cold. When he looked down he could see that both of his cowboy boots had filled with blood. The hitchhiker had pulled the trigger after all.

My dad swerved into the weigh station and jumped out, but his legs wouldn't work. He lay on the asphalt, legs splayed out like a frog's. A worker found him and called an ambulance. The police never found the hitchhiker.

At the hospital, they cut my father's Billy the Kid suit off—the jacket to hook him up to machines, the pants to plug the bullet holes in both legs. The first shot went clean through both legs, and the second went through one leg and lodged in his ankle.

I never see his suit again. The doctors probably ball it up and throw it away in the emergency room. Although I'm sure my father would have found some artistic use for the bloodstained cloth, I guess a bloody suit isn't like saving a cast or stitches.

I never wear my suit again. It hangs in my closet and then disappears like the typewriter, the *Double Fantasy* album, and the hitchhiker. It seems strange that the things that shaped me most could just disappear, especially now since they seem to live with me. Maybe I outgrew the suit. Maybe my father knew that to have a suit named after an outlaw would bring only misfortune, though whose misfortune I couldn't say. Sometimes I think the hitchhiker crawled into the woods and died that day, his bones tattooed with the karma of an underdog.

My father recovers, and, although his soft spot for helping others never goes away, he never picks up another hitchhiker. His legs are fine except for a few shiny circular scars. Whenever we go to the beach and someone asks him about the geometric shapes, he always says, "Scars are God's version of tattoos. God's tattoos come with better stories."

After the shooting, things change. Although you can't tell it from my size or my softness, something deep down within me changes. From that moment on, when life gets hard, I find myself reaching for that Billy the Kid suit, pulling it out of the closet of my mind, covering my skin with the soft denim, and feeling transformed.

In the suit, I feel a lot like my dad, and I enjoy a certain illusion of being that guy he wanted me to become, the one who knows exactly what he wants, exactly what he needs, and where the two intersect. In my suit,

I become the tough guy, the outlaw, the top dog. But I also become some-thing more.

My father's art is a rocket ship, a vehicle that he easily fuels to escape from this world and sometimes to reflect more deeply upon it. Now, I know how to drive my very own rocket ship. As a pilot, I finally have the freedom, like my father, to come and go as I please, and once I find a way to fuel my creative ambitions, I know I'll be on my way to becoming a real artist, too.

5

odd time signatures

chesterfield, virginia
july 28, 1978

THE WEEK AFTER MY FATHER COMES HOME FROM THE HOSPITAL, THE
fuel arrives, and, like most things that arrive in our house, it appears suddenly and without explanation. The previous night there had been an
empty space beside the washer and dryer. Now something there resembles
a rickety, green, upright piano. Such things seem to hatch overnight in our
house—an iguana, a stray dog, a roadkill sculpture. Some arrive and stay
awhile; others disappear.

"What's that?" I say, walking into the kitchen.

"Jeffrey," my mom says. "What did I say about zee makeup?"

"What? I forgot," I say, filling a bowl with Cap'n Crunch, my face still
painted like Peter Criss, the cat-man drummer from KISS.

My mom rolls her eyes and sips her coffee.

"Seriously, is it a sculpture?" I ask.

"It's a pian-er," my father says, raising his beer can. "You play it."

"It doesn't look like it works" I say uncertainly. It looks like it might
fall over like the Leaning Tower of Pizza.

"You think I'd buy a pian-er that didn't work?" my father says.

"I don't know," I say, chomping my cereal. "Pianos are for girls."

"What's the difference?" My father laughs. "You dress up in that girly makeup with your friends and listen to that girly music. I figured you'd like a pian-er, too."

"Michael! Zat's *not* necessary!" my mom says.

"It's heavy rock!" I protest.

"Whatever it is," he says. "Vera, if he don't take to it. I ain't moving it." He leans on his crutches and shoots my mom a look. She sips her coffee and avoids making eye contact with him. An awkward silence fills the kitchen.

"You can make it talk, Jeffrey," my mom says. "If anyone can, you can."

"A piano can't talk," I say.

Laughter from my sisters' room glides down the hall. They're probably making more booger sculptures on the walls beside their canopy beds.

"I have faith in you," my mom says.

"What does a ten-year-old need with faith?" my dad yells as he hobbles out the door. The screen door slams behind him.

"Your favorite song is played on zee piano," my mom says.

"*Mom!* I said I loved the way the piano sounded. That didn't mean I *wanted* one!"

That afternoon, as I remove my makeup, I connect the dots between the piano and what my mom said. Peter Criss sings my favorite song, "Beth," which features a piano arrangement. We now have a piano in our kitchen.

Later that day I spread my orange sleeping bag under the piano, bring my reel-to-reel recorder inside, and rewind it to *KISS Meets the Phantom of the Park*, a TV movie in which the band sings some of their best songs while battling an evil inventor at an amusement park. When "Beth" comes on, I sing along with Peter Criss and imagine he's singing about me, Jeff, instead of Beth. Hearing him tell me that he can't come home right now because he has band practice brings me to tears.

Before bed, I bring my digital radio alarm clock inside my new piano apartment, along with KISS's *Love Gun* album and a few bicentennial

Pepsi bottles. For privacy, I tie a sheet to the top of the piano legs and drape it over the piano bench so it makes a door. When I look out from underneath it, I pretend I'm on the cover of the *Love Gun* album, which shows the band standing between two marble columns surrounded by eleven beautiful girls. That's almost three and a quarter girls for each band member.

The next morning, my father walks by while I'm waking up. His feet and the tips of his crutches go from the sink to the coffeemaker to the cupboard. He stops in front of the piano and kneels down.

"You up, Champ?"

"Hey," I say, rolling over and opening the door flap to my piano apartment.

"Why don't you just push a key or something and see how it sounds?" he says, waving his hands across the keyboard.

I peer out from under the piano. "You don't want to know how it sounds. Look at the top. It's got all your papers and bills and dirty paint-brush pans on it."

He sips his coffee. "Listen. I didn't want to tell you this, but this piano is magic."

"What?" I say, rising up and hitting my head on the underside of the piano. "Mom told me that it was from some black guy that lives in a tool shed." I rub my head, reach up, and touch the side of the piano. A layer of paint flakes off between my fingers, like dried green blood.

"That's what makes it magic," he says.

That night, sometime after midnight, I slide out from my new apartment. I sit down at the bench, place my right hand on the keyboard, and pretend I'm Peter Criss. I hold my breath, and with my thumb and middle finger I push two white keys. The strings inside the piano come alive with the breath of my touch like a human voice. In an instant my entire world transforms. Over my hand the word "Power" magically appears as if written with glowing neon ink. I'm seeing things.

I push the keys harder. The word appears, brighter. I move my hand and press a white key and a black key, and the word "Sadness" appears over my hand. I press again, and the word pulses. I push more keys, and more words appear: Anger, Happiness, Triumph, Distress. Each combination has a new word over it, each a feeling. My father was right. The piano is magic.

I bang on random keys with both hands, my hands bouncing up and down like on a trampoline.

"*It's two in the mornin'!*" my father yells, limping into the kitchen.

My hands fall into my lap. I squint and hold my breath. The words disappear.

"You said you wanted me to play!"

My mom appears behind him in her nightgown. "He's right, Michael," she announces as she yawns.

"He gets this from your Bohemian father," my dad says.

"My father? What's my father have to do with zis?" she says. "He gets this from you."

"Go back to bed," he says, "both of y'all."

I keep track of each specific emotion-note combination in my sketchbook. Some require one hand, some two hands, some involve two keys, three keys, or even six. When I think about how Uncle Friedo wears his cutoff jean shorts way too high, I write in my sketchbook "Funny 13" and draw ten lines that represent the piano keys. Then I put dots on the piano keys to remind me where my left hand and right hand go. Later, I go back, push the appropriate keys, and . . . *wa-lah* . . . instant funny!

My sketchbook soon fills with hundreds of emotion-note combinations: Sadness 2, Disappointment 11, Anticipation 17, and Excitement 4. Like the paints, chisels, and canvas that fill my father's studio, I now have the means to create something of my own. But my father, using his special artist intuition, senses that my combinations need refining, which is why he guides me toward a refinery.

"Get your helmet on. Let's go," my father says.

"Where are we going? Alaska?"

"Don't ask stupid questions."

"How can you drive your motorcycle on crutches?"

"I guess we'll find out," he says.

We drive to Petersburg on Interstate 95 and get off at the first exit. We stop in front of an old house the color of a peeled Russet potato. My father walks me to the door.

"Give me your helmet."

I loosen the strap and hand it to him. "Is this a shrink's house?"

My father pushes the doorbell. A dog barks, and the door opens.

"Are you coming back for me?"

A large black woman with a miniature beard on her chin pushes the door open. Her hair fixed in a bun, she's smoking a pipe. A wave of anxiety rushes through my body.

"Mr. Coleman?" the lady says.

"Yes, ma'am. Mrs. Tyler?"

She nods. "You best be back in twenty-five minutes. Sometimes with the little ones the lesson don't go all that long. Come on in, boy. I ain't gonna bite you."

The deeper we walk into the house, the more profound the smell of french fries becomes. The smell sticks in my nose like wax. Everything in the house is french fried: french fried lamps, french fried curtains, even a french fried floor. She points to an old upright french fried piano in the corner. My father starts his motorcycle, and the sound trails away.

"You sit there," she says, pointing to a bench. She sits in a rocking chair behind it. "Do you play?"

I nod. I hand her my sketchbook, which she takes and sets atop the piano.

"Well, go on then."

I look at my sketchbook.

"Can you play a scale?" she says. She stands up, leans on me, and reaches her right hand onto the piano. Her fingers walk up and down the keys like they're climbing up and down a set of stairs. Her arm smells like french fries. "That sounds good, don't it?"

I nod.

"That's a scale," she says.

I nod.

"It's your turn. You do what I done."

I stare at my sketchbook.

"Ma'am, I would like you to teach me about what's in my book," I say.

She opens the book, but as she looks at it and then looks at me it seems that I've asked her to teach me about something exotic, slightly sexual, and totally illegal. She slams the book shut and places it back on the piano.

"Are you deaf, child? I ain't wantin' you to be a virtuoso. Just push on the dang keys like this," she says, pressing the keys.

I don't move. Her will only makes my need to withhold stronger.

"Why you gotta sit there like a bump on a log? I just want you to play, sweetie. You can do it; just push on the keys."

I spread my hands over the piano.

"There you go," she says. "Go on now, that's right."

Over both my hands the phrase "Expectation = Love" appears.

"That's right, dear," she says.

I stare at the words, and a warm feeling washes over me.

"Go on, that's right."

The less I actually do, the greater her expectation becomes. The colossal creative struggle—the one my father and his friends talk about incessantly—comes to mind: the artist as a young man; the conservative, older, female teacher; a longing for the forbidden because the forbidden leads to freedom.

Before I know it, the grandfather clock in the corner chimes. My father's motorcycle pulls up outside. I smile at Mrs. Tyler. She slumps down in her rocking chair, and her legs push her body back and forth.

For the next three months, our lessons continue exactly this way. I meet Mrs. Tyler, hand her my sketchbook, wait in the warmth of expectation, she slumps, and then I leave. In between these paid periods of silence, I continue to document combinations and teach myself how to play (exclusively by ear) my favorite KISS song.

My parents don't have a clue about what occurs, or to be more exact, what does not occur at my lessons. They hear me playing "Beth" and my combinations, so for all they know everything's just fine. Before my twelfth lesson, though, Mrs. Tyler meets my father at the door and lets him have it.

"Mr. Coleman!" she yells, "they may teach students how to become better players where you comes from, but don't nobody teach piano students who won't push the daggon keys. I am a failure as a piano teacher and a sinner for greed. If it's all the same to you, this musical arrangement is finished!"

Dumbfounded, my father doesn't say a word. Instead, he waits until we're on the motorcycle stopped at a light and yells back to me, "Why wouldn't you play for that old lady, Champ?"

"What for?" I yell back. "I just want to play what's in my head. She can't teach me that. She only wants me to play all the stupid stuff that other kids play."

My father looks away. He gasses the motorcycle and we take off.

———

A week later, near dark, we arrive in a different part of town, standing at the door to another potato-like house.

"Give me your helmet," my father says.

I loosen the strap and hand it to him.

"Is this a better teacher?" I ask.

My father pushes the doorbell. A tall skinny black man with an afro and a mustache in a green disco shirt opens the door and slaps my dad's hand.

"All right," he says.

"All right," my dad says back. "You workin' the program?"

"You know it," he says.

He holds his hand out toward me and says, "What's crackin'?"

"I don't know," I say.

"Shake his hand, Champ," my dad says. I hold my hand out, and he slaps it.

"Lenny," he says.

"OK," I say.

We step inside.

"Your old man tells me you're grouse on the keys," Lenny says.

I laugh and nod. I don't know what he means.

We follow Lenny down a dark hall into a basement that smells like incense. As we step over a tangle of chords on the floor, I see that a full rock band is set up against the far wall.

"Yo, Eddie, Freddie, Scotty," Lenny says. "This is the young cat I was telling you about—Mike's son, Jeffrey."

My dad obviously knows the guys and says hello. They slap his hand and say, "Wassup?" and "What's happening, Tricky D?" and "Say, brotha."

Each of the guys—drummer, bass player, and guitarist—looks just like Lenny: big hair, mustache, disco shirt. I stand in the middle of the room with my hands in my pockets.

"OK, young blood, let's see what you got," Lenny says. He motions me over to the band area. I don't move.

"Play your song, Champ," my father says.

I trip over the cords to the band area, and Lenny lifts me up and sits me on a soft, black rotating stool in front of a tower of keyboards. He pushes some buttons and walks away.

I spread my fingers across the keys and wait. The word "Fortune" appears over both of my hands. I close my eyes and imagine that I'm Peter Criss. My favorite song moves through me, amplified into the room. Lenny begins to sing. The rest of the band plays. *Beth, I hear you callin'. . .*

Half a year later, I'm the youngest member of a rock band called Lenny Incline and the Cosmic Doodads. Under Lenny's expert tutelage, the power of my creative expression has blossomed. Unafraid of my sketchbooks, Lenny teaches me that my emotion-note combinations are called chords. Armed with this knowledge—and the support of my father, who drives me over to Lenny's house every Thursday—the basement becomes my laboratory, and Lenny, Eddie, Freddy, and Scotty become my personal scientific team. I learn about the power of chords, but more importantly I learn about the power that chords have over girls.

I walk onto the stage at Chip n' Dales at the Holiday Inn restaurant/bar for the second time in a month. My bandmates and I are picking up our first-place trophy for playing my favorite song in the annual Bell's Road Battle of the Bands competition.

With the trophy on the table between us, I spend the rest of the auspicious evening sipping soda while squeezed into a booth with the Doodads and a bunch of old ladies in their late twenties. In my own green disco shirt and plum-colored Members Only jacket, I feel like I've just won big at Bingo.

The hook sets deep. Girls like chords, and now that I'm in a band the syllogism makes complete sense. Thanks to Lenny, chords soon become my most powerful form of creative expression. Organized and ordered, emotional and versatile, like a spell or a prayer, they give me a means of self-expression that I never knew possible.

6

the acquisition of skipper

chesterfield, virginia / stamford, connecticut
august 24, 1979

WHEN ROOSEVELT DISAPPEARS ONE DAY, MY DAD TAKES IT AS AN OMEN that without his prized artistic assistant his roadkill sculptures that made him famous in graduate school aren't going to pay the bills in the real world. It marks the end of one era and the beginning of another. My dad needs to make some money, and he needs an assistant. Since the Cosmic Doodads broke up for artistic reasons—which involved a nursing home, a decanter of Baron cologne shaped like a Studebaker, and a candy striper—I've got nothing but time. It's time to step it up, which my father and I interpret in different ways.

"Oh no! Nuuuut again," my mother yells from the front porch. She rolls her eyes for the millionth time, realizing that my dad has drained their joint savings account yet again for some money-making scheme.

"Lissen, darlin'," my father yells from the rented truck, giving his head a little macaroni shake. "This time ain't like the rest. Mac 1 and Mac 2 need speech lessons, and your son needs to have someone pay for his bar mitzvah." He looks at me and winks. I wave. He nods. "This plan is based on necessitation. It's divine. It can't fail."

"Don't worry, Vera!" Uncle Friedo yells from the driver's seat, holding his hand out like a peace sign. "Michael's right. This plan is destined for victory."

My dad gives a whoop and slaps the door. He and Uncle Friedo give their macaroni bowls a tandem shake, and the truck takes off and disappears around the corner.

"God help us," my mom says. "Your father iz a whack job."

———

Three days later, my dad backs the truck into our driveway. He rolls the back door up, and the MACs, my mom, and I are astonished with what we see. The truck is brimming with every boy's childhood maritime dream: torpedo casings, ship's wheels, old life preservers, hatch cover tables, brass portholes, and even pieces of whale skin.

Over biscuits and beans, he tells us how he and his brother drove to Stamford, Connecticut, with a plan to slide into the family business.

"Cousin JoJo calls your Uncle Friedo last week. He says, 'Friedo, say *arrivederci* to your food stamps.' Friedo says, 'Why?' JoJo says, ''Cause we just got a contract to dismantle an entire fleet of World War II ships!'"

On the way home, they concoct a remarkable plan. My uncle, the marketeer of the two, decides that my dad, the builder of the two, should build a life-size ship to sell their nautical bounty.

The next weekend, my father and I meet my uncle and my cousin Roman (the same age and size as me) at the Southside Plaza Flea Market. Uncle Friedo explains how most businesses rent a small 12'x12' booth. We stop at a typical booth made from wooden two-by-fours and draped with white vinyl. It looks like a dirty garage inside, filled with old clothing, statues, and perfume decanters. In the corner, an old lady sits in a lawn chair, knitting. I smile at her, and she smiles back.

"Here's our space," my uncle says, turning around and throwing his arms out.

"Where's our space?" my dad says.

"Right there," he says, pointing to the entrance of the flea market.

"Right where?" my dad says. "There's no booths there."

"Exactly."

Uncle Friedo has rented the entire entrance of the market, nearly fifty booths.

During the next six days, my father builds the ship with my help. On the seventh day, *The Tinker* is christened with a case of Schlitz and two Fanta Orange sodas.

The ship is amazing. I walk across the make-believe dock fifty times, holding onto the rope railings and pretending like I can see the ocean below. On board are a hundred-gallon fish tank, cages filled with live rats, and a stereo system playing an eight track tape called *The Sounds of the Sea*, which has crashing waves and screaming seagulls.

Roman and I spend our first day aboard opening and closing every brass porthole on the quarterdeck, taking turns steering the ships wheel, and even chasing a few cockroaches in the captain's cabin. Regrettably, the boat doesn't catch on. In fact, it scares people. They come to the market for a more relaxed experience: to browse through colored glass knickknacks, eat freshly fried funnel cakes, and play a few games of pinball. *The Tinker* is out of place. As potential customers walk by, afraid to come aboard, a deep feeling of failure settles into my father.

My uncle, though, remains convinced that *The Tinker* is a marketing treasure and will catch on if promoted in the right way. For the sake of our food stamps, my father is convinced as well. Enter Project Thunder.

"Champ," my dad says one morning, "you're gonna be our quartermaster. Put this on." He throws an outfit onto my bunk bed. Within minutes, I look like the assistant manager at Long John Silver's.

"I sewed 'em last night," my father says.

"It feels kinda tight," I say.

Over my skintight black-and-white-striped one-piece bodysuit, I pull on my leather vest and black fry boots. My father adjusts my eye patch. He feels proud looking at a miniature version of himself.

"I feel like an elf, Dad," I say. I put on the captain's hat that looks like it's been squeezed with a vise. "I think I need a beard and a hook hand like you."

"Seamen come in all shapes and sizes, son," he says.

I suddenly feel nervous walking outside dressed like this. Some of the kids at school already make fun of me because our backyard looks like a junkyard. They call me Sanford and Son after the television show about a junkman with the same name.

"Come on, Champ. There's no time to feel like a fake. Your uncle Friedo and Roman are meeting us at the dock at o seven hundred."

In the mirror, I touch the huge pink ostrich feather that dangles off the top of my captain's hat. There's no doubt about it. Though my father lost his prized poultry assistant two weeks earlier, he just gained a slightly taller one. I run out to the van before any of the neighbors can see me.

We board *The Tinker* an hour before noon. Like me, Roman looks like a miniature version of his father. He's wearing a navy peacoat that drags on the ground and a sword in a scabbard attached to clothesline rope around his waist.

"Gentleman," my uncle says with a nod, "prepare for Project Thunder."

We sit at a hatch-cover table and eat McDonald's hash browns while Uncle Friedo briefs us on the details of his new marketing plan.

"See that bell?" my uncle says to me. "On Saturdays at high noon and on Sundays at one p.m. (after church time), you're gonna bang that thing like it's a French whore and yell, 'All hands, ahoy!' Understand?"

I smile and nod.

"Michael, that's when you're gonna run up on the plank and shout, 'It's a duel to the death!'"

"It's a thuel to the theth!" my dad snarls through his hash browns.

"Very good!" Uncle Friedo says. "Roman, that's your cue. You're gonna run out with this wooden box and open it."

Roman takes the box from his father and struggles to open it from the wrong end. Uncle Friedo opens it for him. Inside are two huge flint-lock pistols.

"Michael, at this point we'll meet each other under the EXIT sign, stand back to back, cock the pistols, and like two mad pirates walk ten paces," he says, standing. "*Uno, due, tre!* At ten, we turn and fire. Smoke'll rise. I shout 'Victory!' and when the smoke clears, I want you on the ground, moaning. Here, I want you to bite into this." Uncle Friedo hands my father a ketchup package. "Put it in your cheek."

My dad stuffs it in his mouth and bites down on the packet of ketchup, but nothing happens.

"Work on it," Uncle Friedo says. "One last thing. Before people disperse, you boys need to hand these coupons out. Stuff your pockets full of 'em. Ten percent off anything and everything aboard."

I love the idea. If it means we get to eat McDonald's every Saturday and Sunday, I'm all for it.

And so our duels begin. Crowds gather. My father learns an effective way to bite into a ketchup packet. Sales trickle in. My uncle is excited. My mom is more excited. By Halloween, the ship becomes the most popular destination at the market. As luck would have it, just as we're ready to bump Project Thunder to the next level, we attract our first actual shipmate: The Mysterious Stanley.

The Mysterious Stanley is a bowlegged, bald-headed, cross-eyed, fire-breathing magician, and he's a publicity and promotion dream machine. Huge crowds gather to watch his thirty-minute teaser act in front of our ship. Along with the success of Project Thunder, our inventory is fast declining.

The Mysterious Stanley eventually asks me to work as his assistant. For a few hours each weekend I go back and forth between playing quartermaster/cashier aboard *The Tinker* to assisting him.

Before Thanksgiving, Johnnie comes by the store two weekends in a row with her sisters. I'm embarrassed at first, but she holds my hand when I show her around the ship, and I forget about everything else. By the second weekend, I've become an accomplished hand-holder. The day after Thanksgiving, my father and uncle rent another truck and drive back to Connecticut to re-stock. I no longer feel like my father's sidekick. I feel like a pirate rock star, like the living reincarnation of Roosevelt.

Unbeknownst to any of us, though, mutiny is brewing. Some of the other vendors don't like the spectacle. They're jealous. They think *The Tinker* has removed the integrity of the market. One vendor in particular named Cooley Sr., a Victrola record dealer, files a complaint with the flea market authorities. His son Cooley Jr., a cop, is assigned to the case. Officer Cooley puts *The Tinker* under surveillance. A rumor spreads that having a fake shoot-out is against the law.

"Let's see 'em try to catch me," my dad says within earshot of Officer Cooley. "It's my constitutional right to re-enact a fake flintlock gun duel in front of my ship if I want."

Officer Cooley nearly chokes on his funnel cake.

～～

When our new stock arrives, it includes an entire line of small brass crustaceans. Roman and I hide them in every nook and cranny on board. It's perfect for the holiday season. With bright Christmas lights strung from stern to bow, the shiny, tiny crabs, lobsters, and shrimp reflect the lights brilliantly and throw a dazzling briny holiday cheer into the usual lethargic market.

Fresh hand-cut garland covers the plank, and from every doorway hang clusters of mistletoe harvested with Uncle Friedo's own shotgun. At the ship's wheel, my father has placed a life-size replica of Blackbeard dressed to look like Santa Claus. A concerned mother complained that the sculpture looked too fearsome. My father took the high road and rebutted, "Arrrgh, me matie, would you prefer I shove a burning cannon wick in your hair?"

Along with Blackbeard, nearly half a dozen horrifying kid-size elves have spread throughout the ship, attached to the crow's nest and peering out the portholes. My father constantly tells those who ask that these are Blackbeard's assistants, descendants from a dark tribe of elves with magic powers. Even Uncle Friedo agrees that my father has taken the pirate thing a little too far.

After a fight that nearly comes to blows, my father makes cheery, misshapen green elf outfits for Roman's little brother, Anthony, and my sisters. Through the Christmas season, dressed like banana leaves, they join the rest of our pirate family aboard for a few hours every Sunday and hand out coupons. Sunday soon becomes a delight for both Roman and me, because we take great pleasure in treating our siblings as captives and making them do the jobs that we hate doing.

I have another thing to look forward to on Sundays as well. During the holiday season, Johnnie's sister drops her off after church, and I get to spend my entire lunch break with her. Although I have yet to work out the logistics, getting her under one of the bunches of mistletoe becomes my main mission of the holiday season. This goal will come to haunt me as Christmas approaches.

One Sunday, at the end of one of my magician assistant shifts, the Mysterious Stanley asks me to empty his tin container of kerosene, which he uses for fire breathing. Typically I wouldn't mind making the long walk around the building to the Dumpster. But since I'm expecting Johnnie any minute and Roman and I have concocted a time-sensitive plan to get her under the mistletoe, dumping the kerosene into the toilet in the men's room will have to do.

An hour later, I'm still kissless despite walking under the mistletoe with Johnnie half a dozen times. We're sitting with our feet dangling over the side of *The Tinker*, watching my father begin one of his infamous harpoon-throwing contests below.

"Look lively there if yer bones have any value!" he yells and then heaves his harpoon toward a thick upturned hatch cover table leaning against the outer wall of the men's bathroom.

You can see where this is going. It hits, and the entire side of the building explodes.

"Arrr! This be good grog!" he exclaims.

Seconds after the explosion, Cooley Sr. emerges from the rubble with a black face and a hairdo like Albert Einstein.

With my dad's reputation for extreme marketing, Officer Cooley Jr. doesn't ask questions. He confiscates his hook hand, his flintlock pistol, the torpedo, and the harpoons. He tells the Mysterious Stanley that he has to go and takes my father away in the back of his squad car.

Two days before Christmas, and my father's life as a pirate as I know it is all but over. I feel horrible. My trivial romantic plot has put my father in jail. My sisters will never learn to talk right. I'll never get to have a bar mitzvah. Our Christmas will be ruined. Depressed, I spend the entire day wondering if Roosevelt ever failed my dad on such a colossal scale.

My dad is out of jail in three hours, and at dinner that night he's all but ready to sink the ship.

"Officer Cooley said he was keeping my things indefinitely," he says, stirring the peas on his plate.

"Vhy?" my mother says. "Vhat do they say happen?"

"That old man went in that bathroom to see a man about a horse, and when he unzipped, I dunno. I guess it caused a spark and some kind of peculiar chemical reaction."

Luckily for me and my family, the next morning, at breakfast, my father has a twinkle in his eye. This Christmas Eve twinkle will send *The Tinker* sailing toward the land of financial prosperity and pull me out of my self-induced romantic depression.

Around noon, Coach Walt comes over, and he and my father disappear into his studio. When they come out a few hours later, my father is wearing a tie and a sports jacket, which I've never seen him wear. His hair is pressed flat, and his beard is gone. He looks like a banker.

Coach Walt emerges from behind him, shirtless and wearing a grass skirt. His entire body is painted with tribal symbols, and he is dark, like my father painted him with wood stain, which is exactly what he did. Minwax Golden Oak Wood Stain to be exact.

"Meet Kooroong," my dad says, "my aborigine friend from the Chuck Atoll."

"*Ooobah stew koobast*," Coach Walt says and dances around. His legs look like coat hangers bending and unbending. He winks at me. "Don't worry. It's just me, Coach Walt."

Twenty minutes later, we're standing at the customer service desk at Pet World in Cloverleaf Mall, where my father worked the year before and where we got 73 of our 156 pets.

"The bird manager in?" my dad asks, leaning on the counter.

The girl pushes a button on her phone, and her voice booms from the ceiling. "Bird manager, bird manager, please come to the front. Bird manager, bird manager, please come to the front."

Seconds later, a man who also looks strangely like the reincarnation of Roosevelt approaches us. He has a few tufts of hair on top of his head that look like feathers; he holds his arms by his sides like wings; and he has a large round belly. He looks at my dad, then Kooroong, then me. Part of his cheek starts twitching.

"Kyle, meet Kooroong," my dad says.

The bird manager holds out his hand. Kooroong doesn't budge. My stomach tenses.

We follow the bird manager to the bird room, which is past the dog room, the cat room, the reptile room, and the fish room. Inside the bird room, the bird manager shuts the door behind us, which amplifies the already loud tweeting and flapping and seed-spitting sounds. My dad stands in front of a cage containing a large blue and gold parrot. The parrot walks over to the side of the cage like it knows my dad and bows its head. My dad gives it a scratch.

"*Bootay bootay kiya*," Coach Walt says.

"Are you sure?" my dad says.

Coach Walt nods.

"Kyle?" my dad says. "Kooroong says this parrot is very sick and will die within the next week."

The bird manager turns the color of a Coke can.

"Kooma say. Kooma say ring. Kooma say ringa ringa ding dong," Coach Walt says.

My father and Coach Walt proceed through a number of these exchanges in which Coach Walt says something unintelligible and my father interprets it. Each new phrase seems to hurt the bird manager more than the next, until eventually both of his cheeks start twitching.

"Kyle," my dad finally says. "Let me cut to the chase. Kooroong is the Avian Resources Management representative from the Chuck Atoll. He's in charge of the quality, inspection, and grading of all birds coming out of his country. He knows what you been up to. He knows you been a-wheeling and a-dealing in sick birds since you started. He even knows you been buying his sick birds on the cheap and then selling them at a high markup to your bird lovin' customers, who take the birds home only to have the poor critters die with no money-back guarantee."

Kyle loosens his tie and leans against the cages. His face has turned so red I think he might explode. I'm actually worried for him.

"Go on," he whispers and makes a brushing motion with his hand "Go on. Take him. Just take him."

The blue and gold macaw, which my father immediately names Skipper, rides home in the backseat with me. I'm ecstatic. Because of the circumstances surrounding the parrot's procurement—as far as I can tell no money was exchanged—my father suggests that the "acquisition of Skipper" should be our little secret. I can't agree more.

Perched on my father's shoulder on Christmas morning, Skipper gives my dad a grand purpose and seals his fate as a real pirate. After we open our gifts and sit down to our Christmas meal, my mother gives thanks. "Tank goodness my husband is not in jail spending Christmas."

"Amen," I say.

"Kooma say ringa ringa ding dong," Skipper says.

Skipper joins us aboard *The Tinker*. Both he and my dad become quite the media darlings. Re-stocking trips to Connecticut become the norm, and Uncle Friedo soon decides to move *The Tinker* into its own three-story building.

Thanks to Skipper and my dad's creative intuition, our days of food stamps have come to an end. My sisters learn to talk right. I finally get a kiss from Johnnie, and my mom gets what she's always wanted: a real hero.

I also become ten times the assistant that Roosevelt ever was.

7

the most beautiful sukkah in the entire world

chesterfield, virginia / henrico, virginia
may 10, 1980

IT STARTS WITH ICE-CREAM SANDWICHES AT MY GRANDPARENTS' HOUSE, but it quickly progresses to an argument about my bar mitzvah that ends up with me and my mom in her Galaxy 500 tearing down the interstate. Twenty minutes later, we're standing at the receptionist's desk at the Jewish Community Center. By the time we're back in the car, I'm signed up for Thursday afternoon Hebrew lessons, Sunday school, and Jewish basketball (whatever that means).

The following Thursday, my mom picks me up from school, and we begin a tradition that we'll follow for the next year. We drive to Harvey's, browse the aisles for an instant food item—for instance, a box of instant mashed potatoes, Jell-O Instant Pudding, or Rice-A-Roni, the San Francisco Treat—and select one from the rabbi's two-page list. Buying instant food items with my mom already feels like a family tradition because my father and I have spent so much time browsing for similar products for our trips to the Yukon.

Afterward, my mom drives us to Mishkan Shalom for my weekly Hebrew lesson. I have all kinds of questions about the lesson, but either she can't answer them, or she doesn't want to answer them, so we ride in silence. We turn off Huguenot Road at an oak tree sporting a deflated blue helium balloon and make our way down a long gravel road. As we approach the synagogue, I begin to understand why my mom can't answer my questions.

Mishkan Shalom takes as its disguise a white rancher house in the middle of the woods. Not only do no features distinguish it from any other house along Huguenot Road, but no sign announces its existence, and plywood covers all the windows.

We park beside a rusted green Volkswagen van and walk up to the door. It's worse than when my dad dropped me off for my first piano lesson with Mrs. Tyler. After knocking, my mom gives me a look.

"Come on," she says as she starts walking around the house.

"Where are we going?" I say, scared. "Can't we just leave?"

"No," she says. "Don't you hear that?"

Behind the house, a funny-looking man is bouncing a basketball. He's wearing high-cut gym shorts that give him what we now call moose knuckle, a macho man mustache, a Jewfro, a dirty yellow yarmulke, and black socks that go all the way up to his knees. He is wearing all-season sandals.

He lifts the ball to his chest and overshoots the basket—nothing more than a metal rim attached to a tree—which sends the ball flying into the woods and him chasing wildly after it. When he picks up the ball and returns, he sees us, smiles, and runs toward us.

"Shalom, y'all!" he says, waving. "Rabbi Harry Schmuley. You can call me Rabbi Harry." Yeah. He puts the ball under his elbow, shakes my mom's hand, then my hand, and then wipes his forehead with his arm. The irrevocable smell of body odor immediately sticks to me and everything else in the immediate vicinity.

"You're my first customers," he says. My mom introduces us and holds out a box of Honey Maid cinnamon grahams, but he walks right past us as if he didn't hear her, motions for us to follow him, and continues to talk. "How could I resist a sudden booming bar mitzvah industry? Six bar mitzvahs. Tax-free. No overhead."

He informs us that six families in total belong to Congregation Mishkan Shalom. He's from Montana. He's single. His 365-day contract requires him to teach Hebrew, conduct Sunday school, and coach the basketball team. We shouldn't worry about the synagogue's state of disrepair because the congregation has purchased the land that the house sits on—but not the house itself—so it will remain locked except during bar mitzvahs. As we climb into his van, he tells us that he lives in it and will teach Hebrew lessons and take care of most of his rabbinical responsibilities from inside.

"Don't worry," he says. "I have a very good Johnson & Johnson Safe Travels First Aid Kit."

My mom gives me another look, but I'm no longer scared. I like the rabbi's midget-size refrigerator and the itchy bench seat. Except for the creepy smell of B.O. that permeates everything in the van, it all seems really cool.

"One more thing," he says. "Next week is Sukkot, so, instead of the usual Hebrew lesson and instant food item, I'm meeting all the boys here, and we're going to build a fort," Rabbi Schmuley says.

My mom nods. I raise my hand.

"Question?" the rabbi says.

"Are the other guys nice?" I ask.

"Shoot, yes," he says. "They're a great group of guys."

As my mom and I drive away, the rabbi yells out, "So, bring your working clothes and sleeping bag next week because after we build our sukkah we'll be sleeping in the sukkah under the stars and contemplating what it means to be good Jews."

~~~

Back at my grandparent's house, over ice-cream sandwiches, I tell my grandfather about the fort, spending the night under the stars, and Rabbi Harry. He tells me that the fort is called a sukkah. It can't be more than thirty feet tall, and it must be made of "organic material of the earth but no longer from the earth."

"What do you mean?" I ask.

"Twigs and branches that you pick up off the ground are OK. Lumber and plastic is not so OK," he says.

During the next week, I deliberate over the bare-bones basics of my grandfather's holiday explanation. If a thirty-foot sukkah will make me a good Jew, then a bigger sukkah will make me an even better Jew. The next week, along with my overnight bag, I arrive with my hundred-foot extension cord and my father's electric chain saw.

After saying hello to the parents, the rabbi locks himself in his van to attend to his rabbinical duties, and the rest of us run free in the woods. Within fifteen minutes, I have five new best friends, all gathered around my overnight bag.

"Cool beans," Chamster says.

"No way!" says Jujube.

"Do you know how to use it?" Boobenstein asks.

"I help my dad cut wood every winter," I say.

"Do you think Rabbi Harry'll be able to hear it?" says Boobenstein.

"Are you kidding me?" Jujube says. "He can't even hear his own farts."

Everyone laughs.

"Is Poulan your name?" Abracadabra says, reading the name off the saw.

"You ignoramus," Chamster says. "It's the name of the saw."

"My last name is Coleman," I say.

"Coleman doesn't sound Jewish," says Boobenstein.

"That's because it's my dad's name," I say.

"He's only half Jewish," says Chamster.

"Yeah, but when I tell people my name they always hear Goldman," I say.

"Goldman is Jewish," says Jujube.

"Definitely," Boobenstein says.

"How can he have a bar mitzvah if he's only half Jewish?" says Abracadabra.

"Doofus," Jujube says. "If his mom is Jewish, that makes him Jewish."

"That's the Halacha math," says Boobenstein. "But the Israel Law of Return math says if you have one grandmother who's Jewish, then it makes you Jewish."

"Is your grandma Jewish?" Chamster asks.

I nod. "So is my mom."

"His dad is a Hell's Angel," Jujube says.

"Are you serious?" says Boobenstein.

"He rides a chopper," I admit.

"Cool," Boobenstein says.

"But what half of him will get the bar mitzvah?" says Abracadabra.

Chamster hits Abracadabra, and he falls over.

When I take down the first fifty-foot pine tree to the utter awe of my Jewish consorts, you would have thought that I had killed Goliath. No group of guys howled so loudly since my father scored the winning run during the softball showdown. My Jewish soul immediately grows a few inches.

But no one considers how we'll move the tree once it's down, so my soul immediately shrinks to half its normal size. We try and try but find the task impossible.

"Cut off the branches," Jujube finally suggests.

Once I start cutting off the branches and the guys start running them back to the synagogue, the situation starts looking up.

"Keep 'em coming, Jeff. Rabbi Harry's smiling ear to ear in the van," Boobenstein says.

Once the first tree is stripped, I cut down another and another and another, and we follow the same routine. I cut, and the guys carry. Everything's dandy . . . until Boobenstein's father makes a surprise visit and catches me mid-lumberjack pose: my foot holding down a wily branch and the chain saw chewing and spitting up chunks of pine tree all around me. He looks like he's seen a ghost and promptly reports me to Rabbi Schmuley.

Terrified, I immediately turn off the chain saw. Abracadabra appears and tells us that Mr. Boobenstein is recommending that the rabbi call the police for the destruction of private property. My new friends are of no help whatsoever. I drop the saw and run. I zigzag past trees, trip on tree roots, fall in a hole, and run in a circle before I find myself under Rabbi Harry's basketball rim. I run straight for the oil tank behind the synagogue, leap onto it, and pull myself onto the roof. There I lay flat against the shingles and attempt to make myself invisible.

By now, everyone is calling for me. Butterflies are buzz-bombing my stomach. The more they call, the more powerful I feel.

Finally, everyone gathers around the sukkah, which is nearly complete. Chamster says I probably hitchhiked home. Jujube thinks that I probably fell in an abandoned mine shaft. Mr. Boobenstein apologizes. Then silence descends upon the scene while everyone waits for the rabbi to speak. Mr. Boobenstein expects the rabbi to make an example of me. I have mixed feelings. I know I'm not a bad kid—I'm simply trying to express myself and connect with a spiritual truth in my own way.

"This may very well be the most beautiful sukkah in the entire world," the rabbi finally says. Everyone agrees.

That's when Abracadabra spots me. He waves to me, and I stand up and wave back. Mr. Boobenstein sees me and, assuming that I'm going to jump, starts screaming. Wrapped up in the drama of it all, I pretend like I'm going to jump. I flap my arms and bend my legs and yell, "Ooooooh! Ooooooh! Ooooooh!"

Time speeds up. The rabbi begs me to come down. Mr. Boobenstein runs to his car and calls the police on an early version of a cell phone, which looks like a box of cereal with an antenna. The police arrive and call my grandfather. My grandfather arrives and takes me home, making me sit in the back of his Dodge Duster. As punishment, there will be no more ice-cream sandwiches that night or for many nights to come.

Close to midnight, at my grandparents' house, my grandfather gets up and opens the front door. After a while, he taps his pipe in his ash tray, and then the room to my door opens.

"Get dressed," he says. "You are going with the rabbi."

I climb into Rabbi Harry's van, and we rumble back to the synagogue. He tells me that he is a diehard one-for-all-all-for-one sort of guy. He has made an arrangement with Mr. Boobenstein and my grandfather that I will use a portion of my bar mitzvah money to purchase three new seedlings and plant them the following year.

Back at the synagogue, I join my friends inside the most beautiful sukkah in the entire world. Under the heavens, we participate in an ancient and important Hebrew tradition. The rabbi hands out Styrofoam cups, and we drink unlimited amounts of Fresca. Then he hooks up his tiny black-and-white television to my extension cord, and we watch Steve Martin host *Saturday Night Live*.

8

the hornet conspiracy

chesterfield, virginia / powhatan, virginia
june 11, 1980

WHILE MY MOTHER BOTHERS WITH THE LAST DETAILS OF MY BAR MITZVAH, my father loads his cheek with Red Man, our truck with the Jon boat, and his cooler with enough bait to feed all the fish in China.

Like everything he plans with his go-big-or-go-home Sicilian bravado, this pre-bar mitzvah fishing trip will be memorable, inconvenient, and painful. My last seven birthday fishing trips each ended in some bizarre accident. In one of my old sketchbooks, I've listed each fishing accident according to date, type of disaster, location, and possible long-range consequences to my health.

I eat my Wheaties and drink my morning Pepsi in silence. I don't want to go. My dad, the river, and I have history. The day before a once-in-a-lifetime event isn't the time to flirt with fate and the literal meaning of my transition into manhood.

"Michael, dis trip, nuh-huh. It makes me near-vus," my mother says. "Dju really tink it's a good idea to go fishing the day before his bar mitzvah?"

"Come on, Vera," my dad protests. "You really think a boy should be sittin' around the house cooped up like a bump on a log?"

Put to a vote then and there, I would have cast mine for the bump on the log.

"It'll be the last time I get to take my boy fishing," he continues.

"Vhat do you mean?" my mother says, suddenly surprised. I'm surprised, too. Is this some sort of prophecy? What does he know that we don't know?

"After tomorrow, he'll be a *man*, Vera."

"Oh," she says, relaxing a little.

I spoon cereal into my mouth and chew. It's true. According to Jewish law, come Saturday I will be a man—a variable and abstract idea, kind of like owls to the men who frequent Hooters.

"Besides, look at 'im. He looks like Dracula. Some sun'll do him good." He slaps my shoulder, and I choke.

He's right, though. I am white, very white. I'm literally pale with fear. The last trip ended in the emergency room. A treble hook from a Zara Spook lure impaled my ear so deep that I fear it damaged my esophagus. The doctor's pliers broke as he squeezed them against the hook, and my father laughed while I made sipping sounds like I was drinking hot liquid out of a straw. I can't muster the enthusiasm to go on another painful fishing trip.

But there's another reason. More and more, these sacred trips include large doses of liquid sacrament from eight-ounce aluminum cans. Lately, the cooler has held less bait and more trouble. When I was younger and didn't know any different, midnight jaunts to Harvey's Market and subsequent rides to the Yukon didn't matter. Now my dad's drinking stirs concern deep inside me and causes me more and more anxiety. If there's one thing I know, it's that a drinking person is not himself.

"It vould have to be jus' a short trip, Michael?" my mom says. "He needs a good sleep so he can read his Torah."

My father nods. I've lost. Come morning, we're going fishing.

❧

We park at Bailey's Bridge and slide the *Reel Lady,* our ten-foot ten-dollar Jon boat, into a calm stretch of the James River. The morning fog hangs so thick that we can barely see. As we push off from the bank and float across the surface of the water, it's like we're traveling quietly through the sky. It's not a good sign. The river seems calm, too calm, like before a storm.

As we float on, I imagine that the *Reel Lady* is the envy of the animal kingdom, set to impress every crawfish, bullfrog, and water lily that we pass. Unable to afford a real bass boat, my father—resourceful artist that he is—transformed ours completely. Painted pink camouflage, with turquoise metallic flakes so she looks tough and pretty at once, she reminds me of Faylene Cole, one of the prettiest girls in my math class. Faylene wears lipstick and fancy dresses during the week and spends the weekend in bib overalls deer hunting with her brothers.

Like a woman's purse, *Reel Lady* has dozens of secret compartments: for our rods, the cooler, life preservers, the huge airplane battery that runs the motor, my father's wallet, sunglasses, and truck keys. She even has secret compartments that hold other secret compartments.

I'm not quite sure if it's for aesthetic reasons or pure physics, but on the two bench seats my father has attached two bucket seats on pedestals from his once-prized Chevrolet Corvair. Casting from so high up makes me feel like I'm fishing from a pier on a luxury unicycle.

The *Reel Lady,* like any real lady, is defined by her accessories, though. She comes with a depth finder, CB, radio, two pirate flags, three towel racks, six fog lights, a thin layer of AstroTurf that runs the entire length of the boat, and seven antennae, which from afar look like a drag queen's false eyelashes.

We spend the morning as usual: casting, catching, and releasing a few small bass and removing knots. My father talks about his latest artistic endeavor called *Girl Watchers,* which involves attaching ceramic male heads to hand trucks and placing them around the city. Lost in worry, I dig into a bag of pork rinds. The cooler is making me tense. He hasn't had his first drink of the morning, but I'm worried about when he will. The first drink always leads to the second drink, which leads to the third drink, which will lead to me carrying the *Reel Lady* up to the truck by myself again and driving us home illegally—again.

Around noon, we pull ashore and have lunch. The drink can no longer be postponed.

"Get me a drink out the cooler, Champ," my father finally says, his voice rescuing me from one state of worry and taking me to another.

"You think somebody could know you're Jewish if you don't tell them?" I say, trying to throw him.

"Hellfire, Jeff! I don't know. Is this some kind of riddle?"

My attempt to postpone his first drink with small talk needs practice. The topic is important to me nonetheless. Ever since the Sakovitch sisters lured me to an empty lot with the promise of a French kiss and beat me up, I've been holding onto the feeling that being Jewish connects directly somehow to guilt, shame, and something strangely sexual. Since it happened, Tina Sakovitch's words, "You kilt God's son," keep rolling around in my head. I just can't figure out how she found out I was Jewish.

"It's just stuff I was thinking about," I say. "You don't have to yell."

"I'm not yelling!" he yells. "But I suppose if you got a Jewish name like my friends the Mermelsteins, people'd know. I mean, if you were wearing a beanie or had long sideburns or something, they'd know, too. What's gotten into you?"

"Nothin'," I lie.

"Well, I think you been out in the sun too long. Just hand me a drink. You better grab you one while you're at it. Your momma'll kill me if you get dehydrated."

I open the secret compartment that holds the cooler and reach for a drink. Beside a foam container of night crawlers sit four Fanta Orange sodas—nothing else. I pull out a soda, twist off the cap, and hand him the bottle with a smile.

"You know, I get to have a Hebrew name tomorrow?" I say.

"That right?" my father says, swallowing a mouthful of soda. "I reckon if you're worried you better not pick one that sounds too Jewish, huh?"

"I guess," I say, feeling a little lighter. My anxiety, it seems, has been all for naught.

--~---

With the day nearly over, the electric motor pushing us silently toward the final stretch of river, I make a few final casts and laugh to myself.

"You think maybe we turned a corner with our luck?" I ask.

"Just 'cause you didn't end up with a Zara Spook stickin' out your head?" he says.

"Or because you didn't fall overboard because the seat post broke or the *Reel Lady* didn't almost sink because you forgot to put in the drain plug," I say.

"I suppose," he says, and we share a laugh.

"Last cast," I say.

"Last cast," he says, already slinging his line out. "Make it a good one, Champ. It'll be the last one you make as a boy."

My father begins to reel. I barely pay attention as I bring my own rod forward to cast. My line flies deep into a low hanging tree and disappears. I pull once before I realize I'm snagged. Without a word exchanged, my father intuitively pulls the *Reel Lady* around and heads for the tree. He steers us closer. I reel my line tighter. Then, under the tree, he takes my rod and follows the end of my line into the branches until he disappears.

With my back away from him, I don't understand why he's suddenly yelling about the Democrats. But as my end of the boat moves under the tree, I find myself looking up at a huge empty Winnie the Pooh–size hornets' nest. A great flood of anxiety and panic washes over me.

Thousands of buzzing hornets cover my dad—so many that he looks like he's fallen into a bowl of chocolate sprinkles. As he rolls from one side of the *Reel Lady* to the other, the ball of hornets, like a huge ocean wave, moves with him. When he rolls onto his front side, the hornets form a huge point and move together to sting him on his bottom. As he rolls onto his bottom and yells more things about the Democrats that I don't understand, they sting him on his front.

At long last, he rolls right out of the *Reel Lady* and dives into the river. When he emerges on the opposite bank, the scene pauses. The hornets form a tight black ball that dangles in the air. Then they come straight for me.

First I scream like a little girl. Then I wave my arms wildly, each of my hands slashing through the air as if I'm holding invisible daggers. Like my father, I roll on one side, and they sting me on the other. I roll on my front, and they sting me on my bottom. I roll on my bottom, and they sting my front. Tiny stingers poison every inch of my skin.

"Jump! Jump over! *Jump!*" my father yells.

But I don't. I continue to slash my hands through the dark buzzing dots. Finally, I pull his army coat over my head—which ingeniously traps the hornets inside—and I twist around until I trip over the seat and topple overboard into the river.

When I surface, I doggie-paddle up to my father. Drunk on hornet venom and adrenaline, we hold onto a tree root and laugh. We laugh like it's our last laugh left. Our laughter shakes the leaves from the trees, the crows from the branches, and the clouds from the sky.

As we laugh, the boat becomes a trick horse in a spaghetti western, answering only to the whistle of her cowboy. Mysteriously, the *Reel Lady* floats right up to us, and we climb back in.

We drive home like statues. I keep my hands on the dashboard and stare forward. My dad steers carefully, his arms like a piece of machinery.

"It don't hurt 'less I move," I keep saying.

"Then don't move," he keeps saying.

I don't have it in me to tell him that every time the truck hits a bump it hurts. As I bounce in and out of pain, I think about my fight with the

Sakovitch sisters and how I limped home and cleaned myself up before anyone noticed. I think about what Rabbi Harry said about how the painful fates that befall the Jewish people are often interpreted as signs of God's displeasure. I think about the conversations I've been having with the guys at the synagogue, about their nicknames, about my Hebrew name.

Abracadabra suggested my nickname be Semicolon because if I shortened my middle name, Markous, it would be Mark. "Mark and Semicolon are both very grammar-like," he said. Chamster, had he overheard the suggestion, would have intervened by calling Abracadabra an "ignoramus."

I think about how a mark made by a pencil on a piece of paper—like when I draw—is a lot like a slash mark. Then I think about the word "slash" and how it's made from two of my favorite letters of the hebrew alphabet, שׁ (Sin) and ל (Lamed).

I push my tongue against my teeth and make the "S" sound quietly, thinking that Sin looks like a three-tined pitchfork with a beauty mark, like it could pick up something important and hold onto it with style. I click my tongue and make the "L" sound for Lamed and know, like a lightning bolt, that it easily could destroy anything it wanted.

Then I think about my mom's maiden name, Ashe, and how if I combine her maiden name with my two favorite Hebrew letters it spells, "S-l-Ash." I see each of my hands slashing through the hornets. The name Slash feels more powerful than Markous or even Jeffrey. When I get home, I'll add Slash to my sketchbook's growing list of potential Hebrew names.

I rewind the events of the day in my head. I think about my father's role in my transition into manhood. Somehow it feels like our accident was no accident, but rather his own unorthodox version of "hills medicine."

Since I can remember, this has been how my dad has shown his love for me: By putting me in harm's way somehow he has made me fearless. "You get hit by a pitch," he always said at baseball practice, "you walk it off." "You get bit by a snake," he always said when we hunted, "you cut an 'X' on the bite and suck out the venom."

It's fitting that he rolls out one more lesson on the way to my bar mitzvah the next day. When he sees me pulling at my tie because I'm so swollen that I barely fit into my suit, he looks in the rearview mirror and says, "If it doesn't kill you, Champ, it only makes you stronger." I'm not so sure he knows what he's talking about.

Despite my mom's twenty-four-hour silence to punish my father, the day goes off without a hitch. No one even blinks when Rabbi Harry uses my chosen Hebrew name, Slash, throughout the service. Even Mr. Boobenstein, who publicly declares that I'm proof why mixed marriages don't work, uses my Hebrew name when he shakes my hand and congratulates me.

Later that week, my father and I drive out to the synagogue. In the woods, near where I gave my chain-saw demonstration, we plant a couple dozen seedlings using a tiny, green trowel. This isn't exactly manhood, but it's close, and I'm happy that we've found this new place together.

9

a vue shtet geschreiber

henrico, virginia
august 11, 1981

"How could it happen?" my grandfather asks. He puffs on his pipe, blows the smoke into the kitchen, and hands my name-change form back to my mother. They've been talking about me for the last ten minutes. I'm on my hands and knees in the laundry room, my head against the sliding wooden door, eavesdropping.

"Say it again," my grandfather says.

"Slashtipher," my mother says.

"Slatstoofer?" he repeats. "I cannot believe the rabbi lets him choose that for his Hebrew name."

"He wants to be called Slash," my grandmother says.

"Slats?" he says.

"Oh, come on, Frederick!" my grandmother says. "Listen to vhat your daughter is sayink. His name is Slashtipher. Is like Christopher!"

"How does he come up with this?" he says.

"Come up with this? Look in the mirror. You remember when Marcel changed his name?" my grandmother says.

"You mean our friend Marcel Marceau? Of course. He could not do in the war with a name like Marcel Mangel?"

"And how many times do we change our name when the Resistance put us in prison?"

"But is different. All Jewish men were required to sign the name Israel on all legal documents. All Jewish women, the name Sarah."

"You said to me, 'Hilda, it is no longer just a Jewish fight. It is an artistic fight as well.'"

"Well, what?" my grandfather says.

"Your grandson is a man now. A creative young man."

A few minutes of silence pass while my grandfather puffs. I shift my weight from one knee and onto the other.

—◦—

I remember the silence that filled the lawyer's office. Douglas Young, the young lawyer who handled my name change, was silent, too. Which made me nervous. If he had said, "No," I would have fought for it.

"It's like a demarcation," Douglas finally said. "You know what that is, son?"

I nodded, though I had no idea what he meant. The huge leather office chair started to swallow me. I tried to shift, but my skin was stuck to the leather.

"It's what ladies do," he said, sensing my cluelessness. "You know, when they want to keep their last name when they get married? It's like saying you're half Jewish *slash* half non-Jewish. Don't worry, kid. I get it."

I laughed a fake laugh. I wanted to seem more grown-up than I was. He put his pen to the form to sign it . . . then stopped. "Son, the judge is more likely to accept your name change form if you regal it up a bit. I suggest you add 'tipher' to the end to make it sound more official."

"Slash. Tiffer?" I said.

"One word: Slashtipher."

I mumbled it to myself a few times while he tore open a package of peanuts, emptied them into his can of Dr. Pepper, and raised it to his mouth. I nodded and slid an envelope across his desk that contained my bar mitzvah money.

Thirty days later, the name-change form arrived in the mail, approved and signed by Judge Chapman. It was treated no differently than my dad coming home with a dead llama slung across the front of his motorcycle.

— ⁓

"Jeffrey!" my grandfather yells.

"My name is Slash!" I yell back.

"Whoever you are, come in here."

I slide the kitchen door open and walk up to the table.

"Turn around," my mother says. She hired a seamstress to sew the name "Slash" in yellow silk letters on the back of my jean jacket. I feel like a rock star. My grandparents touch the fabric and then start arguing in French. I stand there with my hands in my pockets, not understanding a word.

"Come with me, little Marcel," my grandfather finally says.

I follow him through the living room, though the dining room, and into the hallway. In front of the bathroom, he pulls a green cord from the ceiling, and the attic door unfolds and crashes to a stop just before it takes off my head. A rush of hot air descends. He climbs up the ramshackle stairs. I follow.

"Stay in the middle or you will fall through the ceiling," he says.

At the top I stiffen my body and stand in place. Male torsos surround us, some draped with fabric, others with half-made suit jackets with thin paper patterns pinned to them. One is wearing a tie, another an unfinished vest.

"What are these?" I ask, instantly sweating. The air is so thick and hot I can barely breathe.

"All these I made," my grandfather says while using his hand like a hairbrush to get the sweat off his bald head. He bends down and moves a stack of fabric. Underneath lies a sewing machine. Other sewing machines lie hidden under stacks of fabric.

"Here it is," he says. He pulls a piece of dirty yellow cloth out from the stack and unfolds it.

"A star," I say.

"I was once required to sew these onto our clothing. I spent the last of our money buying this expensive fabric from India. Only the best. Your grandmother called me crazy. Who would ever think I go to sewing these stars to dreaming about becoming a tailor to the stars?" He gets a faraway look in his eyes and stares behind me. He's gone back or perhaps forward in time. When he returns, he smiles. I smile back. I don't really understand what any of this means.

He takes the yellow star from me and stands. I follow him out of the attic.

Downstairs the cold air makes me feel prickly. At the kitchen table, I sit between my mother and grandmother. My grandfather lights his pipe and places the star on the table. With its creases and folds it looks more like an old handkerchief.

"What is all that stuff upstairs?" I ask.

"Your grandfather wanted to move us to Hollywood," my mother says. "He wanted to make clothing for all the movie stars."

"Who are we to talk about name changing?" my grandmother finally says. She stands and begins to make dinner.

"*A Vue Shtet Geschreiber,*" my grandfather says, laughing. This is his favorite Yiddish phrase. It means, "Where is it written? Who says so?" In other words, who says it has to be this way—why can't it be the other way?

10

high school musical

chesterfield, virginia / williamsburg, virginia
january 7, 1983

ALTHOUGH I'M OFFICIALLY A MAN—WITH A NEW NAME AND CLOTHING
line to go with it—I hold onto my insatiable desire for sports. Much to my
mother's displeasure, the piano didn't prove a strong enough distraction.

Despite the challenges of sipping dinner through a straw for the rest
of my life, which my mom assures me will happen if I ever play football,
I become especially fond of playing tackle football with the Atari gang in
the empty lot beside our house. Accordingly, my dreams bounce back and
forth between sports and art. I'm either leaving the field on a stretcher in
Texas Stadium as the quarterback for the Dallas Cowboys or playing the
entire halftime show in a full body cast as Bruce Springsteen's keyboardist.

My mother comes up with the idea of art sleepovers. These regular
Friday night events consist of me and my guy friends checking out stacks
of football books from the library and then spending the entire night
drawing football pictures.

At the kitchen table, long after my parents have gone to bed, we trace
pictures of football players and live vicariously through our drawings. The
uniforms make the players look like superheroes. I love the way my hand

feels as it draws the face masks, each like a maze and different from the next. I especially love drawing the football players' hands.

My father framed my charcoal drawing of Lynn Swann, a wide receiver for the Pittsburgh Steelers. I copied the classic photo of him from Super Bowl X. As he falls to the ground, his hands reach out for a ball that descends from heaven.

Art sleepovers fail to have the desired effect, however. In fact, they only make me hungry for more football. So when I get to high school, I take the entirety of my love of football—and redirect it. I ask Uncle Friedo for his old silver alto saxophone, and I join the high school marching band.

I start as seventh chair alto sax and finish as eighth—because Charlotte Regalberry transfers into the band from another school—but every Friday night the high school marching band takes the field at halftime. It's the only way to get close to the game that I love. It's a compromise, like starting as a janitor with the hope of one day working my way up to president, but the drawback is far from daunting. It helps me develop my band strategy. I plan to use my position as an alto sax player as a stepping-stone to something greater. Though I can't keep a beat to save my life, I dream with every fiber of my being of joining the drum section.

The only person I tell is Golden Joy, an exchange student from Tokyo. She's one year younger than me and a flute player, first chair. Goldie has beautiful black hair—the same color my father makes by mixing Prussian Blue, Alizarin Crimson, and Burnt Umber on his palette.

"The drummers are the closest thing to football players in the band," I tell her.

We're sitting side-by-side on the sofa in her host family's living room. All the lights are on—two end-table lamps, the overhead light, some sort of wall lamp—and we're watching *Soul Train* on TV, holding hands.

"They look like gladiators going off to do battle in their uniforms," I continue. "Full of bravado, addicted to pain, and thin on brain cells. I mean, compared to them, we look like we're going to work as cashiers at Burger King."

Goldie nods, smiles, and adjusts one of her shoulder pads. She loves wearing shoulder pads in all her shirts even though they've been banned from fashion. (She even wears them in her T-shirts, much the same as a football player does). This is why I have fallen for her.

"That is because the drummers are at least twenty years older than everyone else in the band," she finally says.

With my track record with piano teachers, my dad will never even entertain the idea of a drum teacher. But that doesn't matter. Goldie and I keep my dream alive. It's my dream, after all. There are some things about us that our parents never know.

Luckily, during my sophomore year, at Christmas break, circumstances allow me to capture my dream much like a linebacker breaks through the offensive line and sacks the quarterback in the backfield. Our band is invited to play in the Williamsburg Christmas Eve parade. We meet in the high school parking lot on the frigid morning of the event and board a yellow bus bound for historic colonial Williamsburg. Once there, we unload and walk to our assigned places on the cobblestone street.

In front of us stands a group of World War II veterans: a chipper, glowing bunch of old men in gray-green soldier's outfits and red triangle hats. Behind us sit a dozen Shriners in tiny cars, their chins resting on their knees. Each one is wearing his own uniquely shaped hat that looks like an upside-down bathroom trash can with a graduation tassel attached to the top. Our rambunctious, disorganized Burger King–looking band of fifty teens squeezes in between.

The parade begins without warning. Despite our raspy, jumbled, squeaky start, we settle into "White Christmas." As instructed, we repeat the song over and over during our 45-minute march.

Everything's going along fine as we near the alto saxophone section solo (the chromatic descension) for the sixth time—when it happens. It's hard to notice at first with the sound of the Shriner cars behind us and the sound of the lead veteran calling out to the crowds with his bullhorn, but something sounds amiss. The longer we march, the more it apparent it becomes. The *oomph* we had at the start has died.

Jimmy Tisdale, our tuba player, notices first. He marches sideways and looks back. Pretty soon we're all marching sideways. About half a block away and dropping further away from us with every measure, our drum section—in its entirety—is brawling.

The heavy chrome and brass snares lie strewn across the road. Instead of beating the animal skin drum heads with their thick mallets and wooden sticks, the drummers are beating one another. Elbows pump, fists fly, and every once in a while a swatch of polyester uniform flies into the air. As the rest of us march on, a huge void forms between us and the drummers.

With little time to react, the lead Shriner speeds in front of the other cars and aims his own car directly at the pileup. As he nears, he leans to one side, pulls on the chin strap of his trash-can hat with one hand and creates the most spellbinding four-wheeled phenomenon ever witnessed. His car instantly flips. Defying gravity, he hovers over the drummers as if his car is hanging from a string tied to a cloud. When he lets go of his chin strap, his car magically lowers itself into the head of the bass drum. The undercarriage of his car forms the perfect ramp.

The remaining gaggle of Shriners, seemingly trained for just such an emergency, fall immediately into formation. One at a time, they steer toward the ramp and leap the entire accident. As the Shriners become airborne, the little tassels on their bathroom trash-can hats wave like the tails of comets. Everyone in sight has gone wide-eyed. We have all just experienced a vision as rare as a Loch Ness Monster sighting.

—◦—

After Christmas break, our band instructor, Mr. London, announces, nearly in tears, that the entire drum section has been suspended. We later find out that the brawl stemmed from a dispute over whether Mr. London's Chrysler Fifth Avenue had a straight six or a V6 engine.

My long-awaited moment of retribution arrives. Anticipating his next move like a linebacker watching the eyes of the quarterback, I quickly raise my hand. In an instant, I leap from seventh chair alto sax to first chair bass drum player. I am more than merely a bass drum player, though. I am the entire drum section. The positions for the cymbal player, snare player, and tenor drum player have been deleted. Our new drum battery includes only me and my bass drum.

When Mr. London calls me to the front of the classroom and hooks the drum harness over me, I fall over like a turtle. At 81 pounds, I am possibly the smallest person in the history of the world to become a bass drum player, Mr. London notes, saying, "That's a mighty long time because the history of the world includes the Old Testament, the New Testament, and the age of the dinosaurs."

He sends me down to the shop room. Mr. Jenkins makes me two metal kickstands that fit on either side of my belt so when I march on the field I won't fall over.

For seven glorious weeks, I bask in faux football hero glory. Every song from the "Theme to Rocky" to the Go Go's "We Got the Beat" sounds exactly the same on the bass drum and doesn't require that I know how to keep a beat. I just need to bang my huge mallets against the drum when Mr. London claps his hands.

Then one day the drummers mysteriously reappear. Mr. London demotes me to my usual spot. I never recover. That summer I quit, and everything during summer break becomes the color of a pencil drawing.

Depressed at the loss of my dream, I hide my saxophone in the back of my closet and stack the laundry basket on top of it. I go back to sleeping under the piano. I gorge on Moon Pies and Ho Hos. In my depression, I blossom from an 81-pound weakling into a 90-pound weakling. My mother grows increasingly concerned and asks other teachers for advice.

On the last day of summer, Dick Monday, the varsity wrestling coach at my school, a speech teacher, and my mother's entrusted friend, calls and tells her there's a position open on the squad for a 98-pound wrestler. When he speaks to me on the phone, he tells me that he's seen me at the pool over the summer and considers me the perfect young man for the job.

"Vhat do you think?" my mother says when I hang up the phone.

"I don't know, Mom. I'll have to wear those stupid tights that look like a girl's one-piece bathing suit and those strange ear protectors. They look like a yarmulke thong."

"I am letting you play a danzherous spot," she says. "You should consider that my decision is a gift given from God."

Despite the fashion complications, she's right. I accept the gift.

On the first day of practice, within minutes of taking to the mat, Coach Monday calls us ladies. I'm in love. He makes us run up and down the bleachers until I throw up in my mouth. When he makes us lie under the wrestling mat for thirty minutes, I lose consciousness—twice. I've finally found my calling.

During my first match, I become the only AA league wrestler in known competitive history to be knocked out of his tights during a match. Coach Monday calls it an anatomical enigma, though I don't know what he means. Granted, my opponent only half pulled me out of my uniform as I tried to squirm out of a move known as the Seatbelt Single. I don't remember the rest; I passed out. Goldie says that when Coach Monday sent two teammates to pull me off the mat it caused my uniform to end up around my knees. The same front-porch scenario that greeted Coach Walt greeted Coach Monday. My mother stands on the front porch and says, "Vhat is this?" Coach Monday in a rare moment has nothing but silence to offer.

By the end of my wrestling career, I will become the only wrestler in the history of our school for two years straight to lose every match within the first five seconds. Actually, if you calculate the amount of time it takes to inhale and exhale five times, this is how long I actually spent on the mat during my junior and senior year.

Coach Monday doesn't understand it. I come to every practice. I know the drills. I love wrestling. He loves having a wrestler named Slash on the team. My mom thinks it's my acne medication that makes me weak. I think I know what it is, but I'm not sure until the last match of my senior year.

When I step onto the wrestling mat for my twenty-fifth and final time, I hear a faint sound in the distance, like an evening breeze rustling through the trees. It's soft, barely audible. As I line up before my opponent and snap my head gear into place, the sound hints at something powerful enough to change my destiny, like a near-brush with a category 4 hurricane or a car accident. Within seconds of the ref's whistle, the sound grows so loud, so clear that it blasts into my subconscious and shakes me to my core.

"If you play SPOTS, you vill gat paIr OF LIES!"

Somehow my mother's fear of sports has leapt into my osseous labyrinth, the part of my ear that directs my sense of balance. That Pair of Lies, like a pair of pants, descends upon me and squeezes me like a boa constrictor. Vertigo assails me. Recognizing the feeling from the other twenty-four times doesn't help. My opponent slides his arms around me, lifts me up, and slams me into the mat for the final time.

When the ref raises my opponent's hand to signal the obvious winner, I do something extraordinary: I raise my own hand. Call it wishful thinking. Call it arrogance. But now I understand that grappling with my opponent has become a metaphor for grappling with life. Ultimately, many more obstacles will stand before me and my dreams, but only I can ever prevent myself from achieving those dreams. I look past my opponent and into the stands at Goldie. She smiles at me.

I smile back.

11

premature evaluation

richmond, virginia / chester, virginia
february 26, 1984

M‍Y MOTHER SUSPECTS THAT MY MOHAWK, MY EAR PIERCINGS—DONE
with tacks in Mr. Fetter's geometry class—my recent name change, and
my Devo albums have something to do with it, but it's something I won't
tell her or anyone . . . ever.

"Iz it becaz of yor pee-nis?" Ms. Hellinger asks.

"Is it because of my *penis?*" I say. I shift uncomfortably. My silver
parachute pants make a loud scratchy sound as my hands cover up my
hard-on. I have no idea how she knows.

"Iz it becaz of yor pee-nis?" she repeats.

"*M-m-my penis?*" This is what my mom is paying my extremely German therapist to ask me? Her question sends me tumbling deep inside
myself. I see faces from high school—kids and teachers. Pimples pop like
rotten plums. I hide behind a big rock. My breathing goes shallow. My
heart beats furiously. On the outside, though, I freeze completely. At thirteen, the silence in a freezer like this can be extremely devastating.

"Are you imitating a Popsicle, now?" Ms. Hellinger asks.

My teachers have become concerned because recently I have
become quiet. Very quiet. When Mrs. Nelson, my Spanish teacher, sits

down with my mom during a teacher-parent conference she calls me "too quiet."

"To be honest," Mrs. Nelson says, "he's creeping out some of the other students."

"Zee boys in yor gym class have zee pubic hair, yes?" Ms. Hellinger asks. "Do you tink you feel inadequate because zee boys in yor gym class have zee pubic hair and you do not?"

I feel sick. I count on my fingers, pretending to go over some kind of important list in my head. It's a random tick I've developed as a cover-up. Since I turned thirteen, it's like I've become the mascot for the phrase "Man up." Each and every day of my teen life is filled with 96 percent boner. I feel like I'm being punished.

Three and carry the seven. Equals a four and carry the one. Please don't say the word "penis" again. Three and carry the seven. The counting hides the silence and something even worse—my debilitating shyness around girls.

"Iz it yor penis?" she repeats.

Again, my head jumbles. I see the series of multiple-choice psychiatrist questions, the funny shaped blocks, the triangle pictures to be decoded, the ink spot that I have to describe in three seconds. Confusion and heat wash over me. I stumble so far down the rabbit hole this time that I flashback to a Friday night, two months previous.

It's close to midnight. I'm driving my mom's ugly yellow GMC Pacer across town with my alto saxophone and a flashlight that runs on a square battery. I don't think about how I'm in love with a girl I've never even talked to. I don't think about what serenading her in the cool Virginia grass below her window at her parents' house at this time of night will mean or what her boyfriend might do to me when he finds out. I'm just trying to keep my head as empty as I can for as long as I can.

She's the homecoming queen of my high school—Savannah van Houten—the most beautiful girl in the entire world. We've never even

talked, but it doesn't matter. I imagine the melody of my saxophone dancing against her window like Ren McCormack in *Flashdance*.

Below her window, I affix a tiny music stand to the neck of my saxophone and clip a tiny swatch of sheet music to the stand—"Stars and
Stripes Forever" by John Philip Sousa. I adjust the flashlight in the bell
of the saxophone so it lights up the music. Butterflies flutter. The moon
behind me resembles a sliver of a silver spoon. I play.

With the very first honk, the curtains part in the third-story window,
and a black outline fills the illuminated square. I have no idea whom I've
just awoken, so when the door flies open and someone begins running
toward me I run, too. While I'm running, I wonder why I'm running.
But while I'm running, I can hear that it's Savannah. She's laughing, her
laughter edging up against the back of my neck. It makes the tiny hairs
stand on end. My saxophone is bouncing on my side. The flashlight in
my hand is bouncing light all over the yard, the houses, and the trees. A
lightness nearly lifts me off the ground.

Running is like turning the pages of time. We run in circles in her
yard, never leaving it. I want to run far—but not too far. As long as I keep
running, she won't be able to catch up with me and know about me. That
I'm having trouble making sense of my world. That being known as Sanford and Son hurts more than I ever admit. That being Jewish feels like a
dark secret—even more so since I've recently discovered that my mom is
a Holocaust survivor, which is why she lives in the Jew closet. As long as
I continue to run, it feels safe. As long as I run, I remain the guy who sits
two seats behind her in chemistry class.

Finally, I stop running because I can't run anymore. We stand facing each
other. Our chests heave up and down. She's so beautiful that she takes my
breath away. Her long auburn hair gushes over her chest. I want to fall into
her, into the most beautiful girl in the world with more money and opportunities than I could ever imagine. In this magical moment, all the awkwardness
disappears. In this moment, before whatever happens next, I am perfectly
content and happy forever. I don't want to leave this moment ever.

We stare. I don't say a word. Then I run away. She doesn't follow. I get back into my mom's car and leave.

Back in school the next day and for all the days thereafter, I don't look at Savannah or talk to her. I think about her constantly, wondering at the back of her head in chemistry class if in our moment I was more than an eccentric apparition for her. That's why one day, after I give her a note, she looks at me and calls me the worst thing anyone possibly could call me—weird. That's why I ask my mom to find me a therapist. I don't want to be weird anymore.

—◦—

"You don't know?" Ms. Hellinger says.

I shrug my shoulders.

"It doesn't matter," I say.

"An vhy does it not matter?"

"I don't know." I feel sad.

"You don't know?"

I rub my hands together like I'm cold. "The world is going to end next year anyway."

"So? Vhat if zee vorld does not end?"

"I dunno."

"Zen you tink you must go on living, Mr. Smarty Pants?"

"I guess."

"If you do go on living, vhat do you tink you feel about your pee-nis?"

part two

love me not

12

o' virginity

radford, virginia / chesterfield, virginia
december 28, 1986

RADFORD UNIVERSITY LIES IN A QUIET TOWN NESTLED IN THE New River Valley of Virginia among the green hills of the Blue Ridge and a river that flows backward. Four hours from Richmond, it's far enough away from *The Tinker* that I can safely envision a life beyond faux-piracy yet close enough to home in case I need to re-stock my supplies once I begin to set my own course.

I'm a freshman here thanks to Ms. Hellinger and a chance article in one of my uncle's *Playboy*s. Actually, it wasn't an article at all. It was a list of the top ten party schools in the country, which listed the formerly all-female teachers' college as having a very favorable female-to-male ratio of five to one. With a world of Savannah van Houtens out there, I need favorable odds if I ever plan on sliding into second base and enacting Ms. Hellinger's strategy to "go on living."

Still shy and prone to an embarrassing, round-the-clock hard-on cycle, I spend nearly all my time locked away in the practice rooms in Powell Hall, the music building, channeling all my energy related to dry humping—including: dreaming about the perfect hump, finding someone to hump, and getting dumped by someone I've humped—into writing songs on the piano. I go to classes and eat just to occupy my troubled virgin mind. The pain of a life with nothing to hump overwhelms me. I'm old enough to now realize it, so it feels unbearable.

When I've written enough songs, I spend evenings performing in a local dive bar, just me, my keyboard, and my songs.

> P.S. I'm sorry, and I wish you were here.
> P.S. I'm sorry, and I wish you were near.
> I'll send it on the next express.
> It will get to your address
> before tomorrow.

They rhyme too much for their own good, which is good. No one my age can drink without a fake I.D. so I perform mostly to old people, and old people find simple rhymes classy when they drink. Word about my prowess to woo large groups of Metamucil- and Poligrip-users soon spreads around campus, beyond campus, and eventually to my hometown.

A month before Christmas break, Remington Chapman—better known as Judge Chapman, chief judge for the Circuit Court of the County of Chesterfield—sends me a letter. Not only does Judge Chapman command the entire county court system, he also rules the roost in one of the richest families in town.

His daughter, Sylvia, and I had developed a real-estate relationship. She sat beside me in homeroom in twelfth grade. She had hair so enormous that it had its own fire escape. In the letter, Judge Chapman explains the details of his daughter's upcoming Holiday Reunion Ball. My assignment for the event, should I choose to accept it, involves writing a nostalgic song about high school. For my part, I'll get an invitation to the exclusive affair, a lively audience for which to perform, and one hundred dollars. How can I not accept?

I arrive at the Chapmans' with Goldie on my arm, and we enjoy the illusion of belonging as we walk through the large oak doors of the mansion. I feel taller and smarter. Goldie says her boobs feel bigger. After I hand our invitation to the hired help, the feeling leaves us.

In the main room, we behold a superlative situation: to my right, the most likely to succeed; to my left, the best looking; between them, the most likely to brighten your day. The entire football team from the previous year fills the house, and the former prom queen and king are standing by the punch bowl in matching shiny gray and pink outfits. In an aviary full of soaring birds, Goldie and I feel flightless.

"I'm a mere step up from the black men hired to serve the food and pour the drinks," I whisper to Goldie.

"I feel like a grounds custodian," she whispers back.

"They probably think we should be manning a 4-H booth at the county fair."

We waste no time in planting ourselves on a sofa in one of the lesser, and thankfully uninhabited, rooms.

"I hate guys like that," I whisper to Goldie, referring to Donovan Ryan. "He's had a full beard since fourth grade."

"Here, drink this, and you'll find out if you really hate him," she says. She holds out a crystal cup full of green juice.

I hold the cup with both hands and smell it. "What is this?"

"It's hawk juice."

"Like a hawk that flies?"

"No, silly, I said 'Hulk,' like the Incredible Hulk. You know, the guy who turns green and gets all muscley when he gets mad. My host mom makes it all the time. It's green Jell-O, Canada Dry Ginger Ale, and vanilla ice cream."

I take a sip. "It's been spiked!"

"You'll survive," she says. "By the way, are you a mean drunk or a stupid drunk?"

"I don't know," I say. I take another sip, contemplate it, then down the entire thing. "Stupid, probably. More please."

Goldie winks, walks away, and comes back with an entire tray full of Hulk Juice. By the time Judge Chapman calls everyone into the piano room, my cup has become a telescope.

"Guests," Judge Chapman announces. He is a planet of a man, more than three-hundred pounds with an entire solar system of organs. Before his words reach his mouth they orbit through his entire gastrointestinal galaxy so by the time they reach his mouth they sound like the words of a politician: important, but unintelligible. He introduces Sylvia, who stands to applause. She says a bunch of wistful stuff about high school. By now I'm folded over the sofa armrest like a piece of bacon. She introduces me to silence, and in my attempt to rise I lean against her, which nearly causes us both to fall over.

"You've got to get it together," she whispers.

Someone stands me up. I think it's the former all-star running back. Funny, he never talked to me in high school, and now he's straightening me up and leading me to the piano.

"I'm all wobbly," I say, walking to the piano bench.

"Concentrate on something," he says.

I turn around and look out at the crowd, trying to fix my eyes on something. In the back of the room, I see a swatch of something black moving back and forth. When the crowd shifts, I can see that the swatch is attached to Goldie. She's wearing her long black trench coat. As she moves through the crowd, it opens just enough to reveal that she's completely naked underneath. *Oh Dear.*

"Lean back," another voice says, and I do. Instead of falling backward off the piano bench I lean back into Donovan Ryan. I try to wink at Sylvia but only succeed in closing and opening both eyes. She arches an eyebrow. I spread my fingers over the keys. Dozens of words appear and reappear over my hands. I sigh, press the keys, and begin to sing . . .

Do you remember back in high school,
cold bleachers, watching football,
you thought the wind sprint was your downfall,
but the next game was all you saw.

Words and rhyme flash over my fingers. I close my eyes and let the music flow.

Do you remember back in high school
friday games and the midnight dance.
You were waiting for your first kiss,
and you were hoping for romance.

About ten minutes into a three-minute song, I discover that I'm neither a stupid drunk nor an angry one. I'm a confused, long-winded magician. Fueled by the Hulk Juice and my creative concoction of chord combinations, I suddenly believe that I'm one of them, that I'm here because these are all my former teammates. The Hulk Juice has replaced the reality that I was the big nosed, pimply guy in the bleachers of every football game in my Burger King outfit beating on the bass drum.

Do you remember back in high school,
we had it made back in high school,
those summer days back in high school.
Some things remain the same.

The entire room moves forward, surrounding me in a huddle. *My* teammates close in. The former all-star quarterback has pulled up a footstool. The former wide receiver and the former right tackle have joined me on the piano bench. Our place kicker is leaning against the piano, tears falling down his cheeks. Everyone is singing along with me, "Do you remember back in high school, cold bleachers, watching football . . ."

It's like the coach just called my number in the final game. It's fourth and goal. We're down by six. Coach puts his hands on my shoulder and says, "Go in there, and bring it home, son." I'm so thrilled that I almost fall off the bench. One of my teammates pushes me back on.

Finally, I press the two farthest keys on both sides of the piano, which is how I end every song. I lift my hands and let them fall into my lap. A sense of peace washes over me. In all my years of drawing football pictures, of using the marching band as a surrogate for my love of football, this important feeling continually eluded me. I feel complete.

I turn my head toward the room. All my teammates are crying. The room erupts in applause and my teammates lift me into the air on the piano bench. It's like my bar mitzvah all over again. Instead of singing the "Hava Nagila" they sing the Skyhawk fight song.

> Hail to the Skyhawks,
> blue, white, and blue.
> Hail to the Skyhawks.
> To you we will be true!

"Touchdown!" someone yells.

They set me down with a shower of shoulder slaps, and a smile spreads across my face. I try to mingle, but, as I wobble around the house looking for Goldie and listen to fragments of stories about vacations to Milan, financial freedom, and a wine of the month club, my self-esteem plummets.

"Slashtipher, wait!" Goldie says, her entire chin neon green like she's been drinking from the punch bowl. She suddenly embarrasses me. "Where are you going?"

"Home," I say as I head out the front door. "I just want to go home."

"Can I come with you?" she asks, stepping on the back of my shoe and apologizing.

"Come on," I say.

—◦—

Goldie is driving the GMC Pacer—naked.

"Where's your dress?" I ask.

Apparently she had a problem with nausea in the Chapmans' upstairs reading room and stuffed the dress into a can of the judge's pipe tobacco.

"I liked what you played tonight," she says, steering us into her host family's driveway.

"Thanks."

"I don't feel so good," she says. She holds her stomach and puts the car in park. "I think I drank too much punch."

I nod.

"Do you want to kiss me?" she says.

I don't say anything.

"Did you hear me?" she says.

"All right," I say.

I want to, but I'm afraid.

"Are you going to kiss me?"

My head feels like it's on fire.

"You don't like me, do you?"

"Um, I like you," I say.

"Are you ashamed of me?"

"No!"

"Then why won't you do this?"

"M-my lips are really sensitive."

"So? I'm really sensitive, too."

"So I can't touch anything but food with my lips. The doctor said so."

"Not even for a minute?"

"Mmmm. Well, maybe, for a minute."

"Well, don't wait, or I'll probably change my mind."

My lips touch hers. It feels nice. Her lips are soft like cookie dough. She climbs on top of me. We wobble back and forth, our mouths pressed together.

As we kiss and trade virginities, I hear a sound like my dad's motorcycle. It keeps getting closer. By the time I recognize it's the sound of Goldie's churning stomach it's too late. Goldie shivers. Her tongue swells up in my mouth. She burps, and a green horizontal waterfall shoots out of her mouth and into mine. The force of it twists her against the door. I try to grab her but pull the door handle instead. She tumbles out and pulls me fast and hard behind her. At the bottom of the driveway, we roll under a rhododendron bush. Through the leaves, the sky above swims in circles.

"I like you," she slurs, reaching for my hand. "We're two peas in an alcohol-soaked pod."

I don't say anything. Embarrassed, I walk back to the car with my pants around my ankles and drive home.

Goldie cries for hours the next day because I won't return her calls. She cries the next week and the next month for the same reason. I erase her messages on my answering machine before I even finish listening to them. My method of dealing by not dealing will probably haunt her in years to come along with the memory of a cocktail dress in a tobacco can. A bittersweet trio of firsts will haunt me as well: the first time I felt like I belonged, the first time I went all the way, and the first time I played football back in high school.

13

rules by which a great declaration may be produced

radford, virginia
may 17, 1988

WHEN I RETURN TO SCHOOL, EVERYTHING AND NOTHING AT ALL HAVE changed. I feel confident, but I have no self-esteem. I'm no longer a virgin, but I'm no Casanova. The Radford campus becomes both a gigantic muse and a slap in the face. Full of angst, too shy, and not smart enough to understand how to replicate excerpts of my Goldie experience with another girl, the better part of my next year as a college student leaves me feeling slightly puzzled. As a result, professors, friends, and passing strangers frequently ask me: "Is everything OK?"

Not until my junior year do I fall back on a familiar childhood obsession—reaching altered states of consciousness through sports activity—and finally reach a breakthrough.

Gymnastics class with Dr. Myers leads to a walk-on tryout and a starting position on the men's gymnastics team on the pommel horse. That leads to my debut as a Radford Highlander gymnast, where, at the University of Georgia, I suffer dorsal wrist impingement. All the tendons in my right hand tear during the meet when I fail to rotate my wrist properly during a Direct Stockly. That leads to unconsciousness during the meet, which leads me to write about the experience a week later in an essay for Professor Hoffman's English 101 class. That leads to the Monday that changes my life forever.

"I would like to praise one student for the depth of his honesty," Professor Hoffman announces to the class. She talks about how the reflective essay is similar to looking into a mirror and seeing a reflection of an experience from your past. I'm barely listening. Instead I'm staring out the window at snow flurries in May. As she begins to read the essay, I wonder when this terribly long winter will—

Wait, those words are *mine*.

"My dad got into AA shortly after my tenth birthday. It never made things perfect, but it helped. He still struggles with it, and we sometimes don't get along." As she reads, two girls turn to me and smile. Another laughs at a part not intended to be funny. For the first time since sitting in the booth surrounded by girls after the battle of the bands victory, my artistic work has come to resemble a winning lottery ticket.

"But this story that we share changes things between us," the professor continues. "It engages me in a conversation with the rest of the world, with you. Telling this story won't change the past, and if you retell your own story it won't change your past. What I've found, though, is in telling our stories it changes us and our relationship to what happened, and in the end that's all that really matters."

When she finishes, a silence descends upon the room. Applause rises. I don't really understand the significance of the moment. I simply completed an assignment: writing an essay where I compared the pain of the gymnastics injury and the embarrassment of passing out to the pain I felt when the hornets stung my father and me and the embarrassment of jumping overboard.

With this reward, a distinct connection suddenly forms between how my personal experience and my artistic expression have come to influence this very moment, revealing a truth that my father could never quite explain to me in a way that made sense.

The applause has me hooked. As I retrieve my essay from Professor Hoffman with a handshake, I want more of this praise—a lot more.

"Something told me that you had something like this in you," she says after class.

"Really?" I move aside so a few students can get by. A few other students linger.

"It was just a feeling," she says. "Sometimes it's the quiet, slightly bewildered ones that surprise you the most."

I smile. I like that she can see this part of me.

"Your writing is very unconventional," says a tall guy beside me who reeks of privilege. "It reminds me of Richard Brautigan."

I scribble the name on my notebook, but I'm not sure whether to take his comment as a compliment or a criticism.

"Do you know each other?" Professor Hoffman says.

I shake my head, and the guy holds out his hand.

"Grady Armistead," he says. His chin is weak and his skin is pasty like he's been living in a basement his entire life. He pronounces his name with such distinction that it sounds like he's introducing the president of the United States.

"If you want to learn how writers have achieved what you achieved today on a much grander scale then you should listen to everything this woman has to say," Grady says.

"If you like fishing," Professor Hoffman says, unfazed by Grady's groveling, "you can begin with *The Old Man and the Sea* by Ernest Hemingway." I scribble the name on my notebook beside Richard Brautigan.

High on praise and the discovery of an untapped gift that may hold my ticket to getting a girl, I float to the cafeteria with Grady. By the time we sit down with our trays, I still can't tell whether he's teeming with intermittent condescension or he's just trying to hide his southern accent.

"You've never read a book?" he says. "That's just ridiculous."

"Magazines and stuff," I say.

"D. H. Lawrence? John Steinbeck? Henry Miller?"

I shake my head. "I always thought books were for people who were smarter than me."

"How can you be a junior in college and live a bookless life?"

"I dunno. You know in high school, in ninth grade, when you have to diagram sentences? Well, the first time I drew all those diagonal lines, I knew books weren't for me. It made reading seem like math. I was lucky to have smart friends and CliffsNotes."

"What in the hell have you been doing for three years?"

"*Obviously* not reading," I say.

"I mean, what classes have you been taking?" Grady asks.

"Well," I say, swallowing a forkful of iceberg lettuce covered with French dressing, "P.E."

"Are you joking? Like Badminton?"

"Badminton, Advanced Bowling, Archery."

"Is that your major?"

"I don't have a major," I say. "I'm supposed to make a decision by November, but I'm still not sure."

"Undeclared major, huh?" he says. "We'll just have to remedy that, won't we?"

14

the gateway gig

radford, virginia
september 27, 1988

THIS IS BIG—BIGGER THAN I COULD HAVE EVER IMAGINED. OVERWEIGHT men in suits with various styles of mustaches keep entering and exiting the small office. A man on a walkie-talkie with a mustache like a walrus refers to me as a "perpetrator in the midst of a spiritual predicament."

He has arms like flippers. I wonder if he had a bowling ball for lunch, I think.

Papers are passed and signed. A short woman with a mustache like Frida Kahlo's saunters into the room and announces, "The university president will be here shortly." She turns and disappears.

The outer surface of her upper lip cast a faint shadow like a line of brown paper ants searching for the entrance to their home.

Since winning the English 101 essay lottery, declaring myself an English major, reading nearly every Brautigan book (only after discovering that the house that Grady shares with his bandmates unofficially and self-appointedly contains the entire Richard Brautigan collection that once resided in McConnell Library), and joining Grady's band, I've begun to think in complete sentences. Every moment morphs into a carefully crafted sentence bound for my Pulitzer Prize–winning book. I can't write these sentences down fast enough. A cheap college-ruled notebook has replaced my Moleskine sketchbook. My entire mind fills with nothing but complete sentences.

Even now, in the midst of this predicament, dressed in a periwinkle blue nuclear waste removal outfit and my Baltimore Colts football helmet, the sentences continue.

They superimposed my nose over the golden arches on the McDonald's sign as if I had sneezed the words "Over 99 Billion Served."

Moments ago I was screaming T. S. Eliot at the top of my lungs while Grady pitchforked naked plastic baby dolls from a wheelbarrow into the Radford University campus fountain. The crowd was amazed and confused, the world perfect.

But now I'm a little scared, and my butterflies are restless.

The head of campus security, a barrel-chested no-neck man with a crooked mustache, rough-handles my T. S. Eliot book. The campus chaplain, who has no chin and a mustache like Charlie Chaplin, snatches the book from his hands and mouths the title of the book, *Opossums Book of Practical Cats.* In a whisper, he reads: "Mungojerrie and Rumpelteazer had a wonderful way of working together, and some of the time you would say it was luck, and some of the time you would say it was the weather." He laughs and looks over at me. "Whether or not you end your career as a college student today has yet to be seen."

I shift uncomfortably.

Man didn't kill poetry. Men with mustaches killed poetry.

Without notice, the university president enters the room. Everyone leaves.

His hair is like a bowl of melted soft-serve on his head that his wife wants to lick.

"You must understand that I am very rarely called onto campus for matters such as these," he says, shuffling some papers. He looks up. "Goodness gracious, what on earth are you wearing?"

"The truth is, sir, like I've told each of your men a thousand times already, this was simply a musical promotion for our band."

"A band? What kind of band? Officer Blint says he saw you stabbing children and yelling obscenities at little cats. In addition, his fellow officer confiscated these from the scene."

He slides a handful of postcards across his desk. They say "Vegetation Information" and depict a caricature of man's head, his skin removed to reveal the muscles underneath.

"Is this 'Vegetation Information' some sort of agricultural activity club?"

The president's reaction quickly turns my laugh into a cough.

"No, sir. It's actually a jazz ensemble. Jazz is a spiritual truth."

As he considers my words, he twists the end of a pencil in his mouth. I feel like I'm about to confess things I've never even done before.

His eyes seem to sparkle. It's a familiar sparkly look—the same look I've seen on dogs while they're pooping.

He wants me to explain, but I have no idea how. All my bandmates seem like divinely inspired musicians. Mason, our tenor sax player learned to play in church. While the world of boys played flashlight tag and pulled the wings off butterflies, Grady, alone in a closed-door room, practiced scales on his stand-up bass. How do I even begin to explain my relationship to music?

The university president—the bowl of melted soft-serve on his head—and I have entered a staring contest.

"Son," he says after a long time, "this isn't the sort of thing that I'd normally condone, and I hope the Lord can see more sense than I can see in you right now, but may God grant you guidance on your most enigmatic and unfathomable journey. Good day!"

He pushes the button on his phone, and suddenly a tall, blonde girl appears beside me. She has a large, yellow feather in her hair that looks like corn on the cob. She bends over, and a wave of lavender and patchouli

floats past. The feather floats down against her shoulder. Excitement diz-
zies me. She pulls out a rubber stamp and pushes it against the band's
wheelbarrow, the pitchfork, and my T. S. Eliot book. When she removes
it, the college seal appears.

I retreat deep inside myself. I imagine myself climbing aboard her
back, putting my bare feet in her hands like stirrups, holding her hair like
reins, whispering in her ear that I love her. We fly toward Alaska while I
eat corn on the cob.

"Dr. Washington, should I stamp his helmet?" she asks.

"I don't think that's necessary, Shiloh," he says. "I think that will be
all."

"Shiloh, Shiloh, Shiloh," I repeat to myself. I start singing Barry
Manilow's "Copacabana," replacing Lola and Tony's name with Shiloh's
name and my own.

> Her name was Shiloh.
> She was a showgirl
> with corn cobs in her hair
> and a dress cut down to there . . .

—~—

When she turns to leave she looks at me as if she knows what I'm singing.
The door closes behind her. I immediately miss her, blinking in disbelief.

"Son?" Dr. Washington says. "Son?"

"Yes, sir?" I say.

"You are free to go," he says, reaching out and handing back my book.

"Thank you," I say.

I stick the book and the pitchfork in the wheelbarrow and push it
toward the door.

"One more thing, son," he says. "Next time you have one of these
promotions, come by the office and have our work-study girl stamp your
belongings."

"Yes, sir."

Shiloh isn't sitting at her desk as I roll the wheelbarrow out into the hall, but her perfume lingers. Instead of feeling like I'm missing an organ, like my heart, it feels like I have an extra one. I push the elevator button and wait. The door opens, and Shiloh nearly falls into the wheelbarrow. I move to the right as she moves to the right. She moves to the left as I move to the left.

"What the hell?" she says.

"I'm so sorry," I say.

I move to the right again as she does. I feel faint.

"What are you doing?" she says.

"Nothing," I say, looking away from her. My face flushes. I'm so embarrassed. "It must be the magic of electrons or something," I mumble stupidly. I instantly feel like an idiot for saying it because I don't even know what I mean.

That night I toss and turn, watching a gazillion wallet-size photographs of a sleeping Shiloh spread across my mind's eye. In the photos, her chest rises and falls in a regular rhythm, but then her breathing changes. When I awake, I take out my sketchbooks and write a batch of new combinations for the first time since I was a kid. As soon as I assign one to my sketchbook, another appears: Satiation 11, Completeness 4, Abundance 3.

15

the battle of shiloh

radford, virginia
december 5, 1988

ON THE *EASY RIDER* POSTER ABOVE MY PIANO, PETER FONDA, JACK Nicholson, and Dennis Hopper ride their choppers toward freedom. Under the poster, on my piano, sit two coffee cups, four empty wine bottles, and one wad of purple napkins.

The previous night whirs. I hold my head in my hands and try to remember.

Shiloh walks up on stage as I pack my keyboard. Though she's consumed my thoughts for weeks, I don't recognize her. My bandmates laugh.

"There goes the band," Mason says.

I roll my eyes.

She walks back to my dorm room with me, arm in arm. After I open the door, I linger in the doorway and watch her walk inside.

"What are you doing?" she says.

"Nothing."

At my piano, I open my sketchbook and play the combinations that I've written for her: Passion 17, Love 43. She sits beside me on the bench and leans her head onto my shoulder. I play as she nods in and out of sleep.

"I've never been serenaded, you know?" she whispers.

I think about Savannah van Houten chasing me around the yard, my saxophone bouncing on my hip.

"It's good for you," I say.

She laughs softly. Like her voice, her laugh has a soft southern twang.

"I wrote these for you," I say.

She reaches out and touches my sketchbook. "I like serenades," she says and wraps her arms around me. I play my two combinations again and again. I want to keep playing because I want her to stay this close to me always.

We spend the next four days whispering, touching, kissing, and falling in love. I love the way she folds her long legs under herself when she sits. I love that she makes fun of me for asking so many questions. I love waking up in the morning with her and the way she wraps herself around me like a banana peel. I love chewing on her hair. I love that she holds my toothbrush like a pipe and mumbles funny things to me while brushing her teeth.

After four days, she goes back to her apartment. I don't want it to end, afraid I won't know how to build a bridge back to her.

"Please stay with me forever," I say.

She hugs me and nuzzles into my neck. "I love you. Forever."

❧

Building a bridge back to Shiloh after she leaves my apartment proves more difficult than I could ever have imagined—even more so after I learn that the person with whom I've fallen in love isn't who I think she is. It's extremely confusing.

"When I stop by, she's never home. When I try to surprise her at work, she's never there. When I call her, I just get her answering machine," I lament.

"Did you try her parents'?" Grady says.

"I don't know her last name," I admit.

"Maybe she's a secret agent," says Mason.

"Don't listen to him," Grady says. "Ask that woman with the Frida Kahlo 'stache who works in the office. Maybe she knows."

"I did. She told me it was against university policy to share information about university employees with students. I don't know. Maybe she's not even worth it."

"Are you kidding me? You told me she was a sex machine," Grady says. "I'd give my right arm to spend ten horizontal minutes with her."

"Yeah, but I thought love was supposed to make you feel *more* satisfied not *less*."

"It sounds like you've fallen into a Wilkie Collins novel," Grady says.

"Yeah, maybe you're more in love with the idea of finding Shiloh than you are with her?" Mason offers.

"I have no idea," I say. "Not counting Savannah van Houten, this is the first time I've been in love. It feels exactly the same, though."

"Lucky for you, you have your Pulitzer Prize–winning book to occupy your time," says Grady.

"Yeah, use it for material," Mason says.

"Your prose lurches forward either in wacky, surreal anecdotes or in wide-ranging observations and similes that crash into each other with jarring incongruity," Dr. Ham says as he hands back my blue booklet.

Shifting uncomfortably in the leather office chair, I turn to the last page of the booklet where Dr. Ham has written the words, "See me!" in red pen. The framed photos behind Dr. Ham's shoulder show him with various, important-looking military dignitaries from the Korean War.

"I concur," Professor Franklin says, sipping coffee from a Styrofoam cup. "We think you are either a genius or full of shit."

"Mr. Coleman, you do remember the title of this class is History of European Criticism and Aesthetics, don't you?" Dr. Ham says.

I nod.

"I'm not saying that Thomas and I aren't rebellious by nature," Dr. Ham continues. "It's why we decided to team-teach this class to begin with. But what made you think writing a story about an elephant searching for a long lost girlfriend was appropriate for your final?"

I decide not to tell them about all the sentences in my head or Shiloh or how I've collected more than 130 rejection letters from publishers for my half-finished Pulitzer Prize–winning book. At this point, I'm reveling in the idea of feedback. They used the word "genius" in connection to my writing.

"I don't know," I say.

"Well, sir, then who does?" asks Dr. Ham. "Throw us a bone. You're the writer, after all."

"I guess the words of Hemingway come to mind. 'I know now that there is no one thing that is true—it is all true,'" I say.

Professor Franklin shoots Dr. Ham an inquisitive look.

"Was that the wrong thing to say?" I ask.

"No, no. It's just not what we were expecting to hear," Dr. Ham says.

"You and Poppa spend a lot of time with each other, then?" Professor Franklin asks.

"I spend more time with Richard Brautigan," I say. "But, yes, I guess you could say that Ernest and I are on a first-name basis with each other."

The teachers share another look and a smile.

"One can never tell with these summer classes, Mr. Coleman, whether a student is on the right page with us or not," says Dr. Ham. "It's my conclusion that you are a young man with an exceptional gift. May I recommend that you guard this gift more closely from this point forward."

He extends his hand, and I shake it. I shake Professor Franklin's hand as well.

"One more thing, Mr. Coleman," Professor Franklin says. I stop at the door. "Just so you know, although this class is only pass/fail, had it been otherwise we would have given you the highest numerical grade value possible."

"Thank you, sir," I say.

The tale of my bravado spreads throughout the dorm like an STD. My bandmates think I'm a superhero. By my final semester, though all my frustrations channel into my writing, Shiloh still remains a mystery. I use another chapter of my novel for my final exam in African-American Literature. This time the response is less than perfect. Gilbert Harman freaks out, calls me an amateur, and promises to block me from graduating.

"I assumed that I would see you again before you graduated," Dr. Washington says. "How is the jazz band?"

"Good," I say. "We're playing a full-day concert for the families of the graduating class."

"Yes, I saw that. Congratulations," he says. "It's on the lawn in the quad, isn't it?"

I nod.

"So what is this business I hear with you and Professor Harman?"

"Nothing, really. I thought it would be appropriate to write an essay that read more like fiction. I didn't think it was a big deal."

"You like to think outside the box, don't you?" he says and winks.

"Yes, sir."

"Do you feel as though you answered the questions on the final sufficiently?"

"I do. I mean, in my own way."

As he considers my words, he twists the end of his pencil in his mouth. "Very well. I will handle Professor Harman. He can be a bit thuggish. Worry not about graduating. You are free to go."

My mind wanders back to my first time in the office. Feeling uneasy, I half expect Shiloh to walk through the door.

"Dr. Washington, may I ask you a question?"

He nods and looks up from his desk.

"After I met you the first time, there was a girl working for you— blonde hair, tall."

"It wasn't Caralee, was it?"

"No, her name was Shiloh."

"Shiloh? Mmm. Are you sure? I don't think I've ever had a Shiloh working for me. Are you sure it wasn't Caralee?"

Did I imagine the whole thing?

"She had a feather in her hair?" I say.

"A feather. Have you asked Mrs. Brent? . . . Oh, wait. Shiloh. Extremely tall? Yes, I do remember the feather now—a yellow feather. But she wasn't working for me."

"She was doing work in your office when I met you," I say.

"Just between you, me, and the walls, Shiloh's father is a friend of mine. When she was put on academic probation, I let her work a few hours here in the office as a favor to him. He was hoping that she'd find some direction. I was sorry to hear she dropped out of school and went back to Abingdon."

"You wouldn't happen to know how I could get in touch with her, would you?"

Dr. Washington stops writing and looks directly at me. An invisible door has gone up between us.

Please, please open the door.

He reaches into his desk, retrieves an index card, and begins to write on it.

"An early graduation gift," he says, handing me her phone number. "Good luck."

16

devil moose

anchorage / nikiski, alaska
may 17, 1989

"The captain has asked all passengers to return to their seats and observe the fasten seat belt signs. We will begin our descent into Anchorage in just a few moments." I've heard the announcement, but I'm ignoring it. In the back of the plane, near the bathrooms, in the galley, my minor celebrity status lessens the pain just a little. Two flight attendants are passing around my Polaroid of Shiloh. One is wearing a cute blue flight attendant hat, the other is hatless.

"She's so pretty," Hatless says, smiling

In the photo, a flock of seagulls hangs over Shiloh. Her long blonde hair, blown by the wind, floats above the dark sea and the storm clouds beyond.

"Where was this taken?" Blue Hat asks, touching my shoulder.

"On the Okrakoke ferry. We camped out in the dunes during Memorial Day weekend with my parents." I'm soaking up the attention.

"When's the wedding?"

"Well, I haven't proposed yet. That's why I'm going there. I'm going to give her this." I hold out the shell necklace I've made.

"Does she know?"

I shake my head.

"*Ohhhhhh!*" squeals Blue Hat. "That's so romantic. How did you meet?"

"I wrote my way to her." I explain our meeting, her mysterious disappearance, and the fateful way I found her phone number. "I called her one day out of the blue and sang the song 'Michelle' by The Beatles, except I replaced all the lyrics with the words, 'I love you.' Then my mom called her mom and asked if she could attend my graduation. We sort of just picked up where we left off. The last few months have been the best of my entire life."

The stewardesses smile and laugh. After we land and in the next few weeks, this feeling will help me forget, just a little, that I'm nothing more than a speck of person amid a gigantic Alaskan landscape. As we deplane, the captain leans out and wishes me luck. Did the flight attendants tell him, or is it a prophecy? Maybe he knows that I'll need it to find her, to keep her, to keep me from losing my mind.

I transfer to a cargo plane that looks like a furniture delivery truck with wings. The inside reminds me of the rented white truck that we used to collect the nautical antiques for *The Tinker*. It has neither seats nor belts.

Sitting on my duffel bag in the back of the plane, I hold onto a canvas strap attached to the wall with one hand and the collar of Bosschops, the pilot's golden retriever, with the other. Beside me, a frail couple dressed in crisp L.L. Bean catalog clothing smiles nervously. They squeeze each other and stare at the floor. That they feel nervous makes me feel nervous. Then the deafening howl of the engine fills the empty space between us, around us, and eventually within us. It feels like the engine is rumbling through my bones and maybe even my cells. Bosschops rolls over on his side, closes his eyes, and sighs.

I know how he feels. I don't care that Shiloh and I have spent more time apart than together. I don't care that she hasn't said "I love you" as many times as I have. I don't care that Mason said, "If she's always running away from you and you're always chasing her down, maybe it's a sign that you're not supposed to be together." I don't care that I feel scared right now. I care only about how she makes me feel. With her I feel stronger, more creative, and free.

As we wobble into the sky, I lean against the tiny window, overwhelmed by the unmistakable bigness outside. Massive glaciers and mountains make death seem entirely possible but also possibly beautiful. For the first time, finding Shiloh and repairing my unmistakably ruined heart by proposing to her seem insignificant. If the plane goes down now, I would fall from the sky, a mosquito falling into the ocean: an irrelevant blip. My heart and all that covers it would simply disappear.

Suddenly we hit a pocket of wind that turns the airplane on its side. I turn the strap around my hand until my fingers turn white. The man of the couple emits a scream that the roar of the engine swallows. He puts his forehead against his wife's, and they squeeze each other tighter.

The man, his wife, the pilot, and Bosschops all represent different parts of me. The dependable pilot is steering me toward love and the vast unknown. Bosschops is blithely unworried. The man and his wife reach out to soften their intolerable fear.

The man finally crawls forward and knocks on the door to the cockpit. Bosschops looks up for the first time, but the pilot doesn't hear. Then the man looks back at me.

"*My dice pick!*" the man yells.

"*What?*" I yell back.

He crawls toward me and yells directly into my inner ear: "*My wife is sick!*"

"*Yeah?*" I yell back.

She has gone completely white, the color of printer paper. Her mouth bulges on both sides. She's throwing up but doing her best to keep it down. The liquid oozes out and drips down her chin. It grosses me out so much that I nearly throw up. My cheeks bulge out like I'm going to lose it, but I close my eyes, and the feeling passes.

I need to connect with these people. I reach in my pocket for the Polaroid and hand it to the guy. "The truth is, when Shiloh's dad got her a job in the cannery," I yell, "I was like, 'You should go and do what you need to do. I'll see you in the fall.' But she was only gone two days before I gave my notice at the elementary school where I was a teacher's aide. I put everything I owned into my Subaru Brat, drove it to my best friend Grady's house, and bought a one-way ticket out here."

The guy raises his eyebrows and nods. He looks at the photo completely perplexed. He can hear only about 5 percent of what I'm saying, but I need to say these words out loud. Maybe he needs a distraction like I need a distraction. His wife looks up at me for the first time, spots the window beyond me, and then buries her head into her husband's shoulder.

"I don't have any freaking idea how I can live my life without her. That's some crazy shit, man," I yell. There had been so much to say, but now there isn't anything left. The man pulls his wife closer. I lean back.

When we land on the Kenai Peninsula, the captain cuts the engine, opens the side door, and walks to the terminal—a little trailer attached to a liquor store. Bosschops jumps out and bounds after him. It takes me a moment to realize that we're meant to disembark on our own. The man and his wife continue to hold onto each other as I step over them to get out.

I lug my duffel bag into the liquor store, take money out of my sock, and buy some peanut butter, bread, sardines, and a map. The jar of peanut butter costs $15, the loaf of bread $9, and the sardines $11.50. As I walk out to the road to hitch a ride, the first wave of anxiety hits me. The $725 in my sock won't last two weeks at this rate.

At the road, I unfold the map. I have no idea where in the hell I'm going. I swat a bug and spot the couple now sitting on the runway. The woman is leaning into the man. He pets her. I remember when I stared at the ceiling all night when Shiloh left. Something so simple, so primal as putting my hand on my forehead and moving it back and forth like I was petting myself made everything seem OK—even if it wasn't.

A Dodge Dart pulls over and shakes me from my daydream. A man wearing a pointy fur hat and absurdly thick glasses leans out and says, "Where the fuck are we?"

The passenger, wearing the same hat, says something, leans over, and hits him. The car jumps forward and stalls.

"Do you want a ride?" the driver asks. His eyebrows are long and pointy like wings. Down the road in both directions looks desolate. I have no idea in which direction I'm supposed to go. I get in.

We speed into the airport parking lot and skid to a stop in the soft gravel. The two men go into the liquor store. Maybe riding with these guys wasn't such a good idea. When I glance out the back window, there is nothing but trees. I could be walking along the road for days. The men come back out, pass a bottle of Canadian Club between them, and get back in. We drive in silence.

"What kind of hats are those?" I finally ask.

"Seal," the driver says. The passenger mumbles something.

"I'm going to Cannery Row," I say.

"We're going to church," says the passenger. He offers the bottle to me. I decline.

"You coming?" the driver asks.

Before I can answer we come to a screeching halt that throws me against the back of the front seat and knocks the wind out of me. The car stalls. In front of us stands a huge bull moose. My fear instantly turns to excitement. I roll down the window and stick my head out. His horns touch the fir trees on either side of the road, the tines of his antlers unusually twisted and deformed like two huge, arthritic hands.

"Devil moose! It's a *devil* moose!" the passenger screams. "Oh my God!" He turns toward me, shoves the whiskey bottle into my hands, and begins to climb over the seat. His hat flies into the driver's lap. "Get us out of here! Get us *out of here!*"

My heart is racing.

"God damn it!" the driver yells. He pulls his friend forward by his belt. "You're going to get us in an accident."

The driver starts the car, backs it up, and then pulls forward—but the car swerves off the road, swallowed by tall purple fireweed that brushes the car as we nearly tip over the steep embankment and pass the moose. The moose watches, stoic and undeterred.

"Goddamn it, Davis, you sound like my sister! Quit crying!" yells the driver.

"It was a devil moose," Davis says. "I'm sure of it."

"So what?" the driver says. "Take a drink."

"Here," I say.

He takes the bottle, curls up in the fetal position against the door, and sips from it like a baby. I don't understand the significance of the devil moose, but his reaction can't mean anything good. His sobs eventually dissipate to silence.

Mile after mile of evergreen forest passes by and lulls me to sleep. Visions of Shiloh turn into visions of my father and me on his motorcycle on our way to Alaska.

Hours later, we pull over onto a tiny turnoff on the side of the road. The driver slurps the last sip from the bottle of whiskey, chucks it into the woods beyond the car, and then yells for me to get out.

"Yeah, get out!" Davis echoes.

"Where are we?" I ask, nervously opening the door into darkness.

"The campground," he says.

The car swerves away as I sling my duffel over my shoulder. My flashlight beam hits trees and more trees . . . but no signs, no picnic benches, no grills. It's not any type of campground that I've ever seen.

I feel my way into the woods until intuition tells me to stop. I kneel down, open my duffel, pull out the tent, and begin searching for the poles—until I realize that I've forgotten to pack them. I begin to cry. Tears drip down onto the flashlight between my legs and the flat blue vinyl pancake of a tent. I curl up on the ground and rest my head on my bag. Maybe it was a blessing that my father and I never made it to Alaska. He never packed a tent. My stomach turns. After a while, I unzip the tent, slide my sleeping bag inside, crawl in, and fall asleep.

The next morning I awake freezing cold and wet from condensation. When I slide myself out of the sleeping bag and tent, I see that I've slept on the edge of a cliff. My intuition was right: a few more steps would have taken me to my death. I make a peanut butter sandwich from my squished loaf of bread that I used as a pillow.

—⁓—

For the next three weeks, each morning after I wake, I make a peanut butter sandwich, walk out to the road, and hitchhike to all the nearby towns. I show my Polaroid to convicts in bars, piano players in motels, cashiers at grocery stores, secretaries in cannery offices, and even a cobbler who sells me a pair of boots.

After two weeks, nearly all of my sock money is gone. My daily rounds turn into biweekly rounds, then no rounds. More and more of my time is spent writing at the campground. Inside my tent—propped up with sticks—I am truly a sad, greasy-haired, unshaven sight to behold. I have no idea how I'll ever get home. I'm losing faith, doubting the trip, thinking that proposing to a free spirit like Shiloh with a handmade shell necklace might be like trying to saddle a wild bronco. It might break the very thing with which I've fallen in love, rendering it virtually unrecognizable.

Then one night while I'm sleeping, a car pulls up outside my tent. The headlights blast right through it, waking me up and instilling me with fear. The car idles for a long time while indistinct voices talk. Cigarette smoke infiltrates the air. A car door opens, and someone gets out before the car leaves. Shiloh crawls into my tent on top of me, and we kiss.

"You're crazy," she says.

"I'm crazy in love with you."

We kiss some more.

"Where have you been?" I ask.

"The cannery where I was going to work shut down, so I've been working in one near Cook Inlet."

I take off her clothes. "How did you find me?"

"I called your parents," she says.

She takes off my clothes, and we make love.

The next morning, the El Camino returns and takes us to the cannery where Shiloh has been working and living. The car smells like death, and there's something between her and the guy driving, but I'm afraid to ask about it or even acknowledge it. I move into Shiloh's tent on a wooden pallet out behind the cannery. I sign on to work with the company. We live in a place fittingly called Tent City—full of college kids, criminals, and other assorted weirdos—and wait for the salmon to come.

For the first few days after finding each other, we celebrate our new-found sense of wonderment. Our bodies are once again new. We touch for hours. We sixty-nine almost every night. We take long walks. My body pulses with excitement.

The cannery has work for only six people a day, though, because the salmon haven't returned. She works; I write in the tent. Some people say the salmon may not come back, that the recent oil spills have confused them. It's the worst salmon run that anyone can remember. One guy even says it's the worst salmon run in the history of the world.

One day, plant manager Glenn Gaffey pulls up on his four-wheeler. A cigarette dangles from his mouth, and he's holding a cup of coffee. A cranky, skinny, wrinkle of a man who lives in a dirty Edmonton Oilers jacket, he has a stripe of black grease along his chin.

"Professor," he grumbles at me. "Shiloh tells me you worked as a teacher in the schools."

"I was a teacher's aide," I say.

"Close enough," he says. "Come with me. We've got work for you."

I climb on the back of his four-wheeler, and we rumble through the woods.

"That's the way it works in Alaska, Professor," he says. "If you take a piano lesson, you're a pianist. If you have a Band-Aid, you're a doctor."

He kills the engine and shows me to my new office. In a trailer, a gold plaque on the office door reads OSHA SAFETY CAPTAIN. "That's your desk. The yellow hard hat on it is yours. Wear it at all times. Here's the key to the door, and that phone there is your own personal phone line. Read all the safety manuals, answer all the phone calls, and what you don't know make up."

"What am I?" I ask existentially. "I mean, what's my title?"

"When the phone rings, you're the official liaison between the plant and the Occupational Safety and Health Department in Anchorage. Around here, you're just the professor."

Two weeks later the salmon arrive. Everyone works long hours, getting time and a half for anything more than eight hours a day. Most of the work crew works 72 hours straight. I work 9 to 5 and rarely see Shiloh. When I do, she smells like fish. We fuck, sleep, and eat. I've come all the way to Alaska to sit in an office and wear a hard hat in a trailer.

Distance soon divides us—a distance vast as the land between Virginia and Alaska. I spend many nights alone in our tent, petting my forehead, trying to dissolve the distance. It rarely works.

The distance between us grows so immeasurable that a future without her becomes a distinct possibility. What the male nurse told me a long time ago about a glimmer comes back into my head: "Even if you can just get a glimmer of something nice, it'll help." I dream of Goldie, Ms. Ottenbrite, and Savannah van Houten.

One night, after Shiloh is asleep, I sit up and light a candle.

"What's wrong?" she says, bleary-eyed.

"Nothing. Can you sit up?"

I place the shell necklace around her neck and kiss her on the cheek. She smiles. "What's this for?"

"Nothing."

Near the end of salmon season, just as the weather gets cold, I wander through the plant with my clipboard. I ask some of the pinners in the cannery where Shiloh is. They don't know. I walk back to our tent. She's not there. I ask at the office, and one of the workers says he thinks she's in the plant manager's trailer. Outside his trailer, I hear her singing the lyrics to "Me and Bobby McGee."

She's in his bathtub. My stomach drops.

I want to cry. I want to fall down on the floor. I want to yell "*Devil Moose! Devil Moose!*" I open the door and look in. I want to scream, "*What the fuck are you doing?*"

"Hi," I say.

"Hi, sweetie," she says. "I was feeling sick. I needed to get away from things."

I believe her because I'm stupid. We kiss. I go back to work.

Two days later, on my birthday, she disappears with him. For most of the night, I wander through tent city calling her name like I'm calling for my lost dog.

One of the pinners takes pity on me. "I seen her riding off in Glenn's truck. Somebody said they went into Anchorage. Nobody wanted to tell you."

"Thanks," I say.

"No problem. Happened to me before. You seem too good for that piece of shit anyway."

By the end of the week, I secure a transfer onto a tender boat that belongs to the cannery. I burn the Polaroid the first night aboard and spend the rest of salmon season at sea.

"Don't worry none on it, fella," my bunkmate, Burt, says. "Sadness passes."

"I know. The weird thing is, when I caught her in the bathtub, all I wanted to scream was 'Devil Moose!'"

"Why'd you wanna yell that?"

"I dunno. I heard it from some weirdo I hitched a ride with."

"My mawmaw was Inuit, and her people was always talking about the Devil Moose. When we'd ride out to visit her, right before we'd leave she'd always say, 'Remember, be careful out there on the road, 'cause everybody's riding the Devil Moose 'cept you.'"

"I figured it was something bad standing in your way," I say.

"I guess that's one way to look at it. My old man said when a bull moose is castrated accidentally he'll shed his antlers and then immediately grow a new set. They's usually deformed antlers, and he won't never shed those again. He'll wear 'em the rest of his life. Devil's antlers is what they call 'em. The moose with those antlers is the Devil Moose."

That night, as I slip into sleep, all the post-midnight motorcycle jaunts to Alaska with my father run through my head, each one eerily similar. Our helmets molded against our heads like melted devil antlers, we speed along the interstate, following an inexplicable calling like some internal migration pattern. We stop along the roadside as if blocked by an invisible hand. Without my Polaroid, hope, direction, the shell necklace, or Shiloh, I wonder whether all those trips with him laid the groundwork for this moment, Bohemian ideals—once again—just out of reach.

17

peep show

nikiski, alaska / richmond, virginia
september 1, 1989

MY GRANDFATHER DIES WHILE I'M STILL ON THE BOAT. THEY DON'T
dock for anything—not illness, injury, or death will change their course
once the season begins. One of the pinners lost his hand during Halibut
season. Instead of docking, they flew in a helicopter and sent his hand in
a bucket of ice with the medics.

Each night in my bunk, as we float out along Cook Inlet, I read the
letter over and over again. My mother worries about who will hold our
family together for the Jewish holidays now that my grandfather is gone.
I don't know why it matters to her, but she must be considering it more
and more inside her Jewish closet.

His sudden death creates a hole in my chest that continually caves in.
After Shiloh's betrayal, it doesn't hold solid. My grandfather's death piled
on top makes it unbearable. Knowing that he was always there, living in
his little rancher house with my grandmother, made the world complete.
Picturing my grandmother alone in the house breaks my heart. I haven't
been able to stop crying.

Until the letter arrives, I'm planning to find work on the Alaskan
Pipeline in the Arctic Circle with Burt.

"They feed you real good," he says. "T-bone steak every night's the best medicine for a broken heart."

Each morning, while the rest of the crew huddles around the coffeemaker and grouses to life with a first cigarette, I lie in my cot, writing myself away from my life. Dozens of stories fall out of me about my alter-ego, Dean Tankersly, a character like Nick Adams, a boy whom Hemingway used to chronicle his own life. Before work, I sometimes read a sentence or two to Burt.

"In the morning hours, before the West Virginia heat settled, Dean cast the buck tail spinner past the rocks. Right away the line pulled tight, and the rod felt good and familiar in his hands. When the tiny smallmouth bass broke the water, Dean pulled back. The bass danced on its tail. Both he and his father knew this place well."

After I read, Burt usually pursues a tangent about his own life. "When I was your age, I followed the migrant season. Worked my way across the country picking fruit with Mexicans."

His favorite season was the blueberry season in Maine at the end of the summer. These are my favorite stories to hear. Maine seems so far away. Sometimes his stories and my own are enough to help me escape— but that was before the letter. Heartbreak is one thing. Death on top of heartbreak is something else entirely. When I'm not writing, working, or listening to Burt, all I can think about is finding enough money to get home so I can leave my mistake of a summer behind.

Three months later, Burt offers to lend me the money for a plane ticket home because he knows I'll never ask. He has watched me mope around with my letter and my notebooks for long enough. He says he's in no hurry to be repaid. Sometimes a man needs to take care of things.

By the time I get home, the paper fiber of my mother's letter has begun to unravel, worn thin and delicate from my hands. My grandmother has moved into my old room. She sleeps in the bottom bunk under my Dallas Cowboy Cheerleaders poster: six gorgeous big-haired girls with pompoms, short-shorts, and camel-toe. She has begun to unravel, too. I move into my twin sisters' old room and sleep in a canopy bed with Holly Hobby sheets. My grandmother and I are two baseballs with our leather covers removed, separated by a thin wall, our strings slowly unraveling to reveal our core.

Every night, I cry myself to sleep. Then, sometime after midnight, the sound of bedsprings squeaking in my grandmother's room wakes me. She shuffles back and forth across the floor as if being chased and then she screams, "The Stormtroopers! The Stormtroopers! The Stormtroopers are here!" Then everything goes quiet again.

Most nights, I wrestle to fall asleep again. Sometimes I put a glass to the wall between us and listen for some kind of clue. Often I pull out my notebook and take Dean Tankersly on another adventure or flip through *Writer's Market* to find new places to send my short stories. But once awake, my mind betrays me. Even Dean's company or the promise of publication isn't enough. My mind rewinds back to Shiloh in the plant manager's bathtub. He mounts her like an animal, and then the same confusing feelings arrive with the image: I want to push her away but at the same time hold onto her so tight that she'll never get away.

In the morning, no one ever mentions the Stormtroopers. While we eat our breakfast in silence, I conclude that my grandmother loves *Star Wars*. Sliding into her bedroom slippers each night, she plays flashlight tag with Han Solo and the Ewoks.

When I press the issue with my mom, she tells me that the Stormtroopers are another name for the Gestapo. During the war they did horrible things to my grandmother.

"What do you mean?" I ask.

My mom's stare burns a hole into me, but she won't say. Fragments of stories pieced together reveal that the soldiers raped my grandmother once, maybe more, and maybe more than that.

"But what do you mean?" I ask again. I don't want to know the answer. Possessing this information makes me feel like I've swallowed my own fist. It's a part of me, but I don't want it in my mouth. I want it out so I can see it: on a table, in a fight, shaking in the air. It reminds me of the scene in my head with Shiloh and the plant manager. I need to see it to understand it, but I don't know how to handle it.

Early one morning, just before dawn, the Stormtroopers make a surprise attack. The bedsprings squeak, my grandmother shuffles across the floor as if chased, she screams, "The Stormtroopers! The Stormtroopers! The Stormtroopers are here!" Then everything goes quiet.

As I'm listening against the wall, my grandmother flings open her door, runs down the hall, and leaps down the stairwell—an entire flight of stairs. I don't know what to do. She's struggling at the bottom of the stairs, but my own pre-dawn terror keeps me from opening my own door. I'm a grown man, and I'm terrified. Some irrational part of me thinks Stormtroopers might actually be in the house. But once I hear my father open his door, I open mine. He's already kneeling on the floor beside her when I start down the stairs. Crumpled on the floor, a bloody mess, she's moving her legs back and forth as if trying to pedal away on an invisible bicycle.

My mother retrieves my father's long army coat while he holds a T-shirt over my grandmother's left eye. He puts on his coat and lifts her into his arms. Blood spills out of her and makes dark, wet patches on his coat. She looks like a little girl in his arms. I gently touch her shoulder as if petting a cat.

As he carries her out to his truck, the red sky parts like a curtain. She, folded in his arms, her bathrobe trailing the ground on either side of him, looks like a beautiful angel. My father in his long coat, collar turned up, looks like another kind of angel.

In another time, another place, this easily could have been the climax to a magnificent love scene from the greatest love story ever written. A sad but joyful feeling washes over me. For all my father's dark qualities, he loves the Jews. As a man who has rebelled against nearly every convention society has offered—from how he dresses to the way he raised his family—loving a Jew and her family forms part of that rebellion as well.

My mother and I watch the taillights of his truck disappear down the road. I shut the door and stand by the stairwell as she returns with a roll of paper towels. She rubs the paper on the floor, smearing her mother's blood in our home, until it's gone.

"Go back to sleep," she says. I do and sleep as soundly as I have in a year.

At breakfast, she and I eat in silence. As we're putting the dishes away, my father comes home. After the doctors stitched up my grandmother's eye, they moved her to the seventh floor.

"The seventh floor's where they put the people who unravel," he says, pouring a cup of coffee.

My mother says nothing.

"The doctor said the thing about unravelin' is that it's hard to stop the process once it starts," he says.

My grandmother has become the coverless baseball—one end of her string attached to my old bed in the room upstairs and trailing out of my father's truck all the way to the hospital, all the way to her new room on the seventh floor. My own string stretches to a tent stake in Alaska. My grandmother and I are racing to see who can unravel first. She's definitely ahead.

The nurse calls late that afternoon. The doctors have decided that my grandmother needs to quit taking her medication, twenty pills in all. One keeps the Stormtroopers away (poorly, obviously), but it causes depression, so another keeps the depression at bay, but that one causes insomnia, so another helps her sleep, but that one causes an irregular heartbeat, so another one calms her heart, but that one causes—

"Your mother has big balls," my father says at dinner that night.

"*Meshugener*," my mother says, crying into her peas.

My own heart hurts for reasons too shallow even to mention.

When summer rolls around, my grandmother has kicked the drugs and is living with us again. I take her to her weekly Narcotics Anonymous meetings. Every time we get in the car, she says the same thing. "But I only took zee medications dat zee doctor gaves me." She always defends herself.

I always try to change the subject by making her laugh. "For my birthday, we should take a bath together in our bathing suits. What do you think, Grandma?"

I sit in the hallway during the meetings and then afterward I drive us to Morrison's Cafeteria with her new friends: an ex-con, an ex-crackhead, and an ex-priest. It's like the setup for a dirty joke, except it's not. They tell their war stories; everyone laughs and eats. Each one of them seems to feel good about having left the trenches.

My grandma's new friends understand her.

Soon after, she moves into her own apartment. She asks my father to get her painting supplies out of storage, and she paints for the first time since the war. My father builds her an easel, a drafting table, and a cabinet for her supplies. She specializes in rowboats and houses, beautiful crooked little things set in a colorful and expansive ocean or a stark field, yet full of restitution and love. She loves the watercolor paper, the brushes, and the paints like she once loved my grandfather: passionately, overwhelmingly, and without apology.

18

how to bust your best friend's ass
knoxville-style

chesterfield, virginia / knoxville, tennessee
august 15, 1990

THE GULF WAR STARTS. I GO BACK TO WORK ON *THE TINKER* AND WRITE
at night. I could be this war's writer like Hemingway was for all the wars
he covered. The idea burns fiercely inside of me—I have to share it or
risk burning up, so I visit the recruiting station with a wet dream of the
front lines.

At each of the stations—Army, Navy, Air Force, Marines—recruiters
gather around me like I'm a campfire. I tell them how sometimes late at
night I sit in the passenger seat of my Subaru Brat, pretending that I'm
riding shotgun with Hemingway in the Spanish ambulance. Hemingway-
like sentences explain my inner meaning and make the emptiness of my
life disappear. I will bring my notebooks, and it will be good.

When I've said all that I need to say, it feels like I'm in a movie theater
beside a beautiful girl and I'm about to put my arm around her. They all
think I'm nuts. Goose bumps blossom over the Navy recruiter's entire body,
though, even his eyelids. Only he will guarantee me a position on the front

lines before the war ends. Since I'll only take a position as a medic, like Hemingway, he signs me on for a pending position that will never arrive.

Then Shiloh calls.

"I miss you," she says.

I hold the phone silently, cautiously, but it doesn't help. A vise is squeezing my entire body . . . but my hand won't set down the phone.

"What are you doing?" she asks.

I'm holding a tin can phone, a taut string stretching for miles from the huge crevice in which I suddenly find myself. If I answer, I'm not even sure that she'll hear me.

"Um, I don't know," I finally say.

"Well, after Alaska, I followed the Grateful Dead down from Canada," she says. "I'm back home now."

"In Abingdon?" I picture her calling from the barn at her parents' horse farm, her feet kicked up on her father's desk, surrounded by riding trophies.

"Yeah," she says. "It's been all right."

The feather in her hair is resting on her shoulder.

"Oh," I say.

"The concerts were pretty good. They played 'Tennessee Jed' in Albany. I haven't heard that song in, like, forever. How's the writing life?"

"I'm waiting to hear back from the Navy," I say, wanting to feel important.

"The Navy?"

"Yeah."

Knowing that she's back in Virginia feels like Kryptonite.

"I guess I'll have to come and visit you sometime, before you ship off," she says. "Maybe surprise you."

Her idea of a surprise visit both saddens and excites me, like a possible reunification with a lost limb.

"Sure," I say.

⌁

A few nights later, Grady calls.

"Dude, where the hell are you?" he asks.

"You called me at my parents' house," I point out, "and what's with the *dude* stuff? Are you high?"

"No, man, but you need to get your grumpy ass down to Knoxville, Tennessee, because I've got a new band, The Baconbits, and there's this other band called the Judy Bats, and they just signed with Warner Brothers, and there's a lot of buzz that my band might be next, and it's really happening down here, and—"

"You're high, aren't you?"

"No!" He laughs.

"Are you on speed?"

"I'm excited. This place is exploding. It's like the Manhattan of the South. Listen, you need to grab your stack of notebooks and your keyboard and pack it all up in the back of your Brat and get your grumpy ass down here ASAP."

"You sound different," I say.

"You're the one who sounds different. Listen, what the hell are you working on these days? Music or writing?"

"A new book."

"You doing any music?"

"A little. Mostly writing, though. The book is called *Musth*."

"You and the freaking elephant books."

"This one doesn't have elephants . . . until the end."

"So come down here, and work on it," he says. "Get inspired."

"I don't know. The book is a complete mess. It's spread out through sixteen notebooks. It has no plot, shallow characters, and it's full of incomplete sentences. Besides, I'm just getting used to writing on a computer, and I really need to concentrate."

"All of your short stories are still getting rejected, aren't they?"

"Don't remind me."

"Well, we really need a roommate," he says.

The dots between Abingdon and Knoxville connect in my head. The way Shiloh drives, it's fewer than ninety minutes.

"Um, I don't know. There are no distractions here."

"I know a great music teacher down here."

"Whatever."

"No, I'm serious," he says. "One of my good friends is taking private lessons from one of the Marsalis brothers."

In my head Shiloh is sitting in a small jazz club while I gig with Wynton.

"Let me think about it."

❦

A week later, Grady opens the front door of his house in an area of town called The Fort, bald-headed and wearing a vintage pink woman's winter coat. As he helps me carry in my notebooks, keyboard, amp, clothes, and ten bags of dehydrated food from one of my sister's failed diets, I understand why he sounded different on the phone.

"I'm taking a class called Fundamentals of Buddhist Philosophy," he says. "It's intense."

"Evidently. You look like an outpatient from a mental ward." Coming from me, that's saying something.

"You mean the coat?" He laughs. "It's my version of the monk robe."

"I thought you dropped out of school."

"I did, but The Cannon is letting me audit his class."

"The who?"

"The Cannon. Don't worry, you'll meet him soon enough. You'll thank me for introducing you, and you'll love him for changing your life."

Each morning, after sharing rehydrated French toast mush with Grady and eating his share of the sausage crumbles because he has become a vegetarian, we walk to the University of Tennessee together. I go to the library to write, and Grady heads to his class. In the afternoon, I walk to

Grocer's Row and Dumpster-dive fruits and veggies, a romantic way for a writer to avoid scurvy and supplement a dehydrated food supply totally void of essential vitamins.

In the evenings before The Baconbits begin band practice, Grady and I sit in the backyard and eat rehydrated soybean burgers and salvaged whole tomatoes. During one of these dinners, Grady introduces me to Kadambini Kanan—aka The Cannon. One minute I'm reaching for a tomato, and the next I'm looking at a man with a white-blue beard so long that he could use it as a jockstrap. He appears before us in a two-piece white robe as though he fell from the sky.

He takes my right hand in both of his, stares deeply into my eyes, and says: "The Sema represents a mystical journey of man's spiritual ascent through mind and love to perfect."

I can't imagine this guy getting in a car, going to work, teaching class, filling out a W2 form, or doing anything that anyone does in the normal world. He probably rides a mystical camel around all day while chewing on an enlightened falafel ball.

"Is that a relative of yours?" I ask, indicating a tiny photo attached to a bunch of wooden beads around his neck.

"This is my spiritual master, Bagwon Shree Rashneesh," he says, speaking slowly. "We call him Osho."

The name sounds like OSHA—the Occupational Safety and Health Association—which reminds me of my tiny office in Alaska, which reminds me of Shiloh and the bathtub. I wince.

"Turning toward the truth, the follower grows through love, deserts his ego, finds the truth, and arrives to *the Perfect*."

I feel lost. He seems found. Maybe he can lead me to wherever I need to be. Sounds perfect to me. I'm sold.

Each Monday from that point on, after I finish writing, The Cannon meets me at the library, and we walk to an empty lot beside the old World's Fair tower. We eat baba ghanoush, and he gives me whirling lessons.

He shows me how to root my left foot into the center of the earth, hold my right hand up like a beauty queen waving in a pageant, and then spin in a circle. He obsesses over my foot and hand placement. Every movement must be precise. Through weeks of practice, I build up to twenty minutes without falling. Whenever I fall, The Cannon quotes a Rumi saying like, "Water poured inside will sink the boat, while water underneath keeps it afloat."

Given the circumstances, the lessons feel exotic and slightly illegal, like scarfing handfuls of banana chips from the bulk bins at the health food store. There's no denying the feeling, though. Whirling dispels all my troubles immediately.

"I feel like a kid again," I confess.

"When you return from the spiritual journey known as whirling, you return as a man who has reached maturity and a greater perfection so as to love and to be of service to the whole of creation," he says.

I have no idea what he's talking about.

One night, after whirling lessons, Grady asks me to attend his last Fundamentals of Buddhist Philosophy class. "Everybody has to give a speech. I need you to hit me in the middle of mine so I can demonstrate nonviolence."

"Hit you? I've never even been in a fight."

"Yeah, but it's like you're living in your own story," he says. "Besides, you love attention."

Fair point. I really can't tell the difference anymore between what I'm writing in my notebooks everyday and my actual life.

"Plus, with all the time you spend with The Cannon, you're practically an expert on eastern philosophy."

"Ok," I say. "What do I need to do?"

When he uses the cue word, "Gandhi," it will be like the word of the day on *Pee-wee's Playhouse*. "When the word of the day is mentioned on *Pee-wee's Playhouse*, everyone goes nuts. Musicians come out of the floor blowing trombones, bicycles fly across the ceiling, a black king emerges from the floor," he explains.

"So when I hear the word 'Gandhi,' all hell is supposed to break loose?" I ask.

Grady nods. "But I have to warn you, three guys in my class are martial arts experts. If it comes down to a real fight, you might want to fold."

"You mean run?"

"I mean jump out the window."

Butterflies careen in my stomach.

I'm sitting in the middle of the room, fourth row from the door. I'm not wearing shoes, and I haven't showered in four days, which is part of the plan. It gives me an unusual feeling of power—but it's only an illusion.

A roundish girl in the front of the class—pretty face, nice skin—is reading her speech from note cards. I keep wiping my nose on my arm, also part of the plan. Coughing up some phlegm and wheezing occasionally, part of the plan, too, lands me a few cautious peripheral glances.

A nervous energy descends upon the room. The girl keeps looking at me, or rather looking at my hat, which reads *American Tractor, Feed & Seed*. I'm wearing a matching red shirt with the same words on the front pocket.

She finishes. The room applauds politely.

"Grady Armistead," the teacher says.

Hinting at a smile that almost reveals his secret, he arranges his note cards on the podium and then steps away from it. He defines Buddhism and the philosophy of turning the other cheek. I cough loudly and add the word "bullshit" to the end. Few students look directly at me. I snarl and laugh at myself, also part of the plan.

"As a practitioner of *ahimsa*," Grady continues, "Gandhi swore to speak the truth and advocated that others do the same."

That's my cue! I stand atop my desk and run to the front of the classroom, desktop to desktop. From the last desk I leap at Grady, hand cocked, ready to explode right onto his face. Unfortunately, I time it wrong and don't catch him with my fist. My elbow catches his chin, and I crash into the floor. He doesn't even stagger. I uncrumple from beneath the blackboard. He continues to talk.

"Gandhi employed non-cooperation, non-violence, and peaceful resistance as his weapons in the struggle against the British *Raj*—"

I give him a quick uppercut to the gut, and he doubles over. He sighs heavily as all the air leaves his body. His hand knocks against the podium, and a couple of note cards spill onto the floor. I may have gone too far. But Grady tilts his head up and looks right into my eyes, giving me permission to go further and harder. I rear back.

"Gandhi dedicated his life to the wider purpose of discovering truth. He tried to achieve this by learning from his own mistakes and conducting experiments on—"

My fist lands squarely on his forehead. He slumps back, which surprises me because I've never considered what hitting someone in the forehead might do. My hand is shaking, the knuckles red. My entire body is shaking with excitement.

Knocking him out cold by the end of his speech is also a part of the plan—at least that's what we discussed—but I'm wondering now how this could possibly happen. I've never even been in a fight before, but I'm kicking his ass all over the room and enjoying it immensely. But how to knock him out? Maybe I should whack him on the back of the head with a book like they do in the movies, but that might kill him.

A few students gather by the door with the teacher. They send one person down the hall to alert Security while the rest of the students huddle in the back of the room. Paul Reubens would be so proud.

I look around the room, trying to pick the martial arts geeks out from the rest of the crowd, but no one looks back. I figure I've got time for one more combination before Security arrives. I rub my hands together and take a deep breath. I feel like I could karate chop the podium in half if given the chance.

My eyes dart around the room one last time, spittle dripping down the side of my mouth. A pristine combination of a left jab, a right uppercut, and—deal sealer!—a right hook, sends his head flying back. His eyes roll white as he lands against the blackboard, then slumps to the floor. As I turn to leave, I pass a group of students at the door. I throw a fake punch. The teacher scrambles, and two students fall over the same chair.

At the end of the long hall, a small window spills light from a door like *Ascent into the Empyrean*, the Hieronymus Bosch painting where an angel moves through a plumbing pipe toward Heaven. I roll my shoulders back and forth like I've just won the heavyweight title of the world, and my step has a little extra lift in it.

As I open the door, just as I'm squeezing my fist to feel the soreness setting in, the air of Knoxville greets me. Laughter and applause drift out from the classroom. By the time my bare feet hit the grass, Grady has told them the truth of the matter—or at least part of it. He won't ever tell it all, not even when I see him later that night.

When I push open the front door that evening, a crate of salvaged strawberries and my notebook under my arm, my smile turns to shock. Grady is making out with Shiloh on a blanket in the living room.

"I thought you had whirling lessons tonight," Grady says, scrambling to stand.

I bite my lip.

"Uh, Shiloh came to visit *you*," he says.

Shiloh looks away.

"It was going to be a surprise visit," she says while staring at the floor.

My own head reels, emotionally flung against a blackboard, my eyes rolled white. I feel nauseated. A fat, sweaty silence fills the room and crowds up against me. All my entrances and exits in the house for the past few months flash through my mind. This isn't the first time they've been together. I can barely breathe.

When Shiloh begins to cry, I feel stupid and weak. That's when the incident in the classroom comes into focus. It was more than just a scholarly display. It was Grady's own perverted attempt to even the score, a pathetic form of self-punishment.

I walk out the back door, down the alley, down the road, and onto the railroad tracks. Along the tar-covered railroad ties, I fantasize about the steel wheels of a train flattening me like a penny. Then I mail the pancake of myself far away from Knoxville.

Late that night, at some railroad crossing, I turn down a road that leads into a town. I pass a funeral home and diner along the way. On a pay phone outside a convenience store, I call my parents collect. My father answers. It's the middle of the night, I'm tired, completely distraught, and I have no idea where I am. In tears, I explain what happened.

A long pause follows. For a moment, I think he's fallen asleep.

"If Dr Pepper makes you sick," he finally says, "then don't drink Dr Pepper no more."

19

educating harmony

chicago, illinois
september 30, 1991

"My goal was to get into grad school, somewhere, anywhere, somehow, so I wouldn't have to spend another year living at my parents' house and working aboard *The Tinker*," I tell my therapist, Zinnia Raphael.

"And here you are, three months later, still expecting a marching-band welcome?" she says.

"At the very least, I imagined that Dr. Young would have read my novel," I say. "How was I to know that she hated elephants?"

"How did you envision this exactly?" Zinnia asks. This is a classic Zinnia-ism, in which she makes the idea of an alternative outcome my responsibility.

"I dunno. The dean offers me an afternoon cocktail in his office, raves about my writing. Flattered, I open up about how I ran away to Maine after leaving Knoxville and lived in the blueberry barrens for the summer. He smiles and tells me that I remind him of a young Hemingway. He offers me another drink. I decline. He invites me to stay in his carriage house rent-free, helps me get a scholarship, and then introduces me to all his accomplished friends in the publishing world. Instead, I'm living in

Evanston at the freakin' YMCA, lining up for the group bathroom each morning with methadone addicts."

Ever since I came to Chicago for grad school I've spent nearly all of my weekly therapy sessions discussing the writing program. We've barely touched on the real reasons that I'm here, which include: Shiloh, going to graduate school to study writing instead of music, and my latest crush on a seventy-year-old Swedish waitress.

"Chop wood, carry water," Zinnia says.

I have no idea what she's talking about. "Is that supposed to make me feel better?"

"When you escape one crisis without resolution, you often unwittingly enter into a continuation of the very same crisis in a different location. The script stays the same. The character names change."

"But I've come to Chicago to embrace the love of my life: writing."

She throws me The Look, another Zinnia-ism. She curls both lips into her mouth until they disappear. Like a quick jab, it's a momentary silent treatment to help me draw my own conclusion.

"You're saying that getting my MFA at Columbia College is the biggest mistake of my life?" As soon as I say it, I know that it's true. I left one mistake behind in Knoxville and walked face first into another one.

"No single relationship can be *everything* to you," she says.

I roll my eyes.

"Besides, you'll probably do okay if you follow the rules," she adds.

"I'm learning about writing from a pile of common wannabes and assorted literary heretics who think they're the fucking royal family."

"Or not," she counters.

<hr>

On my first day of classes, Professor Maya sat smugly in her chair, legs folded tightly across each other as she opened her three-ring binder and began the indoctrination process.

"Welcome to NAM™, the Narrative Approach to Becoming a Man of Letters. My name is Professor Maya, and this is not a writing program. It is an acclaimed and trademarked method designed to help you develop your penmanship and provide you with a step-by-step procedure for ensuring that you become a self-sufficient writer.

"NAM is not made available to those in the regular English Studies program or to anyone outside the school. If you are here to study literature or poetry, you must know that these genres are expressly disallowed both in school and out of school. If you are caught writing poetry or attending a literary event, you will be expelled without a refund. Believe me, it will be worth it. You will all be better writers because of it.

"Now, let's rearrange these chairs into a circle. Your entire first year will take place in your chair, a chair without a desk, a chair without distractions."

"I feel so lucky," a student said beside me. "I still can't believe I'm studying here. Just last week I was spreading Miracle Whip on sandwiches for my children, and now here I am in the inner circle of NAM!"

By the third week of classes, I discovered that NAM had mapped out my entire road to writing salvation. Humble 101 was boot camp. I was sitting in a circle in kindergarten with a bunch of freshmen writing about drinking Milwaukee's Best from beer bongs.

"Sometimes the straw that breaks the camel's back isn't such a bad thing," Zinnia says.

"I feel so small and insignificant," I reply.

"Just in case," Zinnia says, sliding a box of tissues across the table.

"What are those for?" I say, laughing, which sinks into sobbing. "All my life I've been given an extremely long creative leash, and now I'm suddenly on a choke chain. It's a formula for disaster. The criticism in class, the isolation, coming home to a lone cot in a rented room every night, my stupid memories of Shiloh, all these hours with you."

Zinnia remains quiet for a moment as I cry.

"It sounds like the ideal, romantic writer's life," she says, smiling. "Even the hours with me."

I laugh through my tears. "It's romantic when you *read* about it. Now that it's my life, it's all my brain can do to keep it together."

"Often things need to get worse before they get better," she says.

"How much worse can things get?" I ask in disbelief.

Little did I know.

20

the complete reference guide for
overly dramatic suicidal artist-types
in 41 easy steps

chicago, illinois
december 11, 1991

IF YOU EVER TAKE A GRADUATE-LEVEL SCREENWRITING CLASS AT COLUM-
bia College in Chicago and your instructor invites you into the hall and
asks you to help out a classmate named Gerry whom you barely know and
who is wearing a trench coat with a homemade parachute attached and is
holding a six-pack in a paper bag under one arm and a fancy silver butter
knife in the other hand while crying, here is the complete reference guide
for how to handle the situation.

    1. Take the overly dramatic suicidal artist-type across Michigan Ave-
nue. If, during the walk, his arms flap around, his trench coat flies up like
a separate piece of skin, and he questions your motives, tell him that you
just want to admire his parachute in the moonlight. This is not a metaphor. Also, obsequiousness works wonders—especially with screenwriters.

    2. Upon hearing that his ex-wife has killed herself by slashing her
wrists and nearly cutting off her own head in the bathtub and his telling

you that he wants you to take him somewhere for the night so he can't hurt himself, know that, although in all likelihood you won't be able to tell if this is a story he's written, an event that has just happened, or one that occurred a long time ago, you should believe that he's going to hurt himself tonight if you don't help. Don't worry too much about the wife story. You know how your imagination can run wild. You have permission to fret for thirty seconds.

3. Think. Think. Think. You know that you can't keep up with him because you're twenty-three and he's thirty-three and you can't offer him the kind of support he needs. He needs a therapist as much as you do. Probably more. Definitely more. You can't remember enough good jokes to last all night. You also can't remember his name. Jimmy? Robbie? Leonard? Buy some time. Pat him on his parachute, look out at the lake, and then say in a calm voice, "A good rule of thumb for trying any new life-taking device is that the tester should consider creating a dramatic soundtrack." Then add: "Every artist should know this rule."

4. Tell the overly dramatic suicidal artist-type that you should both go back to your room at the YMCA, where you can make a mix tape for him and eat ice-cream sandwiches. This is Plan A.

When he suggests a backup plan, tell him that you know a place where you can take him where people can watch him if the mix tape doesn't work out. This is Plan B. So he knows that you're not talking about the 24-hour diner at the corner of Granville and Winthrop, tell him about the piano player who lives at this place, plays an invisible piano, and can write a piece to accompany his jump. Other musicians there play other invisible instruments, like clarinets and triangles, but he doesn't have to know this. Tell him that someone at this place does needlepoint and can make a little wall hanging for him that reads: ARTISTS, DON'T LEAVE HOME WITHOUT YOUR MIX TAPE.

Above all else, keep calm. Don't be alarmed when he begins to admire his butter knife.

5. Once the overly dramatic suicidal artist-type starts to ponder Plan A and seems, for the moment, out of any immediate danger, and once your heart rate returns to normal, develop a rapport by mimicking his gestures. Look him squarely in the eyes and commiserate. Say, "I feel really alone in Chicago, too." Say, "Alone sucks. Alone in a hot room filled with nothing but a pillow, a blanket, and a book bag sucks worse." Say, "I feel like a heart inside the chest cavity of someone who is already dead."

6. When you arrive at the YMCA and sneak him inside, offer him a seat on the floor beside your minifridge. Retrieve the ice-cream sandwiches from the mini-freezer and your pocket knife from the utensil box and say, "You know, I really like your knife and all, but it's probably too dull to cut anything. If you really plan on doing this right, you should try cutting an inconspicuous area first. I suggest a slice along the ankle because then your sock can cover it up if it doesn't turn out the way you want."

7. Sit beside him. Hand him an ice-cream sandwich and your pocket knife. Begin your transition from Plan A to Plan B. Explain to him that your father gave you this knife for your thirteenth birthday, that on it lies the blood memory of your first deer. Recount the hunt and the special feeling you have with the knife as if recounting the memory of your first love. Exclude the vomiting scene at the end. Embellish the details of the hunt à la Faulkner until he notices the special connection you have with this knife. When the reverse psychology has taken hold of him, tell him that it's time. When he asks, "Time for what?" tell him that it's time to go to the special place where they can watch him.

8. Don't worry that neither you nor the overly dramatic suicidal artist-type has enough money for the cab ride to Hartgrove Mental Hospital. He will projectile-vomit a quarter-mile from the loony bin and jump out of the cab.

Note #1 to self: Crazy people like to run.

Note #2 to self: Cabbies sometimes waive fares under certain conditions. (Certain restrictions may apply.)

9. Know that when you arrive at Hartgrove Mental Hospital:

a) Hartgrove Mental Hospital isn't used to walk-ins.
b) It has no signs that read: CRAZY PEOPLE ENTER HERE.
c) It will prove extremely difficult for you and the overly dramatic suicidal artist-type to find a way in; once you find your way in, you have no idea how hard it will be to get your ass out.
d) Upon entering, you are presumed certifiable until deemed otherwise by an employee of the establishment.

10. Give yourself plenty of time to find the entrance, the admissions desk, and the waiting room. Remember how long it can take in Monopoly to "collect $200 salary as you pass GO"? A good rule of thumb: Wander the halls until you hear the sounds of a rain forest: shrieking toucans, flying monkeys, etc. Follow these sounds to the mirrored door with a sign that reads ONE WAY DOOR ONLY. It's one of the many doors that doesn't have handles.

11. Approach the customer service desk in the center of the room. Do not under any circumstances sass the black woman dressed like a UPS driver managing the clipboard behind the desk. She can and will ruin your life. She is the president of the United Fucking Hartgrove Mental Hospital States, which is what someone seated nearby will tell you. She has friends who are bigger than her. Approach with confidence, give her the name of the overly dramatic suicidal artist-type and take a seat, even if she says something stupid and provoking and has a lisp.

12. Do not be alarmed when, every half hour, a buzzer sounds and a red light on the wall flashes on and off as the doors to the left of the customer service desk open like a carnival-ride mouth to reveal a loading dock. The ambulance drivers in starched white outfits merely add to the rain-forest ambiance. They will wheel in a popular menu item coming soon to your local Applebee's: Lost Soul on a Stretcher.

13. When the tiny bell rings, two bouncer women, also dressed like UPS drivers, will emerge from a back room and wheel the new shrieking toucan away.

14. Take a deep breath. Tell yourself that the screams you hear aren't the sounds of the UPS drivers dissecting people. Tell yourself to breathe. There is no need to exchange a glance with or even talk to the overly dramatic suicidal artist-type. Plan B is in full swing.

15. At 3:07 a.m., when the carnival-mouth doors open and an elderly black man is wheeled in holding a watermelon and screaming, "My *bebé!* My *bebé!*" in a Mexican accent, don't laugh. Someone may laugh at you, too, very soon.

16. On second thought, laugh. It will help you start to think that maybe you might be crazy, too. While you wait, pretend to play an invisible piano and think about how you'll have so much more time on your hands now that you're getting kicked out of graduate school at the end of the semester. Maybe you can take a gig as the new invisible piano player at the Chicago loony bin. *Can you believe that? Kicked out? What kind of crazy bullshit is that? As time goes by . . .*

17. While you wait, replay the conversation you had with Professor Bennett, the assistant dean of the writing program.

"What am I supposed to do now?" you ask.

"Why don't you re-activate your Peace Corps application," he says, not even looking up from the *Wallace Stevens Journal.* "Or go back to West Virginia."

You stare at him.

"What do you want me to do?" he finally says, looking up.

"I don't know. Call somebody."

"For the next two months, *I am* the writing department," he says. "Listen, Flash, I think it's all very romantic that you bought a one-way ticket from West Virginia and came up here with your manual typewriter, but there's nothing we can do to help you anymore. We're not allowing you to take classes in our department, and that's final."

18. When asked to approach the customer service desk with the overly dramatic suicidal artist-type and asked to take the laces out of your shoes and put them in a basket on the UPS driver's desk, remember rule 9(d): Upon entering, you are presumed certifiable until deemed otherwise by an employee of the establishment; and rule 11: The UPS driver lady is president of the United Fucking Hartgrove Mental Hospital States.

19. Congratulations! You are just like everyone else sitting in the orange seats. Now sit down.

20. No matter how many goddamn times you tell people that you're not from West Virginia, they don't hear you. When they hear Virginia, they add the "West" automatically.

21. Breathe. It will be 4:37 a.m. when one of the UPS women approaches the overly dramatic suicidal artist-type and takes him away. Call him by his name when he goes because no sound is more pleasing than one's own name uttered aloud. "Good luck, Bobbie." He won't turn around, though, because his name is Gerry. After a few minutes the UPS woman will come back for you.

22. She will lead you into a room that looks like it's used for performing operations. It has a tile floor that makes cleaning up fluids a breeze! The doctor who will enter the room will have funny arms. They will hang off his body like loose rope. He will be able to move his hands but not his arms. He will sling them around like bacon on a griddle. He will sling them onto his lap. He will ask you to sit on the operating table, and his right arm will hang down beside his leg.

23. The conversation between you and the doctor will go something like this:

"Are you here for somebody?"

"Yes, the overly dramatic suicidal artist-type."

"What do you mean, 'the overly dramatic suicidal artist-type'?"

"The overly dramatic suicidal artist-type you just talked with. We came together."

"Ahh, I see. Do you know why he's here tonight?"

"I don't know. He's broken, I guess. Is that the right answer?"

"Excuse me?"

"Broken."

"Broken? Broken in what way?"

24. Now is not the time to provide details about what a big whore you think your screenwriting teacher is, what a big stupid-ass scam he's running in your graduate screenwriting class, that you know he gets a deal from a book publisher before the semester begins to adapt a novel into a screenplay, and he has his students create the screenplay, and at the end of the semester, when the screenplay is finished, he puts his name on it, delivers the work to his editor, and gets the credit and the check. Now is not the time to talk about all of this.

25. Imagine that you are entering the climax of your movie. You're about to stand and deliver the speech of all speeches, which will either have you committed or gain your freedom. Think how important freedom is to you. Think about how free you felt on the back of your father's motorcycle as a kid. Say loudly, "Are we broken when we cannot write? Are we broken when we cannot perform as artists? Are we broken when we filter too much out? Are we broken when we can't filter out enough? Are we broken when asked to resign from graduate school at the age of twenty-three?"

26. It's OK to feel dizzy. It's probably not OK to whisper the word "broken" a few times.

27. The doctor with funny arms will scribble on his yellow pad of paper. He will say, "I think you're having problems with object permanence. This means that when an object is removed from your line of sight, you think that the object has completely disappeared from the universe, that it no longer exists." *No shit*, you will think. Then he will stand up and say, "Take the laces out of your shoes."

28. You will bend over and start to unlace your shoes before you remember that you already took the laces out for the UPS lady with the clipboard in Customer Service.

29. Back in the waiting room, you will take a seat. Now is not the time to feel overwhelmed with sadness, resentment, and expectations that have fallen short once again. Now is not the time to think about how you left Virginia nearly a year ago with a one-way Amtrak ticket to Chicago with your pillow, blanket, book bag, and a vision of how your writing was going to change the world. Remember: This is Plan B. Keep your wits about you.

30. In the waiting room, you will start to realize how completely fucking nuts all of this is. Now is the time to remember that the extent of your relationship with the overly dramatic suicidal artist-type is only real-estate related. It's exactly like when you sat beside Sylvia Chapman in homeroom in twelfth grade. You shared a common through-way between your desks. No more, no less.

31. Now is not the time to remember back to your bar mitzvah days and how the Torah says somewhere that the overly dramatic suicidal artist-type is your responsibility.

32. Now is the time to think about how to get your ass out of here. Get out of your orange seat. Walk away. Leave.

33. When you approach the door, the buzzer will buzz, the red light on the wall will flash, and the UPS lady will point to you and call for Nelson. See rules 9(d) and 11.

34. Nelson will be the biggest black woman you've ever seen in your entire life. When she moves toward you, consider lying prone on the floor and whining like your dog did once.

35. When Nelson approaches, hunch forward, nod, and hurry back to your orange seat. At 6:00 a.m., another dissection will begin in the back room. The screams will be unbearable. That is your sign. Will the doors to open. Imagine a light bulb in your mind's eye. Visualize the doors opening. When the doors mysteriously open, get up and walk out, but walk like you're not hurrying and not excited. Walk like you're walking to the post office.

36. Walk. Walk. Walk.

37. Be afraid to stop walking.

38. Don't look back. Walk out the front door, and walk home even though it's nearly sixteen miles away. Repeat Step 36 as necessary while chanting a mantra in your head to the cadence of your footsteps. In the rhythm there is safety.

39. *Motherfucker, titty sucker, two-eyed bitch. I just dropped some guy off in the belly of a witch.*

40. You may want to call someone when you get back to your room, but you don't have a telephone. You may want to lie down on your bed and relax, but your bed is a stiff cot. Spread some dirty clothes on your cot. Lie down in luxurious comfort, and repeat the last line from "Row, Row, Row Your Boat" until you fall asleep.

41. Near midnight, just before you fall deep into REM sleep, you will have a lucid dream. Joining you on the floor in the darkness will be: your grandfather, your grandmother, and your father—the three most influential artists in your life. Sit up. Your grandmother will take your hand and begin a discussion about time-release cold capsules that helps you understand that this huge tangent otherwise called graduate school is really all about freedom.

"Writing school was a way for you to find a medium of expression that belonged exclusively to you," your grandmother says, taking your hand.

"Your experiences are like time-release capsules," your grandfather says. "Hold onto this experience with the overly dramatic suicidal artist-type. When the time seems right, release it."

"Always consider the rate of distribution," your father says. "When in doubt, take the capsule with a Dr Pepper."

21

the german atonement package

chicago, illinois
january 22, 1992

"HELLO, MY DYEAR," VEL SAYS. THE PENCIL MOLE ON HER CHEEK DANCES.

"Hi, Vel." I slide my notebook and the envelope out of the way toward the napkin dispenser. Vel sets a huge stack of Danish pastries on the table.

"You yoo-sual, dyear?"

I nod shyly and slide forward in the booth, moving closer to the fist-size cinnamon rolls. Amazingly, Ann Sather's, the Swedish diner on Clark Street, still serves these for free.

"You afternoon yoo-sual or you evening yoo-sual?" she asks. Her thin hand-drawn eyebrows pinch a piece of skin between her eyes like a pair of tweezers beckoning me.

"Uh, the afternoon, I guess."

Large cotton briefs hang out of her slacks like a huge flour tortilla. Seeing them embarrasses me but mildly arouses me as well. Am I truly in love with the old waitress, or is it misplaced affection for what she represents?

More than just the Gatekeeper of Free Pastries, she's the only person in Chicago besides Zinnia who knows me by name since I left school. I now wish I had the time to bring up the topic in therapy before I lost my student loan money and, with it, the ability to pay for more sessions.

"Be right back, dyear," Vel says.

As she turns, I turn toward the window and shove a whole huge roll into my mouth. It's like trying to fit my fist in my mouth. I attempt to chew. Saliva drips down the front of my shirt. My cheeks bulge. I squeeze the napkin dispenser and make a concerted effort to breathe through my nose to keep from choking. My back molars move up and down. I try to chew with the right side of my mouth, but nothing happens. The roll just sits in my mouth. I begin to panic.

To hide my predicament, I stare out the window at an industrial swatch of Lake Michigan between a tiny two-foot opening separating two buildings. The water is the color of a gun barrel and still. The sky is the same color and ominous.

Zinnia would call this is a prime example of operating in crisis mode. "Your need to consume anything and everything around you that is good comes from a deep down socialized fear. You just don't think good things will stick around long enough for you to enjoy them," she would have said.

It's true. Somewhere, not so deep down, Vel may decide to take away the free pastries.

She appears with my order: a plate of french fries, a cup of vegetarian chili, and a bowl of chocolate pudding. Pastry juice drips down my chin. Suddenly there's a cinnamon roll faucet running out of my face.

"I see you have new envelope," she says, ignoring my perverse gluttony. "Did you get anything published this week?" She wipes her hands on her apron.

I shake my head and swallow. "Just a letter from home."

"I have not been home since I was very small," she tells me.

"I talk to my parents every few weeks, but I only see them during the holidays," I reply, which makes my relationship with my family seem more than it really is.

"I do not think about home so much," she says. "Can I get you anyting else?"

I shake my head.

"OK, I see you in a little while, then," she says.

Vel and the pastries affirm my addiction to crisis. After she sets the check on the table and gives me her famous smile that practically melts me, I turn toward the window again and push another whole roll into my mouth, beginning the pastry faucet ordeal all over again. Afterward, I take the letter from the envelope and re-read my Uncle Pierre's words to my mother.

Dear Vera,

Ten years ago, I petitioned the German government for everything that had been confiscated from Mommy and Daddy during the war. I filled out an application and sent it in. The German Atonement Package has finally arrived. It has come in the form of a check drawn from a Swiss bank account. Please accept your portion of the money and divide it up amongst your children as you see fit. I have also included a copy of a photograph that was taken of us during that time. Please feel free to share this with your family as well.

Sincerely,

Pierre

I slide the photograph out from behind the letter. On the back, written in black pen, is my grandmother's shaky English translation: "September 1937—Kitchen, Moulin Rouge, Paris, France."

On the front, my grandfather sports long, dark hair past his belt line. He looks like a wild stallion. He is wearing his hat that looks like an upside-down bathroom trash can. He is standing in a chorus line of men, ten others equally eccentric in their dress. Everyone is smiling huge, child-like smiles, like the world is full of possibility. Which at that moment it was—but not for the better.

I flip the photograph over and look at the date again. The math tells me that my mother was just a baby, my Uncle Pierre only six. A scene fills my head of my grandparents, barely twenty, in love, frolicking through the streets of Paris with their new family.

The envelope arrives on the same day that Columbia College kicks me out. I've read and re-read it ever since. At first I don't tell Zinnia about it, because the topic will consume all of our time. If we're talking about the writing program, I won't get to talk about Shiloh and my crush on Vel.

But then the loot fantasies begin. A huge storage unit of stuff arrives in front of my YMCA room. Inside lies a first glimpse into my mother's childhood: stuffed animals, books, portraits, my grandmother's paint-brushes, my grandfather's dance shoes. Then the nightmares begin. By the time I tell Zinnia, it's too late. I only have enough money to pay for two more therapy sessions.

"The money that came with that letter seems too precious to spend," I admit to her. "I don't want to waste it on something frivolous. I feel like I've been given a huge problem."

"It sounds like it's time to ask your family some questions," Zinnia says.

"About what? My mom just says the same thing: 'Your grandfather was a dancer at the Moulin Rouge. You get your music talent from him. Your grandmother was the cousin of Ingrid Bergman. You get your looks from her.'"

The next day I call my mother to talk about it. Silence weighs heavily on the phone. My father says it's none of his business. My uncle won't return my calls.

"Without the drama of graduate school, might I suggest a sacred distraction?" Zinnia says during our very last session.

"What do you mean?" I say.

"I think it's in your best interest to proceed to piece together the silence of 1937 for yourself," she says.

⌇⌇

When I stand up to pay the check, the first wave of dizziness hits. My head rolls beneath my shoulders. Nauseated and hot, I tuck the letter into my coat pocket and lean on the table. Then the floor unexpectedly hits my knees.

Vel calls one of the cooks from the kitchen. He leads me to a chair in a small paneled hallway outside the bathrooms.

"I don't know what's going on," I manage.

"You rest here, dyear," she says. "I tink you have a fever." She returns with a cold dishrag for my forehead. She moves my hand to hold it in place.

The clock above me reads 6:55 . . . 7:05 . . . 7:25.

Close to 8:00, I reach for the large, black rotary phone. I dial the operator and place a collect call to Zinnia. She picks me up and drives me to the emergency room. At the doors to the emergency room I say, "Just drop me off here. Don't wait."

She asks if I'm sure. I don't answer. I lean forward, and soon I'm inside the emergency room. As I sit and wait, a wave of fear washes over me. Other patients look at me, then look away. I have no idea what's going on.

When my name is called, I walk to a cubicle and answer questions. Then, I'm led to a private room. I lie down on the examination table and prop my feet up on the table. The nurse comes in, takes my vitals, and marks them down. With her broad, mannish shoulders and an indistinct glow that resembles a five o'clock shadow, she reminds me of Professor Bennett, the assistant dean of the writing program who sucked the life out of me. She hands me a paper hospital gown and asks me to get undressed.

"Leave all your belongings here. You will need to wear the gown in order to be permitted into the treatment room."

Was that a swastika on her uniform?

After a few minutes a stocky plumber-looking guy walks in carrying a gym bag. He doesn't introduce himself. He unzips his bag and pulls out the largest needle I've ever seen.

"Holy shit!" I suddenly feel much better. "Are you giving me a shot with *that?*"

"Just a small lumbar puncture," he says. "Are you allergic to any medications?"

"*Huh?*" I say. I'm freaked out.

"Just lie on your side. The doc wants a spinal fluid sample." He pushes the needle into a large silver syringe.

"You're going to stick that thing in my back?"

"It won't hurt," he says. "It's just a sample."

"Now?"

"I'll let you know when. First I'm going to rub this cream on you. It'll numb your skin."

I read about spinal fluid when researching whether it was safe to take ecstasy. It's not a bodily fluid that regenerates itself. The idea of him taking something from me that I can't get back just doesn't seem right.

"Can you hold on for a minute? I've got to go to the bathroom," I say.

I lean forward and wobble into the hall. I ask a nurse where I can find a pay phone. She directs me to a new maze of halls. At the phone, I make a series of collect calls. My mom gives me Uncle Pierre's phone number. Uncle Pierre is working at the hospital, so my aunt gives me his office number. I call Dr. Uncle Pierre and tell him about the size of the needle.

"I don't know why this is a remedy for feeling dizzy," I tell him.

"Unfortunately, I must agree with the hospital," he says. Then: "I am extremely sorry."

"That's okay," I say.

"Okay?" he says.

We share an awkward silence.

"Do you know why I apologize?"

"I guess," I lie.

"I will tell you. I'm extremely sorry I did not return your phone calls. I will not admit to you that it was because I was too busy. It is just that I did not want to examine this part of my past. But now let me tell you what it is I think you want to know. Perhaps it will help you now.

"When Germany passed the law that forbid any Jews from participating in the arts, my parents do what a lot of their Jewish friends do. They take their creative energy and join the French resistance. By then, it was no longer just a Jewish fight. It was an artistic fight as well. My parents send your mother and me to live in a Catholic mission in the southern Vichy-controlled areas of France.

"For the next three years, the Resistance sends your grandparents all over France to help Allied airmen shot down over enemy territory find their way to safety. Often, when a town is overrun with Nazis, the Resistance throws them in jail to keep them safe. When it is safe for them to come out, they change their names and fabricate entire histories for themselves.

"But by then, it does not matter. All men are required to sign the name Israel on all legal documents and all women, the name Sarah."

My own name change takes on new meaning.

"One year before the war ends, your grandparents, your mother, and I pile in the backseat of a steamer ship bound for the United States. With us, comes a visitor—a seed of silence. When we arrive at Ellis Island, my father changes our name from Ashkenaz to Ashe to sound more American. Our family is now known as the Ashes, and that is that. Do you have a question or two?"

"Um, no?" I say.

"Okay, then," he says. "I will say good-bye and get back to work."

"Good-bye . . ." I say.

I hang up and sit under the phone. My eyes well up with tears. What to make of this personal history lesson given in such a matter-of-fact way? With one short phone call, I feel somehow less enlightened rather than more. What part of me is actually the Jewish part?—my head, my hands, my heart.

For so long I've felt that my need to push the creative envelope has come from my father, but now I'm not so sure. Now it seems the impetus has roots in some deeper, more sacred place. Zinnia's line about a "scared distraction" comes to mind. Voices and footsteps come my way, so I stand and start walking down the maze of halls. I find the exit and walk into the chill night air, my ass hanging out of my hospital gown.

Walking home in a paper hospital gown somehow makes more sense than feeling dizzy and letting a stranger take spinal fluid out of my back. I never go back for my clothes, the letter, or my wallet.

I toss and turn in a feverish state for the next few days. The resident director at the YMCA makes an exception and allows me to stay in my room during the day. When the fever finally breaks at the end of the week, the great divide—which has split my family in two like a root vegetable too long on the vine—presents itself. Half my family embraces their Jewish identity, and half denies it. My grandfather kept the rituals and traditions alive. My grandmother, disillusioned, became an atheist and rolled her eyes. My uncle Pierre became a Super Jew, promoting all things Jewish, associating only with other Jews who wore yarmulkes during the week, who went to synagogue on the weekend. My mother, like my grandma, became a Closet Jew, hiding all things Jewish, marrying a good ol' boy from West Virginia, and trying to forget the specter of fear that silenced my family.

Marrying my father had formed part of her ultimate plan of assimilation. If Hitler ever came looking for the Jews again, wherever my father might take her would be the last place he would ever think of looking. An artist capable of creating anything, my father could help her make any type of hiding place to keep her safe—even if that hiding place was me.

part three

love me

22

love in boxes

chicago, illinois
september 30, 1993

"LET ME SEE THE COLLAR AGAIN." WHEN GERRY TURNS TOWARD ME, I adjust the white piece of cardboard under his black shirt collar so the staples don't show. He makes the perfect priest: friendly, fit, nice haircut. "There."

As the cityscape blurs past, Gerry spies himself in the El window, smiles, touches his vestigial tab, puts his hands in his lap, and touches his collar again. Since his release from the United Fucking States of Hartgrove Mental Hospital, Gerry and I have become friends . . . or as close to friends as possible with an overly dramatic suicidal artist-type. We occasionally share a plate of pastries together at Ann Sather's. Sometimes our gatherings include conversation; sometimes just pastries. Occasionally, like now, they include favors.

"From the congregation of corrugation," he says and winks. "How's that, Chief?"

The El slows and stops at Berwyn. The doors open. I move the refrigerator box so a pregnant woman can sit down. The doors close. Gerry adjusts the collar, checks his buttons, and brushes his legs with his hands.

"I'm nervous," I say.

"Nervous? You don't have to do anything," he says. "Besides, you should be happy you're not living with the crackheads at the YMCA anymore."

He's right. I should be—and I am. After transferring into the education department and getting twice as much student loan money, a great apartment in an artist's cooperative in Rogers Park, and the perfect job at the college coffee shop where I slice bagels for every beautiful, creative girl in the Windy City, I do have a lot to be happy about.

"But I'm still nervous. I might have to wait—days, weeks, maybe even a month—before I get a reply. You have no idea. Maybe I'll never get a reply."

"You'd think a man who wants to give a cardboard box to a woman would have more important things to occupy his mind," Gerry says.

Daisy's eyes, lips, breasts, shoulders, and smile cascade to mind. Each part is a star viewed from a distant planet through darkness. Once again, Zinnia was right: The straw that broke the camel's back finally arrived. Everything that she ever said to me finally made sense. Out of the darkness came clarity and brightness.

The train slows and stops at Wilson. The doors open. Gerry adjusts his collar, checks his buttons, brushes his legs with his hands, and stamps his feet twice. The doors close.

"You can still see the word 'Zenith' on it," he says, referring to the purple box. "Do you want her to think it's a TV inside, Chief?"

"I want her to think I went to some trouble . . . but not *too* much trouble." Purple paint underlines my fingernails. "I was worried the paint wouldn't dry in time."

For days I haven't been able to eat. I want to be next to Daisy. I want to hold her, kiss her, disappear inside of her.

"Do I look okay?" Gerry asks.

"Everybody likes priests," I say.

"Everybody likes cowboys more," he says. "When I was at Hartgrove, we had two cowboys, and you should have seen the attention they got. The doctors, nurses, even visitors who weren't crazy wanted to be around them."

"Priests are safe. You look safe," I say, chewing on my knuckles. Nervousness and doubt wash over me. "Do you think I should've gone with the cowboy motif instead?"

"I think you should calm down," he says, eerily remembering the end of Step 4.

"I couldn't find a cowboy outfit at the thrift store," I say. It feels odd that Gerry is the one offering me comfort now.

"Chill," he says.

The train stops at Sheridan. The doors open. An old couple gets on. They look at the box, smile at Gerry, and sit across from us. Gerry adjusts his collar, checks his buttons, brushes his legs with his hands, stamps his feet twice, and rotates his neck.

"Here's the strange thing," he says. "I still don't understand why you just didn't do this yourself."

"That would be awkward."

"But you said you only saw her once. She wouldn't recognize you."

"I said I only *talked* to her once," I say. "She comes into the coffee shop for a chocolate milk every morning on her way to work. I don't want her to think I'm a stalker."

"Did you ever think you might have better luck courting a poet or a film student?"

"A poet? How the hell do you find a poet? Poets are afraid of light. What do you do with someone afraid of light? This girl is a lawyer's assistant. She wears a power suit to work. Have you ever seen a girl up close in a corporate uniform?"

Corporate girls are my version of the firefighter fetish that most women have. The train stops at Belmont. The door opens. Gerry adjusts his collar, checks his buttons, brushes his legs with his hands, stamps his feet twice, rotates his neck, and makes a funny noise. His OCD routine is making me even more nervous. Hopefully the weirdo factor won't trump the priest effect.

"This is our stop," I say.

Gerry's tic goes on for so long that the doors actually close on us as we're lifting the box out.

"Are you okay?" I ask.

"I'm fine. Can we just get a move on? I don't know how long I can keep this collar on."

We stop at the bottom of the stairs, and Gerry rubs his right foot against the sidewalk half a dozen times like a bull preparing to charge.

"Listen, ten more minutes, and then you can get naked for all I care," I say. "Just give me ten more minutes."

"Here's my theory, Chief. The world consists of blinks and time in between blinks. You close your eyes, open them, and the world has changed around you. Blink for long enough, and the whole universe may have changed by the time you open your eyes again."

"Is that why you do all those weird things?"

"What weird things?"

I imitate him. "You know, all that."

"With normal everyday blinking," he says, ignoring me, "your life changes and then changes back again. Like a child playing hide-and-seek?"

Unsure of his own simile, Gerry sets the box down and unleashes a new circus of tics. Like a rooster, he goes back and forth from the previous section of sidewalk to the one we're standing on. It's exhausting to watch. But it's something I've had to endure more and more. Since his release from the loony bin, he feels like he owes me.

"Between blinks is the manifestation of our will. Maybe airplanes really don't fly anywhere. Maybe it's just our will that causes them to lift up during an extended blink. The world turns under us, increasing our nearness to the places and moments that change our lives forever."

"Do you really believe that?" I say.

"I think we all know it somehow. I think we all fear the moments that make us feel more alive."

Gerry stops again. He sets the box down. We're standing one block from the law office.

"What's wrong *now*?"

"Why the hell are you giving a box to a girl?"

The tiny door on the front of the box has a fake handle. Wall-to-wall purple faux fur that cost a small fortune lines the inside along with a string of battery-powered blue Christmas lights. It's the most beautiful thing in the world and reminds me that inside every box lies a world of possibility. It represents every box I've ever unwrapped for my birthday and Christmas. A box—rather than a painting, poem, sculpture, or a dozen sunflowers—is the only way I can adequately express the feelings overwhelming my system at the moment. Zinnia would call this an elemental healthy strategy.

The real reason that I'm giving Daisy a box is that I've never gotten over Savannah van Houten's reaction to my serenade. I'm afraid of being called weird, which is weird because I'm doing something weird so as not to be called weird. Zinnia would call this a self-correcting logical consequence.

"I dunno," I say. "Seems logical, doesn't it?"

"No," he says. "Most guys just give a red rose and a Hallmark card to girls they like. But hey, consider the source, you know?"

Across the street from the law office I let go of the box like a water skier letting go of a tow line. I feel so alive that I want to explode. Gerry and the box bob up and down and then disappear into the building.

Ten minutes later, Gerry emerges, his collar undone.

"Was she there?" I ask.

"She put her hand over her mouth when I announced her name to the office. Everybody looked at her."

"Oh my God, are you sure it was her?"

"The honey blonde? Yeah, she's beautiful."

"I told you! Did you say what I told you to say? You gave her the envelope? The letter has my phone number in it."

"Relax, Chief. She'll contact you. It'll be fine."

For the next week, I spend every waking second thinking about her laugh, her smile, her curves. I fall asleep thinking about Daisy. I wake up thinking about Daisy. Then one morning, an envelope appears under my door. Inside on a piece of paper is Daisy's phone number above the words, "Utilize those digits." My lone box, a lost spaceship, has found Daisy's planet.

As a whacky thank-you for helping me with my courtship, I paste Gerry's photo on a piece of paper in the elevator of our apartment building with the words, HAVE YOU SEEN ME? I'M LOST above his phone number. It's meant to be nothing more than a clever joke, the landlord calls him, and they have a conversation that the landlord describes as a Laurel and Hardy routine:

"Hello, I've found the guy in the photo."

"What photo?"

"The photo in the elevator."

"There's a photo in the elevator?"

"Yes, it's a photo of you."

"Of me?"

"Yes, you. Did you know you were lost?"

"I don't think so."

"Well, if you are, I know where you are ..."

By the time I realize that my thank-you joke has sent my obsessive-compulsive friend over the edge, I'm in love. While he loses it completely

in his apartment upstairs and dissolves the tenuous bonds of our friendship, I've got only one thing on my mind: Daisy. One door shuts, and
another opens.

I blink. I blink again. In between, I feel something I haven't felt in
a very long time. Gerry may have been crazy, but he was right about
one thing.

23

love in 12 courses

chicago, illinois
october 20, 1993

I DIAL AND HANG UP. I'M A TEENAGER ALL OVER AGAIN. MY HANDS ARE sweaty. My heart beats so hard that it pushes against my T-shirt.

"Hello?" I want to tell her that I love her. Probably too soon. "Is this Daisy du Maurier?"

"Who is this?" she says.

"You don't know?"

"Carter?" she says.

My legs feel like paper. I have to sit down. "I'm calling because you told me to utilize your digits. Do you know who it is now?"

"Oh my God, yes," she says. She laughs. I laugh. "I'm sorry."

"For what?" I say.

"I don't know. Can you tell I'm nervous?"

She laughs. I laugh.

"Did you like your gift?" I say.

"Oh my God, yes. Do you know, I now have one of the largest collections of purple boxes in the United States."

I laugh. She laughs.

"I did not know that," I say.

"The box is beautiful."

"I'm glad you like it." I want to tell her that I love her. "I thought you might think it was, um . . . well, strange."

"No," she says genuinely.

"So I have a question for you."

"I might have an answer for you."

I laugh. She laughs.

"I was wondering if you'd like to get together on Sunday for a Sunday Love Feast."

She laughs. I laugh.

"It . . . I mean, um . . . the feast will actually include food," I say.

"That would be nice," she says.

~ ~

She's sitting on the steps of the Hare Krishna temple wearing a polka-dotted hair ribbon, a ruffly red cami, and jeans. Her hair is more brown than blonde, but I'm more surprised that she's not wearing a business suit.

We hug. I don't want to let go. She smells good. "Every single thing about you is beautiful," I want to say. Instead, I smile and hold the door open for her. We step into a massive marble hall and join hundreds of others in the food line. Stretching out before us is a row of tables—at least 200 feet long—topped with silver serving trays filled with food.

"Oh my God. You weren't lying, were you?" she says. "This really is a Love Feast. It smells incredible in here."

We move forward in line.

"They do this every Sunday," I say. "It's all vegetarian."

"And it's free?" she says.

"I promise I'm not as cheap as I seem."

She laughs. I smile and hand her a paper plate, and we move forward.

"You know, I know nothing about you," she says.

I hand her a plastic fork, take one for myself, and we move forward.

"Now's probably not the time to tell you about my plastic cutlery fetish, is it?" I say.

She laughs and runs her fingers through her hair. I laugh and look away. We move forward.

"Well?" she says.

"That's not completely true," I say. "You know I can make change for a five. You know I can slice and toast a pretty mean bagel."

"Except that," she says.

"I, on the other hand, know next to nothing about you," I say.

"Ask me anything."

"Really? Twenty questions?"

"As many as you want."

We move forward.

"Are you from here?" I ask.

"Close. Madison, Wisconsin, but I've been living here for the past two years."

"Why Chicagoland?" I ask.

"For school. I go to Loyola."

I laugh. She laughs.

"Why are you laughing?" she says.

"You know I live, like, half a block from Loyola, right?"

"No. Perhaps we've passed each other. Where do you live?"

"On Granville," I say. "Wait, I thought you worked in a law office."

"Part-time. I got the job out of high school. It pays really well and makes me feel like an adult. I have to wear business suits. Plus, they're paying for all my classes."

As the server takes our plates and fills them, I imagine a private fashion show back at her apartment while I eat ice cream with a plastic spoon.

"Are you in graduate school?"

"Undergraduate," she says. "I didn't go to college right away."

We walk to a corner of the marble hall and sit down on the floor. Too nervous to eat, I stir my food in a circle.

"My turn," she says.

I prepare to tell her about my recent student loan bounty, about using it to move from the YMCA to my new apartment in Rogers Park, about transferring from the writing department to the education department for peace of mind, about wanting to leave Chicago as soon as I graduate.

"Why me?" she says.

"Wow," I blush. "You don't waste any time do you?"

"It comes from working around lawyers for the past three years."

"Am I turning red?"

"Are you avoiding the question?"

"Maybe," I admit. "Okay, I didn't want to tell you this so soon, but, besides the fact that I'm overly impressed with your diction, your parents are paying me to cure you of your extremely expensive chocolate milk addiction."

She laughs. I laugh. She hits me. I fall over. We laugh more.

"What?" I say.

"So that's what tonight is all about?"

"Exactly," I say, holding up a spoonful of rice pudding. "Replacing one ad-*diction* with another. Bon appétit!"

After dinner, we walk down to the lakefront. The moon is an overturned bowl, a sliver of waning crest. We joke about the stars spilling out of the bowl. We laugh. We hold hands. We move forward. On a playground swing set, we twist in circles, our feet entangled.

"Do you know what you want to do after you graduate?" she asks.

"I'm not sure. After I finish my student teaching, I have to write my thesis. I'm thinking about moving somewhere in Maine. Somewhere off the grid away from all of this. Somewhere I can fix fishing nets and write."

"So writing is your main thing?" she says.

"You mean as opposed to curing lawyers' assistants of chocolate milk addictions?"

Her leg touches mine and sends a jolt of energy through my body.

"I just meant as opposed to music or whatever," she says. "You said you were really into music."

"Yeah, pretty much," I say. "I had two short stories published this year."

"Look at you," she says.

"No, they were small 'zines. Tiny. One literally paid five bucks. The other sent me a copy of the magazine as payment."

"You don't want to teach?"

My father's voice echoes in my head: *Every artist worth his salt needs something to fall back on if his art don't pan out.*

"I guess it's something to fall back on. My mom is convinced that it's a good deal with summers off and all. I wrote this essay in English class, and it sort of changed my life. With my music and performing, it's always felt like a series of diversions. A one-way ticket away from wherever I happen to be. My stories are more like a truth, an invitation into a conversation. I dunno, maybe I'm just crazy."

A gentle silence descends between the creaking chains of the swings.

"I like the way you think, Coleman," she says.

We hold hands on the way to the L. She thanks me. I let go of her hand at the turnstile and watch her walk up the steps like a child letting go of a helium balloon, wondering why and wanting to follow.

Every second of my walk home, I think of her. Her eyes are soft and strong and know all the good within me. Her smile, a half-smile really, turns up the corner of her mouth just under her right cheek. I love the way she pronounces her words. I want to sit beside her and watch her read her history books, listen to her read aloud, kiss her, hold her, and share this grand feeling of possibility that she manifests within me.

24

baby with the bath water

chicago, illinois
november 1, 1993

"Drive! Just drive!" I say through the tears. "Just get us out of here."

Inside her Honda Civic, I fall apart, my head against her arm. I hold her as tight as I can and cry.

"Oh, sweetie," Daisy says as she puts the car in gear and we pull away from the school.

"This time I hid in a bathroom stall until lunch," I say.

I roll down the window and scream as loud as I can: "WHAT THE HELL AM I DOING WITH MY LIFE?"

The entire day runs through my head: walking through the metal detectors that morning, the ultra-masculinity of the rent-a-cop with the bullhorn separating the boys and girls; the hardcore gangsters in my makeshift classroom with the concrete floor; kids who smell like cigarettes and answer the roll call by giving me the finger; students with their "We don't fake it, we take it! And fuck you if you don't like it!" attitude; teenagers who can hardly read a paragraph or write their own names.

Gunshots sound in the schoolyard again, and we all duck together. The desks screech like fingernails across a blackboard. For a second, the drug dealing, carjacking, raping, and murdering world outside fades away into a moment of connection. In the brief silence, we inseparably face the possibility of our own death. Then the world begins to turn again, and adrenaline, anger, and such immense sadness conquer me—again.

"I know what you need," Daisy says. "I know exactly what you need." She pulls a U-turn, and we head in the opposite direction. "Can't you talk to your advisor about switching schools?"

"For what? Then I'll have to wait an entire year to finish my student teaching," I say. "Where are you taking us?"

Daisy shrugs. "So what? You said yourself that you want to write when you graduate not teach."

"I don't know . . ."

She turns down Taylor Street, pulls over, and parks.

"Where are we going?" I say.

"It's a surprise. Come on."

She leads me to a small white and green shack squeezed between two apartment buildings. Above it, a sign with green hand-painted letters reads: Mario's Italian Lemonade.

"I love you so much," I say.

Daisy orders us a huge container of strawberry lemon ice.

"Plastic spoons!" I say, smiling.

"I know. I remembered."

I poke at the lemon rinds and seeds among the ice.

"It's the real stuff," she says. She leans forward, and we share a kiss. I spoon a bite into her mouth. "I still don't know why you couldn't transfer to that private school on Sheridan. It's a block from your apartment."

"I don't know," I say.

"The education department makes about as much sense as the writing department."

"The thing is, I'm never going to have time to write with a job like this. My mom is crazy. She said I'd get summers off, but you need the summers off just to screw your head back on."

The next night back in my apartment, Daisy gives me a signed copy of *The Good Life* by Helen and Scott Nearing. The back cover reads: "Helen and Scott Nearing are the great-grandparents of the back-to-the-land movement, having abandoned the city in 1932 for a rural life based on self-reliance, good health, and a minimum of cash."

"I thought it might inspire you," she says.

I kiss her on the cheek, she kisses me on the lips. Everything else disappears for a moment.

"But you can only read it under one condition," she says, pulling away.

"What's that?"

"When you end up going to Maine, you have to take me with you."

Her words tug at my heart, indelibly connecting me to her, filling me up and emptying me out at the same time.

25

anatomy of a whirl

jonesboro, maine / township 14, maine / brooksville, maine /
machias, maine
june 11, 1994

"Listen, I need my transcript to say that I've got my master's degree."

"You wrote half your thesis on your guitar," Deirdre, my thesis advisor, says.

"You said you liked the songs, my account's current, I turned in all my library books. I did the work—I need to start looking for a teaching job."

Under the campground sign—Downeast Jones: The Northernmost Easternmost Campground in the United States—Daisy is holding two buckets of blueberries. I bite my bottom lip and mime that I want to pull the phone off the wall. She smiles and mouths "I love you." Her eyes glisten.

I whisper, "I love you," back.

"The dean is having a real problem," Deirdre says. "She doesn't understand why you included fifty pages of sheet music."

Earlier that day, Daisy, in her tank top and green do-rag, and I bent over between the rows of blueberry, our silver rakes sweeping at the berries. Migrant workers sang and laughed in the field with us as they swung their rakes beside us.

"What happened to your dream of fixing fishing nets and becoming the next John Steinbeck?" asks Deirdre, breaking my moment of reverie.

"Everything's ideal in school," I reply. "There's no deferment here. I've got loans to pay off."

But she's right, and I reconsider the spiel I spouted to the whole education department, telling everyone that I was moving to Maine to get a job fixing fishing nets while I finished my novel. I was going to use my degree as a backup plan in case I didn't make it as a writer. It made me feel better than everyone else. But foolishly I expected the acceptance letters from my short stories to keep rolling in after the first two. It's been nothing but rejection since then, and my writing bubble is nearing collapse.

"Dean Broadhead is pretty upset that you re-included that part about oral sex in your thesis," Deirdre says. "I thought we agreed that you should leave that part out."

"The dean is just mad that the word 'oral' makes it sound dirty. She's such a prude."

"Listen, Slashtipher, I'm with you on this. I've told you that from the beginning. Even if no one in the department gets you, I understand what you're trying to say. But there's only so much I can do. You do understand this, don't you?"

"The problem isn't me thinking outside the box for a solution to our freakin' education system. The problem is that Dean Broadhead wants me to write my thesis *over again*. I explained it all in my thesis. The written language screwed up the world the first time. I'm not going to screw it up more by writing my thesis over. It's not my problem that no one in the program can fathom how to teach without using the written language."

"Slash," she says. "You're a passionate man. That's why I'm with you on this, but there's only so much I can do."

I hang up the phone.

"How bad is it?" Daisy says, embracing me.

"It's just fallout. It's not like I haven't been through this before."

My head swims back to Dr. Washington's office and piano lessons with Mrs. Tyler. "It's like fighting bees all the time with school."

"Sounds like it's time to step away from the beehive," Daisy says.

As the sun ascends over the blueberry barrens, Daisy accepts my marriage proposal. I give her a jade necklace instead of a ring. We begin to build a wonderful life together. We move into a tiny, red cottage in Township 14 on Cathance Lake. We heat our bathing water in a pan on a gas stove and deliver rent to our landlord via a boat called *Sotally Tober*. Watching the long, clear sunsets together, we fall asleep to the sound of loons.

In our free time, we browse seed catalogues and develop our spring plans, which include planting a huge garden in the back field, setting up a vegetable and flower stand out by the road, and selling herb satchels. Before the weather turns, we adopt a blue-gray dog and two Manx cats from the local shelter. We name the dog Apartment 613—he answers to Six—and we name the cats Fruitstand and Fathead Junior. They answer to Fruity and Fatty.

While Daisy attends the University of Maine at Machias, I spend my days in a long-term substitute teaching position at the local Native reservation for a teacher on maternity leave. In our tiny home, our tiny life seems perfect. But outside, beyond, signs indicate otherwise.

"You the renter from the Beale house?" the cashier at the corner store says to me one day.

I nod and slide my money across the counter.

"That gray dog up on the hill is yours, then?" she says. I nod. "Pretty dog. You better leash him. He nearly caused a wreck this morning sittin' in the middle of the vortex."

When Daisy gets homes from class that night, I repeat the conversation for her.

"What in the hell is a vortex?" she says.

I shrug.

"I guess we need to start keeping Six on a lead," she says.

"I guess."

The next evening, Six starts barking long before the visitor arrives. I get up to see what all the commotion is about, but there's no car in the driveway, so I go back to my seed catalogs. When I get up again and turn on the outside light, a clean-cut man in a rumpled suit is standing on the porch about to knock. He wrings his hands, bites his lower lip, and tells us his car broke down in front of our house. He uses our phone. Daisy and I exchange glances. His suit doesn't fit properly. His clean-cut look doesn't seem quite right. I offer to drive him home. Before we do, we transfer hundreds of mason jars of insect larvae from his car into Daisy's car. We drop him off, and he shakes my hand by way of thanks. His hand feels like a bar of wet soap. His black Lincoln sits in front of our house for two days. Maybe he was a biology professor who dropped too much LSD. Daisy thinks he was an alien.

Two weeks later, in the afternoon, a navy blue Lincoln breaks down in front of our house. This time an old Passamaquoddy woman knocks on our door. She uses our phone to call her husband and then waits in her car. I walk out to the road and ask if she needs any assistance. The car is full of Native babies.

"I'm not exaggerating," I tell Daisy. "I usually exaggerate, but this time I'm not."

"They were little kids?"

"No, babies—like newborns."

"Weird," she says. "What did she do?"

"She just waited. Then her husband or somebody came and towed her car full of babies away."

"Do you think it's the vortex?"

"I have no idea."

Two weeks pass before the next visit. Daisy and I are lounging by the woodstove on a Sunday. I'm grading papers, and she's writing one.

"I wish I were doing what you're doing right now," I say.

"Writing a paper on how the Australian colonies federated in 1901?"

"Writing *anything.*"

"Even your thesis?"

"Anything except that. They don't tell you the fine print that comes with teaching: Cut your hair, wear a tie, teach ideas you don't believe in. Teaching that Columbus discovered America makes even less sense on a reservation than teaching it off of one."

Six barks.

"But you'll have summers off," she says, mimicking my mother's accent.

There's a knock at the door. Both Daisy and I rush to answer it. She trips me, I tackle her, nearly pulling her shirt off. She kisses me and bites my neck. She turns the handle, and I pull open the door, both of us breathless.

Stooped under an umbrella on our porch stands a frail, elderly couple no taller than two small children, their pants pulled up to their chests.

"Good afternoon. I'm Leroy Spangerberg, and this is my wife, Frances. We are Seventh-Day Adventists from Blue Hill, and we seem to be having car trouble. Would you mind if we use your phone?"

"Come in," Daisy says.

Leroy calls AAA, while Daisy puts the kettle on for tea. Over the next few hours, Leroy educates us about his church and his vegetarian lifestyle. When he learns we're also vegetarians, he sends Frances out to the car, despite our protests, to retrieve a container filled with meatless meatballs made from saltine crackers. Half of a well-oiled relationship machine, Frances follows her husband's request and upon returning heads straight to the kitchen to heat up the tiny vegetarian wonders. By the time AAA arrives, we have new friends, which means something very different for me than for Daisy. It's another notch in my creative community stick, but it augments her homesickness.

"What's wrong?" I say later.

"Nothing."

"Are you sure?"

She nods.

Although we enjoy sharing silence for hours at a time, this subtle shift into a different kind of silence worries me once the thick of winter descends. More of her comments betray that she's missing home and that her classes on the small, snow-covered campus feel more like high school than college. When my teaching responsibilities take a nosedive one day and send me crying in a stall in the faculty bathroom for the first time since leaving Chicago, we discover that neither of us can summon the requisite support for the other. This time, I don't even tell her what happened.

Daisy begins a less subtle approach for an exit strategy: She cries. As with Goldie, I respond by not responding. After distracting her with dumb jokes doesn't work, we spend more time walking aimlessly and silently up and down the aisles at the Walmart in Calais. Zinnia would call this "operating in crisis mode."

"A Green Party representative called me today," I say.

"Oh yeah?" she says. "What'd they want? Money?"

"She asked if I'd give a speech at a fund-raiser for William McGuiverson."

"The incumbent governor?"

"Yeah, she wants me to spark a community discussion on the politics of local education," I say.

"You haven't actually received your diploma yet."

"Does it matter?"

"I guess not," she says. "Are you going to do it?"

"Beats the hell out of teaching," I say, expecting her to laugh or at least look up. She does neither. "The Spangerbergs sent us another package. It's in the spare room."

"They're beating us down with kindness," she says. "More saltine cracker recipes?"

"And a signed copy of *The Good Life*."

"Now we have two copies?" she asks rhetorically.

"They invited us to visit them again. They said they'd take us to the Nearings' farm and introduce us to Helen."

"Scott is dead."

"So I've heard."

"Are you going to do the speech?"

"I have to write it first."

— ~ —

The Grange Hall smells like damp wood and looks like a church that the Pilgrims used for witch trials. A stain in the shape of a body marks the floor. On a long wooden bench sit other guests invited to speak on a number of topics, including politics, the environment, etc. In the program, my name falls just below the governor's: "Slash Coleman on Education: Connections, Consequences and Understanding." I'm so excited I feel like I'm going to throw up.

As I await my introduction, I go over my simple introductory statement again, who I am, how glad I am to be here, the format of my speech. My plan is to speak for five minutes and then give a short whirling dervish demonstration. Some in the audience might think it odd, but hopefully by the end some will join me on stage and whirl themselves. Some might even ask for lessons.

Unenthusiastic at best, the host's introduction makes a perfect notecard rendition of me. A polite round of applause follows, but the room lacks energy. I remove the microphone from its stand. Sitting before me are hundreds of men and women, mostly dressed in flannel shirts and jeans. A man yawns. The Cannon's words come back to me: *The Sema represents a mystical journey of man's spiritual ascent through mind and love to Perfect.* Two women to my right continue their conversation. A strange, incredible, familiar surge of energy pushes through my body. *Turning*

toward the truth, the follower grows through love, deserts his ego, finds the
truth, and arrives to the Perfect.

The memory of Grady's speech in Knoxville compels me to do what I
want to do instead of what I'm supposed to do. I want to knock something
over, cause a scene, providing some kind of relief. So I remove my clothing,
one piece at a time. As I take each piece off and fold it neatly beside me on
the stage, the audience shifts back and forth uncomfortably.

"He's completely naked!" someone finally yells, sending the room
into a frenzy. Men shout. A fight erupts. Someone punches the wall.
Women scream.

I extend my left arm from my side, point it toward the ground. It
extends into the center of the earth, anchoring me into something solid.
This is me, I think, back in Harvey's Meat Market and Grocery watching my father run down the aisles with wonder and excitement. T-minus
three minutes and counting.

I lift my right arm like I'm on a bicycle making a right-hand turn. My
hand is flat as if I'm waving. I pivot on my left foot. I turn in a circle. *This is*
me, I think, back in the parking lot of Harvey's Meat Market and Grocery,
chewing on a Slim Jim, watching my father kick-start his motorcycle.
T-minus two minutes and counting.

Angry men and women slowly whirl past me. Faces, body parts, and
a wall with windows blur past. His security team removes Governor
McGuiverson from the premises. I whirl faster. My penis pulls outward
with an agenda all its own. The shapes of windows and people form a line
of light—a thin blonde line like looking at the horizon. *This is me,* I think,
on the back of my father's motorcycle being steered toward truth, beauty,
freedom, and love. T-minus one minute and counting.

The sounds merge together into a hum. Emotions disappear alto-
gether. I'm floating. It's hard to believe that I feel this good without drugs or alcohol. Then, suddenly, I'm gone. Lost in a whirl, in a
place far, far away. "When a man returns from this spiritual journey

known as whirling he returns as a man who has reached maturity and a greater perfection so as to love and to be of service to the whole of creation."

⌁

"Did you honestly think this wouldn't affect me?" Daisy says, crying.

"I didn't know. It just happened. It's not like I planned it. I wasn't thinking."

"I can't believe you put me in that situation," she says, pulling her knees into her chest.

Feeling helpless, I put my hand on her shoulder. "What situation? You weren't in any situation."

"The hell I wasn't! We're together, remember?"

"Sugar, it was—"

"Don't call me that!" She gets up from the sofa, walks into the bedroom, and shuts the door.

"Babe, come on, please. This isn't the way I wanted to start our morning. Please. It was an emotional response. It was a reaction to their actions. They were being disrespectful. How was I to know everyone would freak out like that? I didn't know they would call the police."

"I didn't even know you'd left!" she yells through the door. "I thought they were lynching you inside. I was worried sick when I drove away without you."

I sit by the door and lean my head against it. "Is there anything I can do?"

"Go away." She continues to cry.

Grabbing my fishing poles from the woodshed, I call for Six. As I untie the boat from the rock, he jumps in. I start the little 5 hp motor, and we head toward a tiny cove. As the sun begins to rise, I cut the motor and cast.

"I don't understand it, Six. I really don't know what I've done wrong."

His gray eyes stare at me.

"I have no idea how to remain true to the creative spirit that calls to me in my heart without somehow getting myself in trouble," I say, reeling back in time to when I cut down the pine trees at the synagogue and hid on the rooftop.

When I get back to the house, Daisy is still in her room. I kneel by the door and knock.

"We're supposed to go the Nearings' farm today," I say gently.

"Are you *crazy?*" she yells through the door.

"It'll be a sacred distraction."

She opens the door and sits back down on the bed, her eyes red and swollen.

"I can call Leroy and Frances and tell them we can't come if you want," I say.

"Shh," she says and pats the space beside her.

I sit on the bed. We face each other, and she wraps her arms around me.

"You have to promise me that if you ever do anything like that again, you'll tell me first."

"But, I didn't kn—"

"Shh, shh." She puts her finger to my mouth. "Promise me that you'll include me."

"I promise you," I say, kissing her. "I love you more than anything."

"I love you, too."

On the way to pick up Leroy and Frances, Daisy pulls into an Irving gas station and stops the car. "I have to tell you something important."

Maybe she's pregnant. Maybe she's having an affair. Maybe she's leaving. I might have to walk back to our cottage. I wonder if I'll be warm enough.

"Wait," I say. "Is it bad bad or just bad?"

"It's pretty bad," she says.

I hold and release a deep breath. "Okay, I'm ready."

"I'm starting to have murderous thoughts about the Spangerbergs and their dog. Isn't that awful?"

Wait, what?

"I want to tie Maxwell up to our car bumper and watch his head zing around as I drive down the back roads," she continues.

I start laughing.

"You think I'm awful, don't you?"

"Want to hear something more awful?" I ask. She nods. "I hate Leroy and Frances, too. I was just afraid to tell you."

"Are you serious?"

"I want to tie Frances up and let live lobsters crawl all over her body until she cries."

"I want to pull Leroy's hat over his eyes, push him down a cliff, and scream 'Stop being so nice!'" Daisy shouts.

"No one has ever, absolutely ever, been so nice that I've been forced to want to do these things."

"Well, after today, we never have to see them or their saltine cracker meatballs again!" she announces.

"Thank God!"

We laugh. We high-five. We hug. We agree to keep it a secret.

By the time we pick up the Spangerbergs and drive to the Nearings' farm, Daisy and I have exchanged half a dozen looks, winks, and quiet laughs. We both feel gratifyingly ashamed of ourselves.

As we pull up to the Nearings' farm, Leroy assures us that he and Scott Nearing were chums, and he's sure that Helen will remember him. After Leroy knocks a few times and Helen waves us in and walks away with barely a "Hello," it starts to look like Leroy's memory of their friendship may be on the blink.

We four stand awkwardly in the kitchen not knowing what to do. We snake our way through the house together until we find Helen writing at a large oak desk.

"You do know it's past visiting hours," she says, not looking up.

"I'm extremely sorry," Leroy says. "I understand if you—"

"The sign that you passed coming in explains that visiting hours were established to give us a certain amount of privacy," she continues.

Daisy and I turn to leave while Leroy and the usually quiet Frances begin to mumble back and forth to each other. Their strange pattern of clicks, whooshing sounds, and facial recognition gestures flashes me back to my sisters' Twinspeak days. It dumbfounds and frightens me a little. Daisy squeezes my hand. Helen stares at me as if to say, "*Did you forget to drop these two off at the circus?*"

After almost a five-minute performance, Helen gets up from her desk and waves for us to follow her. She escorts us through the kitchen to the back door and down an overgrown path. She opens the door to a yurt, and we follow her in, the now quiet Spangerbergs bringing up the rear.

"Sometimes I sit in here for hours," she says, "waiting for the Mothership to beam me up."

I can't tell if she's serious or deadpanning us. Only one way to find out.

"Helen," I say, "do you know much about vortexes?"

"What kind?"

"An invisible antimatter wormhole—something straight out of a *Twilight Zone* episode."

"Has it been affecting you?"

"It's been making him do strange things," Daisy offers.

"A lot of cars have been breaking down in the vortex," I add.

"The lady at the corner store says that she sees Apartment 613 sitting in the center of the vortex every morning," Daisy says mischievously.

"That's how they met us," says Frances. Leroy nods.

Helen makes a strange face. She's still thinking about why an apartment would be sitting in the middle of the road and how we could have met two circus freaks inside.

"Vortex ushers, huh?" Helen says. "If it was me, I would open a car repair shop. I bet you could make a killing."

We all laugh.

"Okay, ladies and gentleman. It's past my bedtime. I must bid you farewell," Helen says, standing.

"Would you mind?" Frances holds out her camera.

"Just one photo, I suppose," Helen says.

Daisy and I stand on either side of Helen and smile. I put my arms around her and smile until the flash blinds us.

On the way back to Township 14, the aurora borealis comes out to lick the sky, alive with unexplainable energy. Red, yellow, and green lights dance through the air, pulling me back to the blueberry barrens of the summer before, filled with the songs of migrant workers and rich white kids pretending to be poor.

"Why are we here?" Daisy says softly as the sky breathes above us.

26

love at first sight or by other routes

machias, maine / township 14, maine / madison, wisconsin
april 11, 1996

My first morning back at school, the principal calls me into his office before the students arrive. "Despite your intentions, you have crossed a line with your creativity."

When Daisy hears that I'm not allowed back into my classroom to retrieve my belongings, she cries. She's hoping I'll understand what she, the principal, and the rest of the world have been trying to tell me all along. But I don't. I'm mad at the entire world for not understanding me.

She misses home even more. She cries more and more at night and during the day. We grow apart, which makes Township 14 seem more remote than ever. I don't know how to deal with her, my life, any of this. I leave the room, the house, for hours, half a day, hoping something will change, but when I return everything remains as I've left it. I no longer feel like I can fly.

Daisy picks a date to move back to Madison. As it nears, a state of temporary perfection reasserts itself between us again: long talks, longs walks, holding hands—but then it gets even worse than before. In an effort to protect myself, I become stoic and cold. She sometimes holds onto me, but I don't hold back. Once again, I respond by not responding.

"I can't understand why you want to leave," I tell her. "This is the only place I've lived where I can really breathe."

"It's the only place where I can't," she says. "Why can't you come with me?"

"Once you find a place out there, I'll join you. When the time is right." The time will never be right.

━‿━

One afternoon I help her pack her car and buy her a gas card to pay for the entire trip. It feels amicable. She's wearing her jade engagement necklace, which she touches before hugging me. Only part of me hugs back.

"I'll call when I arrive," she says. "I love you."

"I love you, too."

She drives off. I stand in the road long after her car vanishes from sight. I am alone: in my mind, in my body, in Township 14. It feels like my heart has fallen out of my body. The downward spiral is immediate. I don't want to be alone. The gravel driveway hits my knees as I begin sobbing. I have no one to talk to, to dream with, to hug.

It's dark when I finally get up, walk back into the house, collapse again on the hallway floor, and scream. I hate that no one can hear me scream. Six licks my face and looks at me sideways. I hate my creativity. I hate my writing. I hate my music. I hate myself.

I cry for days. I quit eating, sleeping, bathing, brushing my teeth. I call Daisy every four hours and leave a message, but she never calls back. Hours turn into days. I call her parents. They say she's renting a room on an organic farm. Days turn into weeks. I call her parents every few days. They have no new information.

My landlord stops by and lets Six outside. His wife brings me food and a pamphlet about suicide. Curled up on the floor, I regret every part of who I am. I cry so much I throw up. I dry heave because I haven't eaten. I hate myself. I hate the world that put me in it. I hate my mother and father.

Then, somewhere in the darkness two and a half weeks later, a feeling hits me deep in my gut. The butterflies furiously awaken. The familiar blueprint for traveling into the unknown takes shape. The time seems right. I pack my Subaru, open the passenger-side door, and Six jumps in. I put Fruity and Fatty in the back with a litter box and some water. A huge piece of birch bark lies on the ground near my front tire, looking like an oversize aluminum can split in half lengthwise. I set it on my dashboard as a totem. The poorly planned trip feels as familiar and disorienting as my trip to Alaska. I need to find her, but I have no idea how.

Everything reminds me of her: the trees, the clouds, the road, and especially Six, Fruity, and Fatty. Daisy found me as I emerged from my darkest, loneliest place and covered me and sheltered me like a blanket. Now that she's gone, now that the blanket has disappeared, my skin has turned inside out. Every breath, every air particle digs into me like a needle.

Twenty-four hours later, I pull into Madison. Following my intuition, I turn down one street and then another. As I pass the Willy Street Food Co-op, she is driving the other way. I honk. She pulls over. We get out and embrace. Her hug doesn't feel the same. I cry. She cries. I expect to feel relief, but I only feel more nervous and sad. She's not wearing the necklace.

"Where's your necklace?" I ask.

"Right here," she says, pulling it out of her pocket. "It broke."

"Where are you going?"

She doesn't answer.

"Can we go somewhere and talk? Back to your place?"

I follow her to a bean farm. We turn down a long road and pass fields and fields of beans. We stop at a barn. Inside the barn, she unlocks a door, and we sit on her sleeping bag on the barn floor. She looks at me wide-eyed. I am deliriously tired.

"Why are you here?"

"What do you mean? I needed to be with you. I tried calling you. What happened?"

Silence.

"Are you planning on staying here?" she asks, looking away.

"I was planning on it, yes. Is that okay?"

"I'll have to ask the farmer."

"Why didn't you ever call me back?"

She doesn't answer, and Glenn Gaffey, the plant manager from Alaska, comes to mind. "Did you meet someone?"

She doesn't answer. Alarm pools deep in the middle of my chest. "Already?"

"Already," she says. "I'm sorry."

I cry. She cries. My body folds into her.

"I need closure," I say.

"How?"

"I don't know."

In the morning, we drive to Lake Mendota. We sit near the shore, the birch bark totem between us. I draw two stick figures on it and a heart between them.

"Rip it in half," I say.

It tears easily.

"Should I throw it in?" she says.

"Wait."

We each take a piece and set them on the lake. They slowly drift apart and then away.

I hug Six for the last time and kiss him on the top of his head. From the camper shell of my Subaru I lift out Fatty and Fruity and place them into Daisy's car. When Daisy and I hug for the last time, I rest my cheek against hers and listen to her breath. I drive back to Maine completely heartbroken.

Once back, I paint EVERYTHING $5 onto a piece of plywood and set it out by the road. My furniture, my fishing gear, my clothes—all of it, five dollars. It all vanishes.

On the morning that I decide to move away—exactly thirty days from now—I walk into the garden completely naked except for a pink chiffon scarf and a five-gallon bucket full of every seed in the house. Like Fred Astaire I dance with the Ginger Rogers bucket, swinging it across the soft raised beds that Daisy made the previous year, flinging seeds over every square inch of the garden. When I'm done it looks like a chocolate-covered doughnut with rainbow sprinkles.

Sitting on the overturned bucket, I admire my work. A certain liberation runs through me. My veins pulse with freedom. Treating our seeds—our dream—so flippantly has given me an uncertain deliverance.

Back in the house lies the scene of the crime, hundreds upon hundreds of empty seed packets collected since the beginning of our dream: Black Beauty eggplant, Golden Bantam corn, Straight Eight cucumbers, Chioggia beets, Looseleaf lettuce, Yukon Gold potatoes, Texas Super-sweet onions, White zinnias (perhaps destined to be more helpful than my old Chicago therapist was), Fireball marigolds, Fancy Dress Petunias, Candy Box impatiens, Shasta daisies, Genovese basil, Common chives, Greek oregano, and more. Crumpled and chaotic, the edges of the open packets are all smiles.

A month later, a potluck has sprouted in the garden. Vegetables, flowers, and herbs commingle in a riot of diversity, close and intimate. The stronger plants will eventually kill off the weaker ones. It's beyond my control.

Everything in my relationship with Daisy has been a performance up to this point, from Gerry's sanctified delivery to the performance at the Grange Hall and all the minutiae in between. Though it offers me absolutely no solace, it occurs to me that to have liberation you must first have a censor, an oppressor. I might avoid the future need to be liberated if I maintain my damn liberation in the first place.

The night before I leave, as I sleep among the smiling seed packets, Hurricane Edouard churns just off the coast, frantically whipping the trees outside.

I dream that an angel falls into the Houston Astrodome. Bruised and bleeding, he writhes on the green AstroTurf, the crowd cheering as he attempts unsuccessfully to lift himself up. His wings are broken. Each time he moves his wings, he grimaces in pain. From high above, in the nosebleed seats, I watch him through my binoculars and then on the big screen in the middle of the stadium. All around, people yell. Some scream, "Stay down!" while others wail, "Get up, you son of a bitch!" The angel hears both, rising only a few inches each time before falling back down.

The next morning I strap my surfboard onto my truck. I drive out to Jonesboro beach, a mile from where Daisy and I spent our first blissful summer. I pull on my wet suit and paddle out into the sea. As the wind whips up to nearly sixty miles per hour, a small north-facing cove provides a perfectly protected wave. Among lobster traps and rocks, I surf until evening, the curl of the waves pushing me and my sadness back and forth along a rocky reef. When it's time to go, I paddle in to where the water is up to my knees. I remove my leash, turn toward the sea, close my eyes, and push my board back out into the water.

It floats out toward the horizon. Darkness swallows the scene. I will have to re-invent myself completely.

27

clean sweep

richmond, virginia
september 5, 1996

EIGHTEEN HOURS LATER, I KNOCK ON MY PARENTS' DOOR AND COLLAPSE
at my father's feet. "I need your help," I say, crying. For the first time
since I was a boy, he lifts me up in his arms and carries me to my room. I
apologize over and over again. For once, he says nothing about Dr Pepper.

Over the course of the next few months I help him aboard *The Tinker*
and read *Zen and the Art of Motorcycle Maintenance*. On lunch breaks,
I take his little Honda Rebel on short drives through the back roads.
It's satisfying to know that I could lose control of the motorcycle at any
moment and demolish myself. It helps take my mind off of Daisy, the
sound of her voice, the color of her skin, the smell of her hair, what my
body used to feel like next to hers in the morning. Every cell in my body
acts like a mirror that captured a miniature replica of her.

In the evenings, I sit in my father's studio and watch him paint. We
say very little. I just watch. The familiar smells of fiberglass resin and oil
paint are comforting. I'm not sure what part of the past few months is a
dream and what part is reality—writhing on the floor for weeks, dancing naked in the garden while flinging seeds, riding waves while dodging

rocks and lobster pots. Sometimes I swear the AstroTurf angel was me. Sometimes I think I remember looking in the bathroom mirror in Maine, reaching around to my scapulae like a yogi, feeling for the tiny stubs on my back where my wings once attached.

"Slash?" my mother calls down from the studio steps.

"Yeah?"

"Phone!"

"I'll get it down here!"

"Slashtipher," a male voice says.

"Hi."

"You don't know who this is, do you?"

"No."

"So what's your next move?"

"Who is this?" I say.

"Do you want a hint?"

I take the phone outside into the backyard.

"From the congregation of corrugation," he says.

"Gerry?"

"You got it, Chief!" he says.

I immediately remember our falling out and regret it. I apologize, but Gerry says it's not needed. He has moved to Portland, Oregon, enrolled in massage school, lives in a mansion with ten artists, and teaches masturbation workshops. He asks about Daisy.

"Since she left, it's like my heart grew wings and flew away."

"The good ol' dark night of the soul," he says. "I know that place better than anyone. It sounds like you need either a karmic reconstruction station or a huge distraction, Chief."

"Actually, at this point, I wouldn't mind having both."

"Good. I've got just the remedy."

28

courtyard with lunatics

portland, oregon
march 15, 1997

I'M TWENTY-NINE YEARS OLD AND RIDING DOWN HAWTHORNE BOULE-vard on my Pee-wee Herman bike. It's been a little under seven months since I lost my wings and less than a month since Gerry invited me to move into the Ivon Châteaux.

The white mansion on the corner of 44th Avenue and Ivon Street looks like a gigantic hardened marshmallow. More than four stories tall, it squeezes between two tiny houses on half a lot, which makes the marsh-mallow appear to be wearing high-water pants and a suit jacket that doesn't fit. It's my new personal wing-reconstruction laboratory. Although I crawled in, I plan to fly out. I've still got a long way to go.

I still cry during the day—a lot. I still cry in the afternoon—a lot. The most random things set me off: a familiar smell, an uncertain breeze, car horns honking, never the same thing twice. I still look for Daisy in crowds, often mistaking someone else for her. I still have trouble falling asleep, and I often wake up in the middle of the night missing her. Even though I'm living in a house with ten roommates, I still feel incredibly lonely—a lot.

Thanks to their urging, I've been living my life like a subcontractor hired by my heart to fill every second of every day with whatever is necessary to mend my wings. I'm enrolled in massage school, taking classes at a yoga studio, carrying crystals in my pockets, and trying my hand at making a living as a sculptor.

It's also why I'm biking in my latest attention-getting outfit. It's a near-perfect cure for my recent and insatiable desire for human interaction that doesn't actually require talking to human beings. It's unusual to want to be close to others but simultaneously not to want to be close to them.

My outfit includes: Clark Kent glasses (sans lenses), a powder blue tuxedo (with ruffled shirt and a tiny sky-blue bow tie), and my Baltimore Colts football helmet (with deer antlers attached to the top). A perfect throwback to my gladiator days, it makes me look like something both beautiful and poisonous from the animal kingdom. It draws attention without the need for any time-consuming conversations.

In my bike basket, a dozen blue delphiniums are billowing in the wind alongside *The Amazing Ashra's Simple Love Spells* (with the "Return to Me" spell to bring back a lost love dog-eared), a chocolate bar (organic), a purple potato (also organic), and a bag of spelt flour. Zinnia would call this the perfect recipe for a "dysfunctional and unsober" moment—and I'm loving it.

I hang a left beside the huge red-and-green-neon Bagdad Theater sign and pull up beside a Dumpster. For the past few months, following my father's sage advice, I've been Dumpster-diving materials for my current sculpture project: creating 3-D representations of the Western Zodiac. I stand up on the pedals and peek into the Dumpster. That's when I spot him, facedown.

Seconds later, the Dumpster's steel ladder helps me into a pile of trash. Up to my knees in soggy black bags, I reach for his shoulder, instantly fulfilling an important prophecy foretold by my high school guidance counselor, who swore my career aspirations would never rise above those of a garbage man. If he could only see me now, he'd know that rescuing a life-size papier-mâché black man in a shimmering sharkskin suit from a Dumpster feels just like being a Peace Corps volunteer. When I finally push the trash bags aside and turn him over, half his face is missing.

"Mister, you are coming home with me," I announce.

I lift him up on my shoulders and climb out of the Dumpster. Perhaps, turned into a mermaid, he'll represent Pisces, or with a mane and a crown regally represent Leo the Lion. In the more practical meantime, how to get him on my bicycle? I try the obvious. I set him on my seat, but when I climb on he slides off.

"Behave!" I command.

I lift him over the handlebars, and, careful not to crush my flowers, I wedge his ass in my basket. We ride away.

At the the corner of Division and Hawthorne, a truck pulls up beside me, and the couple inside laughs.

"Where do you think you're going?" the woman says with a smile.

Before I can answer, the light turns green, and I pedal away. They honk, triggering a flurry of honking horns and waves. I hang a right on Division and pedal furiously with the traffic while thinking about *Great Expectations,* starring Ethan Hawke and Gwyneth Paltrow, which I've just seen for the twenty-third time.

At the Châteaux, as I lift the paper man up by his waist, his name comes to me: Don Ivon de la Ivon Châteaux. *Perfecto.* I grab my flowers, book, chocolate bar, purple potato, and bag of flour and let my Pee-wee Herman bike fall to the ground. I kick the side door open with my foot and descend into the basement.

On the way, I trip over the recycling bins and months of empty rice milk boxes, stepping over a pile of laundry to make my way into the far left corner of the basement, my art studio. A dozen doors removed from doorways throughout the house partition it from the rest of the space.

Attached to each door is a distinct configuration of the zodiac, sculptures made from wire, wood, watches, hubcaps, and Barbie doll parts. Each weekend I put the sculptures in a box and take them downtown to sell in a booth at the Portland Saturday Market.

But one door is different. Its gold frame holds a reproduction of a Goya painting called *Courtyard with Lunatics* that depicts, among others, two nude men fighting outside an insane asylum while wardens beat them with clubs. "Goya painted it after a mysterious illness left him physically debilitated and permanently deaf," I explained to Gerry when I adorned the door.

"It seems like some strange personal muse, Chief, is it?" Gerry asked.

"I guess," I responded. "My father reproduced a mammoth version for his graduate-school thesis. It was more than thirty feet long and took up an entire wall in our house. It's sort of always been my personal symbol for sustenance."

Now, inside my studio, a sense of power overwhelms me. It reminds me of my father's studio. Since giving up music and writing, I'm finally responsible for creating my own reality. For once it doesn't feel like escape. It feels instead like desire mixed with the unknown, like promise, like hope. These doors make me feel safe. I have the power to open any one of them and step into a world of possibility and my creation.

I lay Don Ivon de la Ivon Châteaux on the workbench, pour some flour in a salad bowl, mix it with water, snatch the morning newspaper from the recycling bin, put on a Prince CD, take off all my clothes, and open my love-spell book. I squeeze a few squirts of glue into the bowl, rip the newspaper into strips, and dip the strips in the bowl. Prince just needs my body from dusk until dawn.

I cover Ivon's face with gooey strips. Some of the paste drips down his suit, which I wipe away with the back of my hand. As the concoction hardens, I shape his eyebrows, the curve of his mouth, his cheekbones, and his nose. An hour later I stand back and revel in my accomplishment: I've not only rescued this man from a Dumpster and surgically reconstructed his face, but I've given him a second lease on life as the house talisman. Watch out, Madame Tussaud. This very well may be my new calling.

Prince wants to be my fantasy, and maybe I could be his, are my thoughts as my roommate Ranajay walks into the basement with a load of laundry. Ranajay, a photographer, attends massage school with me. He lives upstairs in the room beside mine. He's going through a phase right now where all his girlfriends are strippers. At night, when he's having his threesomes, fourgies, and so on, I sometimes listen at the vent, imagining what it's like to be him: a lanky, redheaded twin sleeping with strippers with an exotic nickname thanks to his recent life on an ashram.

He spies my project, then sees that I'm naked, and starts to laugh. "Oh Lord!"

He said exactly the same thing two weeks ago when he saw me riding across a major intersection downtown buck-naked in a shopping cart, my clothes folded neatly beneath me. Something about this latest phase sets me free from the cage of clothing that has trapped me my entire life. Clothing (or lack thereof) seems to be the new frontier for now.

"I'm not even going to ask," he says.

"Good. Come over here."

"Oh, God!" he says, jumping back. "What *is* that thing?"

"Meet my friend, Don Ivon de la Ivon Châteaux!"

"Was that in the package you got from Virginia?"

"No, but this was." I reach under a door and pull out a *Great Expectations* movie poster, a T-shirt, and the soundtrack.

"You've got to be kidding me. You're still wasting money on that crappy movie? It hasn't gone to video yet?"

"I've been going every Monday, Wednesday, and Friday for the past thirteen weeks, and plan to go every Monday, Wednesday, and Friday until the movie goes to video." I've tried to explain the connection that I feel with the movie too many times. None of my roommates understands.

"I told you, the movie starts out with the artist as a young boy making sketches in a Moleskine sketchbook."

"I still think it's an expensive vice," he says.

"Watching Ethan and Gwyneth hold hands at the end of the movie gives me hope."

"What, that Daisy will return your phone calls one day?"

"According to this"—I hold up the spell book—"she'll be coming for a visit sooner that you think. I have faith."

Indira rushes downstairs while sipping from her tiny yogurt dish and dances as she sings along to the CD: she doesn't have to be rich to be his girl; she doesn't have to be cool to rule his world. She loves Prince. She twirls in a circle and trips over her own feet. Her white robe flows out like a mushroom, and she laughs.

Indira is in a phase right now in which she drinks her own pee from a tiny yogurt cup, eats strawberry jelly sandwiches exclusively, and trains to be a stripper. In the mornings, after she practices stripping in the living room, she pees into a cup and then drinks it. I can't imagine she pees more than a teaspoonful each morning, and with her two left feet none of us can imagine that she'll ever make any money as a stripper. But she says that Dr. Chen, her Chinese herbalist, claims that drinking *jinye,* bodily fluids, and following your bliss will harmonize one's yin and yang, which may help cure her uterine cancer.

"You, too," I say, beckoning her over with my finger.

"Oh, God!" she says, jumping back. "Who is that?"

"It's Ivon," Ranajay says flatly.

"It's Don Ivon de la Ivon Châteaux," I correct him. "I rescued him."

Indira kneels down beside the paper man, wiggles her hand under his shirt, and rests her head against his chest. "He'll need a heart to survive," she says, looking up.

"Got that covered," I say, holding up the purple potato.

"Artists are like dogs," Ranajay quips. "They can poop anything."

Ranajay grabs Indira's hand and pulls her up. They dance and twirl and bump and grind around me. After a few minutes, they take off all their clothes, too.

As I continue to work on Don Ivon's face, the side door opens, and Brogan enters. A broad-shouldered oil painter from Nacogdoches, Texas, he uses the other half of the basement as his studio. He walks over with a handful of paintbrushes and a bucket of gesso and says hello. But when he spots the naked shenanigans, he turns away.

"Wait," I say. "I need you, too."

"I ain't gettin' nekkid," he says.

"You don't have to," I say. "Just come in and stand over there."

"What have you been up to?" Ranajay asks, twirling Indira under his arm.

"Yeah," Indira says, nearly breathless. "How's the love climate?"

"Olivia's boyfriend came back from Peru," Brogan says in his charming Texas drawl. "Caught me mountin' her. Chased me through the house with a plant stand. I ain't been to work since."

"Sorry to hear that, my friend," I say. "I need you to stand over here."

"Iapetus!" Mitchell yells from the top of the stairs. Mitchell is Indira's boyfriend and another roommate. Iapetus is his eight-year-old daughter—named after the third largest moon of Saturn rather than the Titan son of Uranus and Gaia—and our youngest roommate.

As he walks into my studio, he rubs his hands though his mop of black hair and smiles when he sees Indira and Ranajay standing there naked. He hands Indira a strawberry jelly sandwich, kisses her on the cheek, and starts taking off his shirt.

"Good God!" he says, jumping back. "What is that thing?"

"That's our new roommate," Ranajay says.

"And you are not having sex with him," Indira adds.

Mitchell shakes his head. He's going through a male prostitute phase, making his living by giving old gay men hand jobs for $1,000 a pop.

Together, Mitchell and Indira are going through a phase where they like to have sex in public.

"Is my daughter hiding down here?" he asks.

"No," we all say.

"Can you stand beside Brogan?" I ask.

Mitchell puts his arms around Brogan and kisses him on the cheek. Brogan winces and feigns pain. Prince tells him to act his age and not his shoe size. Maybe they could do the twirl. Ranajay twirls Indira. Mitchell twirls Brogan. When the song ends, my roommates leave my studio one at a time and disappear upstairs.

Later that night, I open the love-spell book and continue to follow the directions. I carve the purple potato into a likeness of Daisy, cutting the top open and putting a piece of the chocolate bar inside so that whenever she thinks about me she'll think sweet thoughts. "Once the transformation from potato to effigy is complete, it is necessary to keep the symbol in a closed container." Indira did say that he'll need a heart to survive.

I remove Ivon's tie, unbutton his shirt, and pull both back. My fingers push into his chest until they hit the galvanized chicken wire that covers his entire body just below his papier-mâché skin. After cutting through it with wire cutters, a soft nest of the delphiniums goes into the hole, on which rests Don Ivon's new heart. I pull the wire back into place, mix up another batch of papier-mâché, and seal the surgery wound.

After midnight, I paint Ivon's face, button his shirt, and adjust his tie. I scoot my stool closer to the workbench and rest my head on his chest as I take his hand. "I really miss her," I say, my eyes welling up with tears. He doesn't say anything; he just stares at the ceiling, his freshly painted burnt-umber eyes glistening. "I know it's crazy, but I really miss her."

He knows exactly how I feel—abandoned by someone who once loved you and still loving that person even though that person doesn't love you back. According to the spell book, Daisy will arrive within three months or two new moon cycles.

I lift Don Ivon onto my shoulders and carry him upstairs. I hide him in Ranajay's walk-in closet, spending nearly thirty minutes adjusting him so it looks like he's reaching for a shirt on the upper shelf. I'm fast asleep six hours later when one of the strippers screams and bolts downstairs. Two more scream, then Ranajay joins the chorus, shouting, "Call 9-1-1! Call 9-1-1!"

I've not only taken a dozen years off my roommate's life but, according to the spell book, I've also just sent a very clear subliminal message to Daisy, requesting that she return. From that moment on, Don Ivon sleeps in my bed.

Three months later, I'm eating raisins with Mitchell at the kitchen table when Ranajay walks in.

"Slash," Ranajay says, "There's someone here who would like to see you."

Behind Ranajay stands Daisy. Behind Daisy stands a guy I've never seen before. Speechless, I choke on a raisin.

"Surprise!" Daisy says. "I know, the last person you'd ever think you'd see again, right?"

"What are you doing here?" I say, unable to move.

"I was hiking the Pacific Rim with Ronald, and his Westfalia bus broke down. Slash, this is Ronald."

Ronald's jeans look store-bought new. His shirt is tucked in and buttoned up too high. He leans against the kitchen sink and wipes his bald head with a handkerchief. He is everything I'm not. He probably works in an office selling life insurance, descended from a family full of life insurance salesmen. Suddenly I'm back at Sylvia Chapman's house— before the Hulk Juice—an invited guest in my own home. Time stops. That all-too-familiar bohemian pulse surges through my body. The butterflies rage.

Ronald extends his hand in slow motion. I reach out with both of mine, but instead of shaking his hand I reach for his face. I clasp his cheeks, pull him toward me, and kiss him full on the mouth. It happens so fast that he can't pull away.

"Nice to meet you," I say.

The room is silent. Ronald stares at the floor. What just occurred instantly disappears into a black hole. Not even Daisy acknowledges it.

"I wanted to know if I could stay here for the night until Ronald's bus is fixed?" she says.

"Um—" I say.

"I'm staying with a friend," Ronald mumbles.

"Sure."

Ronald leaves. He is a braver, more secure man than I. I wouldn't have the courage to let my girlfriend have a sleepover with her ex. Then again, I did just plant one on him, so maybe he's not worried so much.

Daisy and I go upstairs. We sit on my bed, Ivon between us.

She sees my massage table in the middle of the room. "Is massage school going okay?"

My head leans against the wall, a million miles away.

"Are you okay?" she asks.

I shrug. This is what I want. This is what I need. This is what the past few months have been all about.

"Do you want to help me out?" I say.

"Sure," she says.

"I still have to give another massage for homework this week. Can I give you one?"

"Oh. I don't know."

"It's homework." I need a reason to touch her, to know that she's real, to feel something that I used to feel.

"I don't think it's a good idea," she says.

"It would really help me out."

"I don't know . . ."

"No?"

"Okay," she says.

"You're sure?"

"It's for homework?"

I nod. "I'm going to leave the room, and you get undressed and get under the sheets on the table."

"Do I have to take everything off?"

"Whatever makes you feel comfortable."

The soft rustle of her clothes as they leave her body drifts outside the door. She's finally here, and I'm finally here, and—something isn't right.

"I'm ready," she yells.

Her body rises and falls with her breathing. When my hands touch her shoulders, I start to cry. Suddenly everything feels wrong. I try to stifle my tears, but they fall on her back. I wipe my face, take a deep breath, and tell myself that I'm okay. But I'm not. I start to shake. I fall apart completely. Nothing she can do or say will help.

That night, we sleep in my bed together, clothed, Don Ivon between us. The next morning Ronald honks from his VW bus. At the front door, Daisy and I press together our foreheads when we say goodbye, holding each other, unable to do anything more. She leaves. I cry all week. Recovering a second time is twice as hard.

But after a week I'm done. With my new creative family surrounding me, a part of Daisy that I thought would never leave me finally leaves for good. Insulated by my art, I no longer cry during the day, I no longer cry in the afternoon. The familiar smells, the uncertain breezes, the car horns honking all belong to me again. Now, when I wake in the middle of the night, I wander down into my studio and create things that never existed before, things that belong to me, things that will never leave.

29

the rise and fall of the great corn bread warrior

rhododendron, oregon
july 11, 1999

MOTHERSHIP BUFFALO LIES AT THE FOOT OF MT. HOOD—ONLY A FEW hours from Portland, one of the most beautiful spots in the entire world—but regret, sexual excitement, and fear render me oblivious to it. My dorm room at the commune hides me, crying quietly and carefully, from the kitchen crew. Being in my room during unapproved hours is strictly forbidden, and the walls are thin as tortillas.

A dull bulb dangles forlornly from a single string, illuminating the four plywood walls. From some far corner of my mind comes Zinnia Raphael's voice: "When you escape one crisis without resolution, you often unwittingly enter into a continuation of the very same crisis in a different location."

Maybe this is why I can't appreciate the forest for its trees. Although this doesn't feel like a continuation of the same script, the situation, more than a little messy, has confused me since meeting Raleigh Shanahan. When we met fewer than twenty days ago on Delta Flight 5578, she insisted that the Annual Eternal Loving Polyamorous Summer Retreat would change my life. Obviously I didn't sense any red flags.

"You'll love it," she said. "It includes delicious vegetarian cuisine, engaging conversation with free-thinking creatives, and gobs of beautiful, intelligent people who share a commitment to the mode of intentional community."

On the front of a brochure for the retreat, a group of pretty people stands in a field. The caption under the photo reads: "It's the kind of authentic sharing that creates the possibility of love and intimacy." Raleigh's sense of reality, much like our meeting, resembles one of those scrambled Magic Eye images: perplexing, difficult to confirm, and following a completely different set of rules.

Flight 5578 was scheduled to fly from Washington, D.C., to Portland, Oregon, but fog forced it to land in Salt Lake City. Airline officials told us, deplaning shortly after midnight, to go into the terminal for a hotel voucher. Wearing a pair of tennis shoe roller skates, I was carrying my art portfolio and my Baltimore Colts football helmet. Raleigh was standing behind me in line. When she bumped into me, I lost my balance and fell, my art portfolio spilling at her feet. She fell in love with my art, and I fell in love with watching her fall in love with my art.

Twenty minutes later, we were sitting cross-legged atop my bed at the Marriott, butterflies bouncing around in my stomach. Somehow my dream life and my real life had intermingled.

From the back, front, and side—even down to her personality quirks— she looked the spitting image of Daisy. I nearly hyperventilated when I connected the dots. She had the same soft, wholesome face, the same thick caramel-colored hair with blonde highlights, and the same small nose and high cheek bones. The only difference was that she had a jacked-up Amazonian figure like a car with large tires in the rear that tilts forward.

Gracing her arm was a tattoo sliver of moon just like the waning bowl Daisy and I saw over Lake Michigan. Only this time it reminds me of a fingernail, the rest of the finger hidden in the sky somewhere. The same exact moon was hanging in the sky when I parted the hotel room curtains. It seemed like destiny. We were like holograms that night: One part of me wanted to reveal one part of her and vice versa. When I emptied my pockets and spread my magic stones across the madras bedspread—rutilated quartz, moonstone, obsidian—it didn't surprise me at all to watch her pockets reveal her own magic stones: topaz, bloodstone, tourmaline.

She had also been visiting family for the holidays. She lived on a commune about three hours away from Portland. The Mothership Buffalo sounded a lot like the Ivon Château. Both of us had been living in our respective communities for two years. She always wanted to be a famous astronaut and travel into outer space. I always wanted to be a famous artist and travel to faraway places. Her father, a southerner, had taught at Princeton. Mine, a good ol' boy, had attended the country's top art university. Her parents hosted wild parties at her house, where as a child she often mingled with the cast of *Star Trek* and *The Muppet Show*. I grew up in my father's art studio, and my babysitters were eccentric painters, poets, and bohemians.

By dawn we were spooning. She had no idea that I, curled around her, kept imagining that she was Daisy. It was like finding a two-for-one relationship coupon. We lay on the bed and kissed, our legs wrapped around each other. We kissed and kissed but nothing more.

The next morning an even thicker fog covered Portland, so our plane diverted to Seattle, where we flirted, talked, and practiced yoga in the terminal. There was something so brand-new, yet so familiar with Raleigh. But there was also something urgent and intense in our connection. I already wanted it to be tomorrow, next week, next year with her. I already wanted her to sleep in my T-shirt. My spare toothbrush already wanted to live at her house.

As she slept on my shoulder, I touched the sliver of moon on her arm and whispered, "God, thank you for bringing Daisy back to me." When we finally landed in Portland, two days after meeting, I was already in love—even if for the wrong reasons. Back at the Château, I tried to concentrate on my final semester of massage school, painting, and the questionable health benefits of drinking pee.

But nothing worked. Raleigh was Daisy was Raleigh was Daisy, and I wanted Daisy back. In my studio, I decided to create something to bridge our connection. I made a large book, big as a card table, the pages hand-sewn with an upholstery needle and kite string. Inside, my oil pastels told the story of Astronaut Girl, whom, like the Moon, a lonely young artist boy once observed from Earth. I covered the book in purple faux fur and over-nighted it to her.

The book arrived just in time. She called to thank me on her way out the door to Mexico, driving down there in her Ford Escort, named Michelle, with a few friends from the commune. For the next few days I couldn't sleep, unable to think of anything but her. Raleigh was Daisy was Raleigh was Daisy, and I wanted Daisy back. The blueprint smacked me again, which hadn't happened since Shiloh. *This is me,* I think, and suddenly I'm back in Harvey's Meat Market and Grocery waiting for my father to gather our goods. The need to go somewhere—anywhere—to fill the unmistakable hole inside me was overwhelming.

I made a huge papier-mâché moon, in the same phase as Raleigh's tattoo. When I sold a sculpture that weekend at the art market for the exact price of a one-way ticket to Baja, the decision was obvious: I jumped on a plane to find her.

The blueprint once again had me on a plane chasing down a girl, following the template for fulfillment based on travel and the unknown that my father helped me concoct. How would I ever find her? Ten years had passed since I made the same trip to find Shiloh. On this trip, I didn't even have a photograph, just an empty place in my heart, the need to replace something that I'd lost, and a papier-mâché moon.

"*God,*" I prayed as we descended over a field of orange poppies into Mexico City, "*please don't let the Mexican banditos kill me.*"

How I wish I could rewind my life. If not to before the plane ride, then at least to before my decision to take the bus to Mothership Buffalo.

"*Where is he?*" Jaco screams outside the dorm. My entire body tightens. Fireblossom follows him. "This is definitely not allowed!"

Whispering shadows flit under my door. Fireblossom swings it open, Jaco right behind her. I immediately sit up. Fireblossom, the assistant to the lead cook, has a Jewfro that's seen better days. Her wall-eye considers the wall behind me while her other one attends to the task at hand.

"Come with us," she says.

Jaco shines his flashlight in my eyes and then swings it down to the floor. He has a funny eye, too, but he isn't wearing any clothing, which is more apparent. I follow Fireblossom and Jaco's bare ass and flashlight through the dorm and along the forest path, scared out of my mind. They bring me to the community kitchen. Scabs of fluorescent light illuminate the rustic wooden counters. What once seemed like a room for the creation of vast amounts of nourishment now seems like an interrogation room.

"Sit there," Fireblossom says.

"And think about what you've done," Jaco adds before they both disappear.

In front of me sit five pans of corn bread—evidence. The kitchen has filled with its sweet, delicate smell.

After a few minutes, the double doors swing open, and Jaco enters followed by Fireblossom followed by Sundancer. The weekend ringleader, Sundancer, a pale older woman with a soft face, has salt-and-pepper hair and breasts that would have sagged past her belt if she were wearing one—or anything else for that matter.

"Corn bread does not aid in promoting the ever-important emotional lightness of being necessary in helping participants release the anchors of their attachments," Sundancer announces.

"Eggs and buttermilk are forbidden during this retreat," Fireblossom says.

"Where did you get access to the ingredients?" Jaco asks.

"From the pantry," I say.

A bungee cord appears to connect Jaco's penis to some sort of voice-activated sensor. It bounces up and down whenever anyone talks. My eyes try to resist the distraction.

"Why did you run away?" asks Sundancer.

"I don't know."

"That answer won't work here," she says.

I look at the floor.

"Look me in the eyes. What are you feeling right now?"

"Scared."

"Scared enough to run away?"

"Everyone freaked out after I made the corn bread. They said I ruined the weekend. I should be sent home."

"Come with us," Sundancer says.

In the kitchen office, Daydream, the assistant workshop leader and commune elder, joins us. Naked like the others, she is by far the soggiest of the group. She looks like she's been soaking in a hot tub for decades. Even her eyelids and fingernails droop. Everyone huddles around her, referring to me as "the student," while a debate ensues as to whether to serve the corn bread or compost it.

Although I certainly understand and try to respect their ambiguous rules about eating, I don't understand why a simple apology can't fix what I've done. The longer they refer to me in the third person, the more scared I get. What kind of example do they intend to make of me for what is becoming a more reprehensible sin by the minute?

"This is a really good example of how the student can choose in each moment to act from his vision rather than from his damage," Sundancer says.

"But every student has the choice to spread that message, and it is up to him or her to make that choice," Jaco counters.

Their huddle transforms into a circle. They clasp hands, close their eyes, breathe deeply, and begin a visualization that involves cerulean blue. Their eyes remain closed for so long that I think they may have fallen asleep.

After a while, I sit on a milk crate, fold my hands, and stare at a bird clock on the wall that emits the sound of a different bird each hour. After twenty minutes, the Downy Woodpecker calls seven o'clock, and they open the circle. They have made a decision.

"Rather than waste the nourishment," Daydream says, turning to me, "we will serve it."

Everyone leaves the room except Fireblossom. To make amends for ratting me out, she probably has something to say. She puts her hand gently on my shoulder and whispers, "Americans will put up with anything provided it doesn't block traffic."

I have no idea what she's talking about.

Nodding and smiling, I follow her back into the kitchen, where we cut the corn bread and bring the pans into the dining lodge with the other pans, full of meatless tempeh meatloaf.

In the lodge, fifty people have gathered in an "ovalish" around the food. I join the ovalish, and a hand on either side grabs mine. "Thank you for your patience with dinner," Sundancer says. "As we are all discovering, every moment here is a lesson in being present. When we let go and trust in the present, our history, our patterns, and our limiting ideas no longer have a hold on us. This allows us to experience freedom."

"Amen!" says the girl holding my hand.

"Ho!" another person chimes. (Earlier in the day I learned that this is not an insult meaning "You hooker!" but rather some kind of Native American term of agreement.)

"Today, there was an experience in the kitchen," Sundancer continues. "One of our students used ingredients forbidden during our journey here.

These ingredients aren't forbidden because they do harmful things to us, they are forbidden because they weigh us down and keep us attached to the very things we are here to learn to let go of."

"Amen!" someone says.

"After considerable discussion, we have decided to allow the meal to be served. You should know though, that in every moment, we are all free, and all choices and ways of being are available. We saw how much energy we expended trying to protect you from this, and in the process we realized that we were actually suppressing ourselves. This is a learning process for me, too, and I want you to know that I am continuing to learn that letting go is a choice made moment to moment and that we always have the ability to let go, no matter how unpleasant the circumstances."

One of the naked students in the circle raises his hand. "I just want to say that I'm noticing now how much energy was released when you revealed yourself."

"Thank you, Starman," says Sundancer. "Okay, so that's all I have to say. If there's nothing else, we'll have Julie lead us in song."

Everyone begins to sing.

> The gospel train is coming.
> I hear it just at hand.
> I hear the car wheels moving
> and rumbling through the land.

The ovalish collapses after the song as I realize that I feel too humiliated to eat. I sit down at a table and stare at a container of wheat-free tamari, feeling absolutely horrible for ruining so many potential breakthroughs.

But something interesting happens midway through the meal, something palpable in the room. After days of subsisting on nothing but Holocaust-like rations of raw vegetables, spoonfuls of seed, and air, a soothing contentedness spreads throughout the room. My fellow students gorge themselves on my bread, eating it like it's their last meal on Earth. All five pans disappear in less than twenty minutes.

When I leave the dining room, I feel like the kind of hero imprisoned for a murder he didn't commit who does good upon his release. Even the mood in the kitchen during cleanup improves—probably because the cleanup crew isn't starving to death for the first time in three days.

But as I wander along the tiny dirt pathways of the commune, my feelings about all of this gather in the back of my throat. I want to scream, but I know I can't. The attention it would attract wouldn't be the right kind. I'd like to run away, but I'd probably get lost in the forest for days. I'd like to talk to Raleigh, but we're not allowed to have contact during the retreat.

So I do the next best thing: I break into the yurt that has the pay phone and collect-call the Château. The phone rings and rings. I hang up. I call my cousin Chester in Arizona. "I'm not doing very good," he says. His voice betrays that he's been crying. He tells me that he's been working in a sex shop while his girlfriend strips in a peep-show booth.

"For months, I've been slinging a mop and pulling a bucket around to the plastic booths, mopping up cum while dirty old men watch Ida shove zucchinis in her pussy and bananas in her ass, and clamp clothespins on her nipples."

"That's horrible," I say, thinking back to all the times Shiloh left me feeling completely insignificant.

"I just figured it would hurt less," he says. "At least, here I'm close to her, rather than at home alone thinking about her being in a peep box."

As he tells me the story, a tree is falling on the roof of his proverbial house, the entire tree, roots and all. My stomach tightens in a knot, and I bite my lip, wondering about Raleigh and my own tree. I tell Chester about my predicament, about the corn bread, about seeing Raleigh two nights ago cuddling on the floor with Jaco, and how it made my stomach drop.

"The mixing bowl, wooden spoon, and the corn bread might be a slightly different version of the mop, bucket, and peep show," he says.

"Misery loves company," I say, hearing voices outside the yurt. "Crap, I have to go. I love you."

I hang up and sneak out the door just as a dark shadow of people walks by.

"Everyone must report to the Mystical Dimension room in ten minutes," a voice echoes.

"Yesterday," Sundancer says in the small room that looks like a church basement, "you learned that milling about the room means walking openly and without purpose until someone takes your hands. Then you learned how to look deeply into another person's eyes to witness them. We are now ready for the next evolution in milling.

"Mill about. Then walk up to a fellow student, look them in the eyes, and say, 'Is there anything you are wanting or not wanting right now?' The listener should answer the speaker's question thoughtfully and with honesty."

I begin to mill. I tell the first person I encounter that I'm craving a cheeseburger from the McDonald's dollar menu. The girl gives me a funny look. I let go and mill about. A man walks up to me and hugs me. I hug back—too tightly.

"You sure have a lot to give," he says.

When I let go and turn to mill, another girl immediately embraces me. I hug back—too lightly.

"You don't have a lot to give, do you?" she says.

"Stop!" Sundancer announces. "Find four others to whom you are drawn, and one at a time tell the group your deepest secret."

I tell my group that my mom is a Holocaust survivor and that my family is Jewish, which I've never told anyone. I can hear my mother's voice in the background, *Don't tell anyone you're Jewish. They will find you. They will kill you. You will die.* In her Jewish closet, she is eating a McDonald's cheeseburger and holding one out for me.

While I'm speaking, I keep thinking that when I'm done a huge weight will lift from my back. But when I finish, I don't feel any different. Absolutely nothing has changed.

Just before dawn, Sundancer announces: "Each of you will now get the chance to be *seen* by the rest your community. One at a time, each of you will come and stand on this cinder block to be witnessed. Community members will respond to what they see."

Judgments and faults blindside the first two participants who stand on the cinder block.

"I see someone who is afraid of the world," one person shouts.

"I see a woman who is crying out to express herself," yells another.

When I step up on the cinder block, I stare at the wall beyond. My arms dangle by my side. I tense my stomach, preparing for the worst.

"You have such a nice, warm smile," someone says.

"You have a heart of gold," says someone else.

"You are so giving that it is inspiring to be in your presence."

I don't understand. I've stepped onto the cinder block expecting the worst and received the opposite. The compliments keep coming. My reaction blindsides me. My eyes begin to leak. As more people say nice things, I begin to sob. I sob until my body collapses, my cries so loud that they feel like screams.

At first the facilitators decide not to intervene. I heave uncontrollably for fifteen minutes. Then others in the room begin to cry. At some point they lift me up, carry me into another room, and set me down on a little blue foam mat.

Everything is a mess. Every fear I've ever experienced, every moment of terror, anxiety, depression, or pain wells up and pushes itself out from the depths of my heart. I feel the fear of death as I swerve into the night on the back of my father's motorcycle. I feel my stupidity for not believing my friends when they tell me that Shiloh is a slut. The pain of losing Daisy comes back, and I see myself lying curled under the back porch like a dog about to die. I regret the way I treated Goldie, pushing her away simply for wanting to love me. Everyone I've ever wronged, everyone who's ever wronged me, they all untangle and float away.

An hour later, two elder women with gray hair sit beside me. I've cried for so long that my legs have fallen asleep. To help me stand, the women massage my legs and unfold them. I feel ninety years old. One woman holds my hand as I lean on her shoulder. She says that the others could hear me crying through the walls.

"You've held a lot in, and now it's found a way out," she says.

"You sounded like an Alaskan Malamute," the other one says with a warm smile.

"I feel like I've been reborn," I say, leaning on the women as they help me into the other room.

"Once you identify an attachment," Sundancer says, "like wanting control, wanting approval, or wanting love and you let go of it, you quickly discover that letting go is a physical, visceral experience that can't be faked. When a person lets go, their posture straightens, their body opens, and they became luminous."

Sundancer glances at me. The room goes silent. I rejoin the circle without celebration.

"It's time to put our energy and attention into getting what we truly care about," she says. "It's time to be relationship warriors and to commit ourselves 100 percent to creating alive, powerful unions with the people we love."

On the last day of the workshop, a man called the Goddess comes in. He looks like Tony Robbins in drag. When Sundancer calls my name, I go to the front of the room where the Goddess dances around me and pretends to pick invisible objects off my shoulders. He is giving me my karmic GED.

~~~

Driving back to Portland, I eat an entire bag of Fritos, a Burger King Whopper, and chew through an entire pack of Hubba Bubba. Indira greets me at the door of the Ivon Château with a hug.

"How was it?" she says, sipping from her tiny yogurt cup.

"My tree is smaller," I say.

She laughs and takes another sip.

"The thing with trees on your back is that you can't really cut them down. You kind of just have to starve them and wait for them to die," I say.

"That's how I cured my cancer," she says.

"So I've heard," I say, winking at her. "I was thinking that the best starvation diet is one in which you do things you wouldn't normally do."

"I ate jelly sandwiches on Wonder Bread until my body didn't recognize me anymore. For someone else, it's something different. I take it your tree got confused?"

"Confused and then sad. I created an entirely new ecosystem this weekend. The roots of the tree no longer recognized the host that it was feeding on. Sadness kills everything."

30

beauty & voluntaries

eugene, oregon / portland, oregon
december 5, 2000

ASTRO AL—A TOOTHLESS, AGELESS MAN—WEARS A PURPLE VELVET
robe that bears an aroma of manly musk, hippie dust, and the magical
forest outside Eugene, Oregon, where he lives. I am seeking his advice on
a wedding date. Raleigh and I have exhausted ourselves trying to come
up with one on our own. We referenced and cross-referenced the Mayan
calendar, the Chinese zodiac, Rudolph Steiner's bio-dynamic calendar,
the Ephemeral chart, the *Old Farmer's Almanac,* the western zodiac, and
the Moon phase chart. We fought over it at the kitchen table, on the
living-room couch, on the front porch, in the car, at my massage clinic,
and even while hiking.

We didn't dare give a date to my future mother-in-law until we had
talked to Astro Al. Raleigh was away doing an ever important silent
retreat at Breitenbush Hot Springs, so I went alone.

She was always away when it came time to make important decisions
related to our relationship, and it always gave me a kind of stomachache
whenever I went to make these decisions. It felt exactly like jealousy. Here
I was, filled with dread at making the wrong decision and jealous that I
couldn't be out in the woods with a bunch of naked people.

In his yurt, Astro Al is sipping a drink made in his Vitamix, consulting his tomes, and smacking his gums. "Aha!" he says while clearing his throat. His eyes bug out of his head. I can't tell if he means this salutation for me or as some third-person epiphany, but either way it's not going to be good.

"Leo Scorpio," he says, referring to me. He never remembers people's names, only their sun sign and rising sign, using these as names. "There are two things you should know about yourself. One, you are susceptible to hallucinogens. Don't do them. Two, your astrological makeup gives you a zodiacal predisposition toward extreme, surreal, and dramatic situations. Quite simply, you are wired for intensity and inconsistency. If you don't become an EMT, an army medic, or the on-call manager of a suicide prevention hotline, I suggest you do something with your life where you can channel this energy."

Astro Al had just reached into my soul and found the instruction manual for the remote control of my life. As I stare past his dreadlocked comb-over to his sequined outhouse in the field beyond, everything about my life suddenly comes into focus.

I can finally see the proverbial speed bump that knocked me out of 45 monogamous relationships in 8 states and 2 countries, that threw me into 112 different apartments and tossed me into 90 day jobs. This is why others thought I had lived nine lives by the time I was nineteen and forty lives, now, by the time I'm thirty-three. He explained the weirdo magnet attached to my sternum that attracted all kinds of strange events into my life and people into my heart. Before now, there had been no explanation. But now, in this moment, my life separates into two entities: my life and an explanation for it.

"Aha!" I say back as fat tears roll out of my eyes.

Astro Al responds with his own "Aha!" and we go back and forth in an epiphanic ping-pong match.

By the time Astro Al finishes, the front of my shirt is soaking wet. Lost in his prophecy, I don't connect the dots, though. The intensity to which he spoke refers not only to my life, but also to my future marriage. Not good. Not good at all.

31

love fight club

As RALEIGH FUMES BACK TO OUR HOUSE, I PICK UP HER ENGAGEMENT ring, step onto the bus, sit down, and yell out the window: "I don't need your freakin' fight club anymore. I've got one of my own, bitch!"

She has no idea what I'm talking about. It sounds like something stupid I would say in the heat of an argument. Little did Raleigh know that, instead of going to my massage clinic on the ritzy side of town each day to make rich, divorced, slightly overweight women feel better, I was fighting the CEOs of some of Portland's largest and most well-respected companies in my office. For months, my massage table collected dust in my clinic closet next to large containers of unopened massage oil and linens still in their sealed packages.

"We'll see what Caryn has to say about all this!" she yells back.

Since Raleigh and I departed our respective communities and moved into a small apartment, nearly all of our time together has fallen under the shadow of weekly couples counseling with Caryn Whitman, our sexological love spirit intimacy coach, who is helping us to disguise our fights as adrenalized conversations that end in great makeup sex. As a result, my distance would make a desert hermit look like a club promoter, and Raleigh understandably resents it.

"For many couples, the excitement and rush of an angry encounter is often described as the only time they feel a connection," Caryn says later that day at our weekly session. "Does this ring true for either of you?"

"You can say that again," Raleigh says.

Eight hours apart have done nothing to quench her anger. I nod.

"Have you been working on letting go of some of your resentments, Raleigh?" Caryn asks.

"No!" I answer for her.

"Whatever," Raleigh says. "You're the one with the resentments."

"Is that true?" Caryn says, referring to me.

"She's deflecting," I say.

"Now you're deflecting," Raleigh says. "Do you have an answer?"

"Yes," I say.

"Yes, what?" Caryn says.

"Of course I have resentments," I say.

"Would you care to elucidate?"

"Well, I mean—"

"I can't wait to hear this bullshit," Raleigh interrupts.

"Raleigh, please," says Caryn.

"The biggest is her kissing problem," I say. "She has a habit of kissing guys on the mouth."

"Are you serious?" Raleigh says.

"Raleigh, please," says Caryn.

"It began almost as soon as we met. The day we left Mexico she kissed an old man who sold us a blanket. You should have seen the guy. His eyes got as big as two corn tortillas, and he almost fell into a cactus. He seemed very pleased that he got to first base for selling her a blanket."

"How did that make you feel?" Caryn asks.

"Like my stomach was hooked up to a helium tank. It started rising up to my head. I thought I might faint . . ."

"Is there more?" asks Caryn.

I nod. Raleigh shifts uncomfortably. I roll my eyes.

"The End of Days Kiss came about two months later. My roommates at the Ivon Château held a going-away party for me, and she kissed each of my roommates on the mouth."

"They were pecks," Raleigh says.

"It was a lip gang bang!"

"Pecks!"

"Then why did you disappear? For hours?"

"It was twenty minutes."

"Three hours later I finally find her in the carport slow dancing with my roommate to Bryan Adams's '(Everything I Do) I Do It for You.'"

"Oh yeah, crybaby? Well, you're supposed to be a man, and a man is someone who rushes up to his woman and says, 'My girl doesn't slow dance like that with anyone but me,'" she yells.

"Well, you're supposed to know that it's not okay to do that to someone you love."

"It was an innocent dance," Raleigh says.

"An innocent dance doesn't make someone lock himself in a bathroom and cry," I say.

"This didn't cause you to break up?" Caryn says.

"He tried," Raleigh says.

"I went down to my studio, ripped twenty pages from my art pad, taped them together, and wrote her a twenty-two-foot breakup letter."

"I asked him to give me another chance," Raleigh says.

"I've given you *nothing* but chances," I say. "You've given people nothing but kisses. Ask Mitchell how many kisses you've given him, and you kiss Paul on the mouth hello every time we see him."

"That was once," she says.

"Once at the Bagdad Theater. Now he conveniently pops up all over town." A bell on Caryn's table dings. Time to go home.

"All right you two, that's all the time we have. I want you to keep the lines of communication open. Slash, when you feel resentment building, see if you can journal your feelings. Raleigh, I want you to share your thoughts with your loved one a little bit more."

That night at dinner, we don't enjoy our usual pre-food ritual: holding hands, closing our eyes, visualizing the food's energy, and giving thanks to the universe. We scowl and scoop forkfuls of kale and brown rice into our mouths in silence until the doorbell rings.

"It's probably for you," I say.

Raleigh gets up from the table.

"Are you teaching here tonight?" I ask, referring to her private prenatal yoga sessions.

She doesn't answer.

"It's for you," she says, returning.

Napoleon aka Doug Ackerman (one of my clients) is standing in our front hall. He measures six-foot-three inches tall but stands at only five-eleven-and-a-half because his trapped anger has bent his spirit, causing his chest to cave in and his body to lurch forward. Even when he straightens up, he doesn't recover the missing four and a half inches. His bones are so gaunt they protrude where they shouldn't, and he wears a perpetually sad face with sunken eyes.

"Uh, Napoleon. Wow. Hello. What are you doing here?"

"Do you have some time?"

I glance down the empty hallway. "Uh, sure."

"I don't mind paying you," he says.

"No, it's not that. Come on." We meander through Raleigh's herb garden and stop beside a large pile of cow manure. "What's going on?" I say while looking him in the eyes.

"I've been eating a lot while watching TV again," he says.

For some reason, this extremely skinny man has convinced himself that he's fat.

"Um, do you think it could be because there are so many food commercials?" I say, biting my bottom lip and wondering how the fight club might work beyond the safety of my clinic.

"I don't know," he says. "Watching TV tends to be an escape from my reality, so I'm thinking that overeating is helping me cope with my jolts back to reality."

A rusty rake, a yard gnome missing a nose, and a five-gallon bucket filled with rainwater occupy the yard. *Mental note: Avoid those areas for safety reasons.* During our last session, Napoleon pushed my head into the sink and cracked the faucet housing. *Second mental note: Call plumber.*

"Do you think the food commercials take advantage of your vulnerability?" I ask.

"I dunno," he says.

I glance up to the house, expecting to see Raleigh peering out the window. She's not. It's more likely that she's sprinkling all-purpose cleaner onto my dinner. Napoleon looks like a sad *Tyrannosaurus rex*, his sad arms curled up in front of his sad chest.

"Are you ready?" I ask.

He nods.

I instruct him to kick the cow manure and lead him in fire breathing, which involves sucking large amounts of air into his nose and blowing it out of his mouth really fast. Next, I grasp his arms and squeeze them extremely hard. *OK, here we go.*

"Your father thinks you laugh like a girl," I say, staring directly into his eyes. "It was your fault that your mother stuck you in the shower as a three year old when you vomited your spaghetti up in the middle of the night."

The litany of insults continues as usual, and I expect the usual buildup: near-anger, break, repeat. But Napoleon peaks right away. He gazes at me in a way I've never seen before. Suddenly I fear for my life.

He charges me, and I take off running—first through the herb garden and then around the house. Twice. By the time I muster enough sense to run inside I'm screaming like a little girl, Napoleon only a step or two behind. We squeak down the hall, and I leap into the bathroom just in time, locking the door and wedging myself against it.

"Motherfucker!" he yells, pounding. "*Motherfucker!*"

Near midnight, Raleigh knocks on the door. I've fallen asleep against the tile floor. I pull myself up, touch the grout indentions on my face, and let her in. She kisses me on the head as she goes to brush her teeth.

In bed, I pull her engagement ring from my pocket and put it on her finger. "Here," I say, romantically, before struggling to pull off my pants.

"You really do have a fight club, don't you?"

I nod and then reach under the bed for a stack of manila folders.

"Project Strongbox," I say.

"'Are You a Victim of the Anger Bee?'" she reads, flipping through various pages. "'The 59 Faces of Anger,' 'A Better Argument without Getting Angry'—what the hell are all these?"

"Handouts for my clients," I say.

"My God, you're serious, aren't you?" she says.

I nod. "It grew out of an accident with a massage client last year. He offered me an extra hundred dollars to cuss him out and wrestle him to the ground."

"Did you?"

"Of course."

"So that whole thing with that tall guy in the backyard wasn't just one of your Andy Kaufman things?"

"Nope."

I tell her how satisfying it is to witness people who never thought they could get angry fly into murderous rages. I work only with people who have the inability to get angry. I instruct my clients to insert the words "motherfucker" and "kill" into my anger management scripts. During meditation, instead of guiding them into relaxation, I tell them to squeeze their toes, legs, and ass cheeks as tight as they can while visualizing themselves as a hot dog burning over the hot coals of an outdoor grill.

"People sign up for this shit?" she asks.

"Not just regular people, CEOs of large corporations," I explain. "You know that guy you saw chasing me in the backyard? He's the CEO of one of the country's largest property and casualty insurance companies. Three months ago, he had no healthy outlet or even the ability to express his anger. Can you believe his progress?"

"Why are you telling me all this? Haven't you heard of client confidentiality?"

"Napoleon's not his real name. All my clients get a new name. It's part of the process."

"But . . . what the hell gives you the idea that it's safe to bring home this kind of work?"

Here we go.

"What do you mean?" I ask.

She gives me a look.

"You want me to stop?" I say.

"You want me to leave?"

"It's not that easy. A lot of people depend on me."

The look continues.

"Besides, it pays really well. I'm actually paying down the premium on my credit cards."

We sit in silence for a moment. The steam in her cerebral tea kettle rises.

"Where the hell did you come up with this dumb-ass shit?" she asks.

"I used the free eight-week anger management course that I took through the county as a foundation and built it from there."

She shakes her head, completely misinterpreting my good intentions, like the rabbit squeezer in *Of Mice and Men*. It's disgusting.

"That course saved me," I say.

"The naturopath saved you," she counters.

"No, the naturopath speculated that it was suppressed anger. She said, instead of getting angry and releasing my feelings, I was holding them in, and they were eating away at me. My anger management instructor said the stomach cramps and internal bleeding might be from a wheat allergy, and *that's* when I went back to the naturopath, who diagnosed it."

"Are you kidding? What the hell are you talking about? Your anger instructor had you convinced you were gay!"

"Polymorphously perverse," I correct her. "Seeking pleasure through all available orifices isn't the same as being a homo."

She pulls the covers off and turns toward me.

"I'm kidding! I'm kidding," I say, flinching. "Don't get all worked up!"

"Worked up? Worked *up?* Do you have a fucking short-term memory or what?"

"Why are you yelling at me?"

"I'm not fucking yelling! *You're* yelling! Don't you remember anything about those crazy-ass angry people?"

"I don't know."

"You said some guy threw his mother-in-law off a balcony, some lady stabbed her boss in the neck, and some postal worker with a tattoo on her face went . . . postal!"

"I remember them all," I say.

"You want those kinds of people coming around the house?"

"My clients aren't like that. Listen, the epitome of sketchy, dangerous, expressive anger surrounds us all the time. Otherwise, a bunch of people literally being eaten away inside by the inability to get angry surrounds us. Consider me a superhero ridding the free world of IBS."

"What?"

"Irritable Bowel Syndrome."

"I know what IBS is! I was a biology major. You're fucking whacked! I can't believe that I'm engaged to a complete idiot—and now you're laughing at me? You're laughing at your future wife?"

"It's nervous laughter."

My laughter breaks the camel's back. Her ring comes flying off again. She leaves the room, and when she returns something large barely misses my head. I sleep in the utility room. Sometime around dawn I sneak back into bed, and we have great makeup sex. Then we make waffles and devour our subtle resentments.

My mouth full of masticated waffle, the terrible offspring of thought and memory bursts into my head—much more dire than my admission of Project Strongbox. Two thin tracks mar Raleigh's herb garden, one mine, the other Napoleon's. They immediately nauseate me.

When Raleigh is in the shower, I sneak outside to survey the damage. As quickly as I lift her crushed plants, they fall. The lifeless carcass of her crushed Stevia plant—an herb that tastes like sugar—lies in my hand like the body of a baby bird. She will never forgive me for this.

32

the days run away like my wife's hair over the hills

kauai, hawaii / portland, oregon
september 24, 2001

WHAT WAS I THINKING WHEN I AGREED TO SHAVE MY HEAD WITH HER?
"Without hair," she had said, "we'll be able to love each other more
fully."

I believed her.

Waking up in a hotel room on the shores of Kauai, I begin to doubt
myself as I watch her sleep. The Hawaiian sun crawls into the room and
illuminates her hairless head on the pillow. Her mouth hangs slacker and
wetter than I remember. Her breathing sounds louder, her body larger, her
head smaller, her shape lumpier.

"Without material constraints," she had said, "we can train ourselves
to look beyond mere physical appearances."

I believed her.

The clock indicates that we've been married fewer than seventy-
two hours, and our marriage has already hit a speed bump. The hairless
woman sleeping beside me in no way resembles the beautiful girl who
walked down the aisle. I've married a big bald man. Astro Al would

have called her bald head a visible sign of the end, much like when I was the ring bearer in my uncle's wedding and fell backward off the church stage. By the time the neck brace came off, he was filing the divorce papers.

Realizing the depths of my shallowness, I pull the covers around my chest. A little blue-green lizard scurries across the floor and up the nightstand and makes its way over to the pillow right in front of my new bride's mouth. It looks at me, then looks at her mouth, seemingly contemplating whether going inside is a good idea. In my head, it says, "*Quite a unique and troublesome upper-middle-class dilemma, isn't it?*"

I nod. Having an imaginary conversation with a socioeconomically sensitive lizard isn't exactly how I imagined the first morning of my honeymoon.

Raleigh wakes. I kiss her on the cheek. She looks at me like she did in Salt Lake City when we met—like I'm a gift. My expression hides a complete blankness that hides disappointment hiding shallowness—like she's a re-gifted gift. She throws off the covers and bounds into the bathroom like it's Easter morning. She laughs while looking in the mirror. A few minutes later she comes out holding two fresh luau leaves in front of her breasts.

"Take a picture of me like this!" she squeals.

I grab the camera and look through the lens. She smiles, but something's amiss. Behind her smile lies something not quite right, like her mouth is full of cavities, like she's trying to swallow that she knows what I'm thinking.

By the time we rent the surfboards and get down to the beach, my silence is bothering even me. I'm supposed to teach her how to surf. I wade out without her and paddle far beyond the breakers.

Either Hawaii has failed us, or we have failed Hawaii, a virtual impossibility. With couples holding hands, couples in matching Hawaiian shirts, couples kissing, old couples, young couples, and military couples, Hawaii has a gift for curing relationships even on the brink of disaster. But I feel like a fraud. We're a couple of frauds. Why else would we have flown all the way to Hawaii to test ourselves?

I come clean on the drive back. "Some people just don't look right with a shaved head."

"Is that right?" she says, pulling over and turning off the car beside what appears to be miles and miles of sugar cane.

"Get out," she says.

I do. She pulls away and then stops. She gets out, takes a picture of me, and speeds away.

On my long walk back to the hotel, I think. Our marriage might be a hologram. If I decode one particular part, it might reveal secrets about the whole. Weeks before, Raleigh felt passionately about changing our last names to Tu Tu Moon-Bear. The ensuing argument in the town magistrate's office about what a husband should or shouldn't do and what a wife should or shouldn't be ended poorly, and we nearly called off the wedding. Her mother cornered me in the kitchen and said, "Raleigh says you didn't want to share a name with her." A funereal sorrow takes hold of me.

—◦—

The next day, we pull up to the ranger booth at Na Pali Coast State Wilderness Park. The ranger tells us that the park is closed because a serial killer is targeting young blonde women.

"You've got nothing to worry about," I say to Raleigh.

The walk back to the hotel is twice as far this time.

—◦—

I run into Astro Al at the Urban Onion, a little cafe attached to a health food store back in Portland. As he slops up some kind of brewer's yeast gravy with a piece of spelt bread and it drips down his chest and onto his purple robe, he says that he knew my marriage was doomed from the start. He couldn't warn me because it contained an all-important catalyst that finally would help me attain the fulfillment of my destiny: the creation of *The Bohemian Love Diaries*.

I have no idea what he's talking about.

With his usual straightforward imprecision, he likens my imminent creation to the creation of a famous Capricorn Scorpio, meaning Sam Walton, the guy who created Walmart. "Mr. Capricorn Scorpio created a place where people could fall in love with shitty stuff, stuff they never thought they needed, stuff that falls apart, stuff that doesn't last, stuff that has a complicated return policy—a waking dream where fulfillment, consistency, and permanency are shelved directly beside the illusion of fulfillment, consistency, and permanency."

Apparently Sam Walton and I are cut from the same cloth, bookends working in a similar profession, senior partners in some sort of cosmic architecture firm run by Cupid.

Right before we part, Astro Al tosses me a profound piece of advice as frivolously as you would toss a fortune cookie across the table at the end of a Chinese meal. "The sound of a heart breaking is the sound of a heart breaking open," he says. "Don't let your heart close to begin with, and you won't have to break it to get it to open up again."

I never see Astro Al again.

━╌━

Six months after Hawaii and nearly two dozen photos of me walking alone through cane fields with the weight of the world on my shoulders, we separate. Raleigh moves into an apartment thirty-three blocks away, a number only significant because one night, just to get a dose of "the hair of the dog that bit me" I walk to Raleigh's apartment barefoot. Afterward, a newly minted phase of liberation begins.

It doesn't take long to get used to farting freely or holding my spoon like a Neanderthal when eating my cereal or doing both at the same time. I move all the drinking glasses into the medicine cabinet and all the bathroom supplies go in the utensil drawer. I even make a fort in the living room by turning the sofa on its end. My life becomes one big private joke about freedom.

By the end of my first season of freedom—after hitting on all my single girl friends yields no results—I crash. Without so much as a glimmer in my subconscious, I feel unbearably alone. I miss her terribly. Astro Al's advice floats back to me. "The sound of a heart breaking is the sound of a heart breaking open. Don't let your heart close to begin with, and you won't have to break it to get it to open up again."

The next morning I book a session at a nearby tattoo parlor and get a huge green flower tattooed onto the center of my chest. Symbolically analogous to open heart surgery, it's the most painful thing I've ever paid for. For three hours, I lie on a lab table while Astro Al's advice bleeds permanently into my skin.

The next day it feels like a broken soda bottle has scraped my chest raw. In New Seasons Market, searching for a homeopathic salve called arnica, I spot Raleigh in the overhead mirror. At first I don't recognize her. Her hair has grown back. She doesn't recognize me. A beard now covers my face. For a moment we see each other as hirsute strangers. By the time our brains register the connection, it's too late to run away.

She looks into my eyes and takes a deep breath.

"I'm not sure what to say," I say.

She shrugs.

"My arms feel awkward hanging by my side," I say.

She smiles. I smile. She takes another deep breath.

"Hi," she says.

"Hi. I miss you," I say and lift up my shirt.

Her eyes well up with tears.

During the next few weeks there are simultaneous phone calls to the florist and lots of flowers—tulips, sunflowers, oriental lilies. I give them to her. She gives them to me. I paint a picture for her, she writes a poem for me, we exchange letters, and we meet for a post-separation date.

"If we could erase it all and start over, it might work," I say.

"Like in the movies?"

"More like a ritual where we burn or bury everything that ties us to the past."

"Our wedding photos?"

I nod. "Maybe the toxic smoke from the photo paper will destroy enough brain cells to make our love life a lot less complicated."

"We could bury our wedding gifts," she suggests.

"What about the Vitamix?"

"Maybe we'll stick to the things we don't like."

"Our wedding rings?"

"Most definitely," she says.

The next week, what we don't bury we burn. With very little of what makes a couple—no shared last name, no joint bank account, no material possessions, no kids—we at last can re-create ourselves and our relationship.

33

bohemian love baggage

portland, oregon / pendleton, oregon / cody, wyoming /
cheyenne, wyoming / jackson hole, wyoming /
woodward, oklahoma / dodge city, kansas /
winchester, kentucky / victor, west virginia /
richmond, virginia
june 1, 2002

"It lasted just long enough for us to buy *Nolo's Essential Guide to Divorce.*"

"That's a shame," my father says, pulling another piece of luggage off the baggage carousel. "I liked her."

As I reach for his bag, he throws another, which slams into me. He turns back to the carousel, oblivious. Since my divorce and flying him to Portland to help me move back home, the air between us has felt unusual. He only returned one of my calls before we solidified our plans. From week to week, when I called home, my mom kept telling me that he'd changed his mind. One week he was coming, the next he wasn't.

She warned me about his new style of dress, but his appearance still shocks me. He looks like a renegade extra on the set of a spaghetti western. He's wearing too-tight wranglers tucked into colorful knee-high Lucchese boots, rusty spurs, a belt buckle as big as a manhole cover, and a rigid new bandana around his neck. A Tom Mix hat swallows his whole head, and a mustache conceals his entire mouth.

"They let you through gate check like that?"

"Yeah, why?" he says, slinging his duffel bag over his shoulder.

"No reason."

Already tense.

On the way to the parking deck, a family stops us for a photo. I take the picture. I think my father looks funny, but no one else does. They love it—and I love all the attention he's drawing. As he puts his guitar into the back of my pickup, he says, "We're still fixin' to stop in every rodeo town along the way, right?"

"I guess." My mom persuaded him that he could use our time together as a creative research trip.

"There's no guessin' to it. I need photos for my new series of cowboy paintings."

"I guess we're stopping then."

He climbs into the cab. He has no idea that I already know about his "secret situation." My mom and I have discussed nothing else for the past few months, including: his cell phone records, the cost of the private investigator she hired, her plan to throw all his belongings into the front yard before he returns, and her theory that his new fashion choices most likely come from the girlfriend.

"He dresses this way when he reads the paper, mows the lawn, and drives to Costco," my mom said.

"Is that why he's only returned one of my calls?"

"He's pathetic. He just can't be away from her."

"He's not drinking again, is he?"

"What do you think?"

"So no meetings?" I said, referring to AA.

"Meetings with her."

"Great. So when I told him it would be a father-son trip like the ones we used to take to Alaska, I wasn't far off."

"Hardly."

"For once, I have a real need to be with him," I said. "I mean, how often do a divorce and a subsequent cross-country trip happen?"

"You can have the bastard."

At first, it seemed important to be with my dad—ideal and natural, like going fishing or hunting. But now it's hard to assimilate my mother's feelings about what he's been doing. Hearing how his new relationship has hurt her, it's hard not to take her side. But taking her side without knowing the full story doesn't feel right.

My father unfolds the atlas in his lap, puts on his reading glasses, and draws his finger along the map. For once I'm the one holding the blueprint, pointing us in the right direction, guiding us. But he seems intent on shaping our time together into something less than the sacred journey I want.

"For tax purposes, we can split everything down the middle—the driving, the food, and the gas," he says, more pragmatic than sacred.

"Whatever you want, Dad."

I'll have to choose my battles along the way.

The first day of driving unfolds like a twisted job interview with a frenzy of questions and answers. "What are you fixin' to do on the East Coast?" "Maybe open a massage clinic or a taxidermy shop." "What are you fixin' to do if you can't get a job?" "Maybe work aboard *The Tinker*." "Where you plannin' on livin'?" "Home seems like a good option" and then I whisper silently to myself *"since you're getting kicked out soon."*

The questions continue in rapid fire until his cell phone rings. "Hero" by Enrique Iglesias blares from his pocket until he answers. He leans against the passenger window, shifting uncomfortably and using a careful, soft tone with vague terminology. He's pretending that it's my mom. But he should know that I know better. Unless he miraculously has become some kind of tech wizard since I saw him, he has no idea how to change the ringtone on a cell phone.

"Your mom was wondering how the trip was," he says after he hangs up.

After the lie, silence settles into our trip. He falls asleep and snores while the rolling boil of a gentle anger bubbles up inside me. He has no idea the tension even exists.

That evening in Pendleton, Oregon, I pull into the parking lot of a seedy motel and promptly lock the keys in the truck. Wanting to avoid an argument, I walk toward the motel pretending they're in my pocket. Anything might set him off now that he's back on the wagon. Until he comes clean about his girlfriend, he's probably doing all he can to keep his usual drinking demons at bay.

"What?" my dad says, standing by his door.

"Nothing," I say. "Come on."

"Wait, I need my phone."

"Get it after we check in."

"Open the damn door. It'll take two seconds." His anger is already rising to the surface.

"Can't you wait until after we check in?" I feel like a puffer fish blowing myself up.

"Throw me the damn keys."

For a moment, it feels as if we might get into a full-blown fight in the parking lot.

"I can't," I say, squaring my shoulders with him.

"Quit your crap!"

"I'm not." I fold my arms. "I locked the keys inside."

A transformation instantly ensues, something I haven't seen in a long time. My father's emotional response leaps to another part of his brain, the part that loves problem solving and knowing the answer to everything.

"You stay with the truck," he says, walking away. "I'll call the locksmith and get us checked in."

He's gone for what seems like hours. He's probably getting wasted somewhere. I sit on the tailgate, watch the occasional car pass, kick at the ground, and wish on a shooting star for my parents to find a way back to each other. It never seemed to matter very much, but now that everything in my world connected to relationships is vanishing, they need to stay together more than I might ever admit. I rearrange the luggage in the truck bed.

When I pull out my duffel bag, it accidentally opens a small compartment on the side panel of the truck. Squeezed inside is an old Borax box, and inside that are two clumps of hair. They belong to Raleigh and me, saved from our ritual in Hawaii, and we meant to bury them.

In the camper shell light, the greasy clumps remind me of our ritual. We shaved our heads on a prickly rock that jutted into the ocean, like a twisted piece of burned metal from a car wreck, purple, blue, black, and a touch of rust with edges sharp enough to cut our feet. We climbed onto it carefully. Raleigh laughed and rubbed her head as she tossed her hair into the ocean. She was throwing away the most important part of herself, the part of her that reminded me of Daisy.

I stuff the hair back into the Borax box and dump it in the parking-lot trash can. When Raleigh shaved her head, she shaved the place where I could always hide my sadness and disappointment. Part of me never let go of Daisy, even now. I wonder if my father, in some small way, feels something similar now that he's replaced my mother with someone new.

When he returns with our room key and word about the locksmith, something strange hovers between us. He's sober, but his secret overshadows and undermines his gesture to help. Guilt rather than a genuine interest in doing something nice compels him. It's a dangerous animal, and, given any attention at all, it may turn on me.

On the second night of our sacred journey—in a lodge in Grace, Idaho, while eating an elk burger—my father looks across the table and finally confesses. "I'm in love with two women, son, and it's a hard road to ride."

Until now, my secret, which was knowing his secret, has given me some unquantifiable amount of comfort. Knowing only one side of the story gave me the choice to feel however I want to feel. So his confession betrays me in a way, like I've just watched him hit my mother. My stomach knots.

"She's got this big horse farm and the deer—you should see the deer in the field behind her house . . ." As he continues, the rolling anger steams up inside of me and burns. My silence barrels toward him like a wall, but my skin, throat, and hands feel like they're on fire.

For the first time, my father's selfishness reveals itself for what it really is. He's oblivious that he's hurting my mother. Their love was never shaped by tender kisses or affectionate touches, but there were always gifts, flowers, drunken poetry written on the walls of our house. Their love always seemed deep, consistent, and passionate. Now I'm not so sure.

Back at the motel room, the silence continues. He undresses and whistles. For him, all burdens have vanished with his admission of guilt.

By morning my anger has transformed into sadness and even more silence. At breakfast I am silent. At lunch I am silent. When we gas up I am still silent. By evening my silence becomes rage. As we walk into a casino restaurant in Browning, Montana, the lines of loyalty begin to break.

As we're seated, his phone rings. He smiles at the waitress, excuses himself, and says, loud enough for the waitress to hear, "Order me an ice tea."

As he walks past a wagon wheel above a stone fireplace, the burn nearly engulfs me. The waitress introduces herself as Stacey and rattles off the specials. I hear only her name. She's tall and plain, but pretty in her way, and reminds me of a stretched-out version of Raleigh. I raise two fingers.

"Two ice teas," she says, scribbling on her pad and disappearing.

When she returns with our drinks, my father hasn't returned. I ask her for more sugar. She brings a jar. I want to dump the entire container into his glass.

"Is that your brother?" she asks.

I shake my head as I shake the sugar into my glass.

"Who peed in your cornflakes?" she says. She's probably used to talking to cowboys who flirt back.

As she turns away, her apron brushes my arm, and it reminds me of my divorce proceedings. In the courtroom before the judge—divorce papers laid out on a thick oak table—Raleigh inches away from me. It might as well have been miles. When she turned to leave the courtroom, the papers in her hand brushed my arm. That was our final touch. When was the last time my father touched my mother? True love may be as unattainable as my dad's plans to get us to Alaska.

Stacey returns twice more, and I finally place our food order because I'm too embarrassed not to. I order an elk burger for myself and elk steak medallions for my father. Just as Stacey returns with our food, so does my father. He touches her shoulder, and they share a smile. I want to knock the smile off his face.

"Just in time!" she says.

"That's the way I like it," he says.

She winks at him, laughs, and touches her hair. As he sits, she asks if there's anything else she can get us.

I hate him. I hate his girlfriend. I hate his cowboy shirt. I hate his plate of food. I hate his now watery glass of ice tea.

He picks up his fork. "What's this?" he says.

I suck my cheek between my teeth and bite down as hard as I can.

"What's wrong?" he asks.

His question releases something inside me. A tiny pin just popped the stretched balloon. Here we go.

"Listen, you son of a bitch. I appreciate you trying to be my friend and all by telling me all this bullshit about you-and-your-girlfriend this and you-and-your-girlfriend that, but you're still my goddamn father, and as my father you're disrespecting my mother by telling me all this crap."

My outburst catches us both off guard. It's the first time I react to him as a man instead of the six-year-old I tend to become in his presence. His silence emboldens me to charge forward.

"It's complete *bullshit*. I'm not your friend. I'm not your drinking buddy. I'm not your goddamn therapist. I'm your son. Your goddamn *son*. What you're doing isn't fair. It's not respectable. It's not goddamn right. When we get back, I'm giving you a month to tell mom the truth and own up to it. It's not fair to disrespect her like that."

He nods silently. It's the first time he reacts as a vulnerable six-year-old instead of the impatient know-it-all he tends to be.

As I lift my glass to my mouth, my hand shakes, spilling tea onto my chin. I wipe my face with the back of my hand and notice that neither is burning anymore. For the first time since my divorce, a sense of power infuses me.

Stacey puts the bill in the middle of the table. "You cowboys all right?"

We both nod. He pulls the bill across the table. When I take out my wallet and offer my share, he refuses.

Something substantial has changed between us. Neither of us speaks a word, but, when we stop for gas, he pays. At the motel, he pays again. I am once again his son, but a different kind of son now—an adult son, an empowered son.

In our droopy motel beds, a dim lamp lit between us, the television flashing an episode of *The Gilmore Girls*, the realization hits me that I know what it means to be in love with two women, too. My dad, shaken and unhappy, is writing in his sketchbook. I want to say something to make it all go away. Instead, I turn off the TV and brush my teeth. Now lacking an underlying anger, our silence brings a new kind of discomfort into the room, worse because both of us feel it. By the time I climb into bed I can barely stand it.

I know what it means to be in love with two women, too, I think. I whisper the words aloud.

His pencil stops moving. "What's that?"

"Nothing," I lie.

Is the number of lies a person can tell finite? We have no roadmap for this. Perhaps we'll linger in silence for days.

"What do you love about her?" I finally say. It's strange to ask this question, considering everything that's just happened, but if I want this trip to turn out differently the only way to get there is by steering us in another direction.

"Pardon?"

"What do you love about her? Your girlfriend?" I say, staring at the ceiling.

He puts his pencil down. "You don't have to do this."

"I know."

"You—"

"I want to know," I say.

He thinks for a minute. "Well, it's not what you think. It's not about the sex."

I shrug.

He takes a deep breath. "For starters, she fishes."

"Do y'all go together?" I say. I feel awkward, but the question feels right.

"Hell, no. She has a kayak she takes out alone on the Mattaponi River." He closes his sketchbook and sets it on the nightstand. "You'll never guess what she fishes for."

"Catfish?"

"Alligator Gar fish," he says.

"No shit?" I prop myself up on one elbow.

"No shit." He smiles. "Remember when we used to catch those down in Powhatan?"

This is clearly the first time he's talked about her with anyone. As his secret world merges with mine, transforming his own world into something bigger, he seems relieved.

"You'll never believe what she uses for bait," he says. I shrug. "She floats balls of upholstery thread on the surface of the water. When the fish hit it, it gets caught in their teeth."

"That's pretty wild."

"She weaned me off Cheetos." He laughs.

"What about Skittles?"

"No more."

I laugh. "What about McDonald's?"

"No more!"

It's like being a kid again, having a sleepover in my bunk beds with one of my friends. One of us makes a statement, and the other one responds. We laugh. It goes quiet, and then it starts all over again. This is the relationship that I wanted to have with him.

"She wants me to start doing yogit?"

"You mean eating yogurt?"

"No, that stretching stuff."

"Oh, you mean yoga."

"Whatever the hell it is, I ain't doing it."

A few hours before dawn, darkness stretches over us and covers us in sleep.

The next day I open up to him about my problems with Raleigh. For once he listens rather than judges. For once, his answers genuinely interest me. I show him my tattoo at a diner counter when we stop for lunch. He draws on a napkin a similar pattern that he calls *The Flower of Life*. When he orders a Dr Pepper, I tell him how much I hate Dr Pepper because of him. He laughs.

For the next few days, we drive off the beaten path so he can fill his camera with rodeo photos. We climb under bleachers, sneak into barns, ignore No Trespassing signs. At night, we take out our Moleskine sketchbooks and write together. He helps me bleach my hair blonde in a hotel room in Billings, Montana. We play guitars by a lake in Yellowstone National Park. When he leaves to call his girlfriend each day, he tells me the truth.

On Father's Day, I find a farmer in Jackson Hole, Wyoming, who rents us two horses with the freedom to stay gone as long as we like. "I'll come looking for you if you don't come back by morning," the owner says.

On the last leg of the trip, we drive to Victor, West Virginia. My father steers us into a holler. When the road dead-ends, he points to a stack of wood and cement barely visible on the side of a grassy knoll.

"That's where I grew up," he explains. "It was a dirt-floored cardboard chicken shack."

Cicadas sing in the high grass. What must it have been like to be born on the side of a hill in the middle of nowhere to two parents who wouldn't have understood the first thing about art, and one who didn't speak English? Standing beside him, I understand for the first time why he went to such extremes with his artistic choices—forging creativity and imagination to escape a life of black lung in the coal mines—and why he chose to make bohemian ideals such an important part of his life. Yielding to anything was irreconcilable.

Understanding him for the first time helps me understand my own artistic decisions. When we pull back onto the highway and head toward Richmond, I want the rest of our trip to move more slowly, like the last few pages of a good book.

Back home, he confesses to my mom. A month later, she kicks his pussy-whipped ass out of the house. He moves into his pickup, and I move into the house.

"I feel sorry for him," I say to my mom.

"He doesn't need any sympathy. Your father made his own bed."

By the end of the year, he moves into an art studio in the basement of an old elementary school and begins a new series of paintings based on transformation. He melts beer bottles in a kiln with cicada shells. I rebuild myself aboard *The Tinker,* spending time with my nephews, fishing, living simply, healing my heart, and paying off my debts.

"Your father has wanted to live the life of a tortured artist since before you were born," my mother says to me.

"Is that what I'm doing, too?"

"Iz it torture to live with your mother?"

"No, just humbling—and sometimes embarrassing. I mean, it kind of kills my dating life."

"So tell your dates that you live with a roommate," she says pragmatically. "It's nothing to be ashamed of. In Italy, all the single boys your age live with their parents. Enjoy it. It'll be gone in a blink."

She's right. In a blink, a year goes by. I move into my father's art studio, and he moves back into the house. A few sessions with a hypnotist convince him to give up his girlfriend for good, and he and my mom become giddy newlyweds again. I feel incredibly grateful. If they can come back from the brink of broken, there's hope for me as well. I take it as a sign.

To prepare myself for the dating world once more, I start seeing an astrologer named Mr. Brimmner and create a profile on OKCupid. Mr. Brimmner is the Wall Street version of Astro Al. He wears expensive dark suits and sports a much more sophisticated comb-over.

"I'm not sure I'm on the path to finding lasting love," I say during one of our sessions. "The last three girls I've met online have all been named Vera. That's my mom's name. Am I missing something here?"

He looks at my chart. "It looks like, in each of your previous relationships, you've had a propensity to fall in love with your lovers' baggage."

"Is that a real condition?"

"I don't think so. However, it looks like you subliminally sought what you found attractive in Shiloh, Daisy, and Raleigh based not only upon what they packed in their bags at the moment you met, but the condition of their baggage as well."

"So I have some kind of baggage obsession?"

"I would say it's more like a Bohemian Love Baggage fetish. But it all starts with an inquiry into your own baggage. For instance, does the zipper on your own baggage stick? Do the wheels on your baggage squeak? Does your baggage open up without a struggle? According to your chart, I'd say your baggage was repaired once already—hand-sewn with dental floss and slapped with a lump of duct tape."

"Yeah, but didn't I inherit my baggage from my parents?"

"You can't keep blaming the salesmen who sold it to you. When you refuse to take responsibility, you're only cultivating your victim karma, which will never allow those three Asian men who came back as chimpanzees in the forest for your sins to ascend to their rightful position in the food chain. It's time to let it go and set them free, lest you end up in the tree with them."

I have no idea what he's talking about. "How do I fix it?"

"In accordance with your present astrological omens, I encourage you to cultivate a succulent kind of receptivity, a meticulously naive experience that will allow you to pierce, enter, and thus repair your Bohemian Love Baggage with divine power. Do you understand?"

Subsequent explanation will only leave me more confused, so I leave Mr. Brimmner's fee in a tiny red envelope and wish I could find Astro Al to explain it all to me using simpler abstractions.

That night, squeezed between a bunch of blank canvas that my father left behind in the studio, I discover all the mementos he saved from our cross-country trip: photos, receipts, and, inside his Moleskine sketchbook, his own poetry and song lyrics.

My father's birthday is a week away, so I pull my laptop open and stay awake until morning scanning each item and uploading it to a website that will allow me to create a hardcover book from the images. Beside a photo of a cowboy holding a newborn calf in Cody, Wyoming, I place his lyrics to a song called "Got My Mojo Workin'."

rolled over this mornin'
hung my head down an' cried
saw her lyin' there
with lust in her eyes

moved to my left
an' took it as a sign
lordy, I gotta stop drinkin'
that whiskey an' wine

Under a photo of a young cowgirl riding a black horse in the rain, I put a stanza from his poem "It Don't Get No Better."

What makes a house grand
ain't the roof or the door.
If there's love in a house,
it's a palace for sure.

The lyrics and poems were written for my father's girlfriend, which makes this a bittersweet process. My mind's eye wanders back to our trip, watching him scribbling madly away in his sketchbook, talking to her on his cell phone. Then something surprises me. In one poem my mother's name appears.

I miss you, Vera, like summer heat,
and, my friend, if you come with me
this last time,
I will make sure
as I take your hand
never to play God
with our love again.

The poems and songs were all written for her. Even when it looked like he was moving away from my mother, he was trying to find his way back home to her. It's an incredibly important realization. How many opportunities did I miss to rectify my own relationships because I never noticed this profound yet simple idea? Sometimes we get lost. Sometimes we find our way back home. Sometimes we don't. My eyes well up as I realize how this little, last-minute art project has filled me with more optimism and inspiration than I've experienced in all the days since my divorce.

The morning birds begin to sing outside. As I push the PAY NOW button on the screen, an image of my father holding his cell phone in one hand, talking to his girlfriend, while holding a pen in his other, secretly writing about his true love, oddly comforts me.

His own girlfriend, like many of mine, served as some sort of phantom limb, replacing something ostensibly missing in a previous relationship but ultimately missing inside himself. His art and writing give me further proof that loving someone because she replaces someone or something else isn't love.

I turn off my laptop and fall into contented sleep. *This is me,* I think, and I'm back on my father's motorcycle once again, hurtling into the unknown. Perhaps his blueprint for escape contained the ultimate wisdom all along.